D0154533

# THE LAST DEFENDERS
# OF THE LAAGER

# THE LAST DEFENDERS OF THE LAAGER

Ian D. Smith
and
F. W. de Klerk

*Dickson A. Mungazi*

*Foreword by Donald G. Baker*

PRAEGER

Westport, Connecticut
London

**HOUSTON PUBLIC LIBRARY**

R01207 04912

**Library of Congress Cataloging-in-Publication Data**

Mungazi, Dickson A.
   The last defenders of the laager : Ian D. Smith and F. W. de Klerk
/ Dickson A. Mungazi.
      p. cm.
   Includes bibliographical references and index.
   ISBN 0–275–96030–7 (alk. paper)
   1. Smith, Ian Douglas, 1919– .  2. Zimbabwe—Politics and
government—1965–1979.  3. Apartheid—Zimbabwe.  4. Prime ministers—
Zimbabwe—Biography.  5. De Klerk, F. W. (Frederik Willem)
6. South Africa—Politics and government—1989–  7. Apartheid—South
Africa.  8. Prime ministers—South Africa—Biography.  I. Anti-
Apartheid Movement.  II. Title.
DT2984.S65M86      1998
968.91'04'092—dc21
[B]          97–39772

British Library Cataloguing in Publication Data is available.

Copyright © 1998 by Dickson A. Mungazi

All rights reserved. No portion of this book may be
reproduced, by any process or technique, without the
express written consent of the publisher.

Library of Congress Catalog Card Number: 97–39772
ISBN: 0–275–96030–7

First published in 1998

Praeger Publishers, 88 Post Road West, Westport, CT 06881
An imprint of Greenwood Publishing Group, Inc.

Printed in the United States of America

The paper used in this book complies with the
Permanent Paper Standard issued by the National
Information Standards Organization (Z39.48–1984).

10 9 8 7 6 5 4 3 2 1

*To Edward Mazaiwana, humanitarian, educa-*
*tor and true son of Africa, whose contribution*
*to the development of Africans is invaluable.*

# Contents

# Illustrations

# Foreword

Ian Smith in Rhodesia and F. W. de Klerk in South Africa were viewed as strident racist leaders who would fight to the bitter end to preserve their white racial dominance systems. Both leaders, however, not only negotiated with black leaders to resolve the racial conflicts in their countries but also, and more significantly, negotiated the end of white minority rule and the transformation of government to the African majority—without the prophesied racial Armageddon or the toppling of the white regimes in a civil war. It is these two leaders, then, Smith and de Klerk, who are of key interest. Their actions in acceding to and bringing about what in reality were relatively peaceful revolutions (for what else can these massive changes from white minority to black majority rule be classified as) are almost inconceivable in the eyes of many observers. What is thus significant about Dickson A. Mungazi's study is his probing exploration and analysis of the last two leaders of these white racial bastions, Ian D. Smith and F. W. de Klerk.

Neither conflict, be it the low-level civil war in Rhodesia in the 1970s or the escalating uprisings and rebellion in South Africa in the 1970s–1980s, was strictly a racial confrontation, for in each country a small minority of Africans, for numerous reasons, supported the white minority governments, including some blacks who served in police forces and the military. Thus, despite the ongoing and certainly escalating conflicts in both countries, and despite the fact that white control was becoming increasingly tenuous, the reality was that neither white government was on the verge of being toppled or overthrown by the conflicts or uprisings.

Thus, in the eyes of most whites within those countries, and a view adhered to by the white government themselves, was that possible defeat (or their overthrow)—at least in the near future—was *not* a certainty.

What is therefore extremely significant, given these circumstances or conditions, is that the white political leaders, Smith and de Klerk, resolved and opted, even though begrudgingly and certainly not at the behest of their white constituents, to negotiate a resolution to their country's conflicts. Their intent may have been solely to grant a few limited concessions, and the fewer the better, to blacks, but their negotiations ultimately led toward the termination of white minority rule and the establishment of black majority-ruled governments. Thus, without the racial Armageddon envisioned or defeat in a war, white racial hegemony ended. Objectively, white leadership may clearly have recognized that in the long run the possibility of defeat was possible, but it was also clear that at that point in time the situation was not hopeless and that a protracted conflict was possible. But given the prevailing circumstances and conditions, both leaders, Smith and de Klerk, opted to negotiate a settlement, one that led to the ending of their white racial dominance systems. For these reasons, a study of these two leaders, their choices and policies, is significant, and it is this analysis that Mungazi undertakes.

Mungazi's study, however, is not limited solely to the policies of these two leaders, for he recognizes, and therefore analyzes, how their actions were the consequence of historical developments, particularly the policies of earlier white governments. What was particularly important in preserving white power and keeping Africans subordinate, he shows, was education policy, for it had two major functions: first, that of restricting and structuring education so that blacks, limited in their skill aquisition, could not compete with whites within the economic sector; and second, that of inculcating within blacks, via indoctrination, the notion of their own inferiority and the supposed inferiority of African compared to European culture. The goal of both of these factors was to create within Africans a form of dependency, be it in terms of limited skills or attitudes, making it thereby difficult for them to contest against the white dominance system. Thus education played a major role historically in keeping Africans within a subordinate position in both Rhodesian and South African societies. Africans, as the author notes, increasingly came to recognize the major role of education in political and economic development as well as in the perpetuation of white power, and as a consequence education increasingly became a focal point in their demands for change.

A critical example of this, in the case of South Africa, was the government's effort to restrict English-language training in African schools (replacing it with training in the Afrikaans language), a step perceived by Africans as an attempt to restrict their job opportunities within an economic system increasingly based on use of the English language. Protests and demonstrations, prompted by the language issue as well as other government policies, precipitated the 1976 Soweto uprisings by high school students, demonstrations that soon rippled outward and occurred elsewhere in South Africa. Soweto, along with the earlier 1973 Durban strikes by African labor and the emergence of the Black Consciousness movement especially among (though not limited to) black college students, marked the beginnings of civil unrest, rioting, and rebellion. That, in turn, set the stage for de Klerk's emergence as the white's political leader, and in 1990, he would free Nelson Mandela from prison and commence the negotiation processes that would ultimately lead in 1994 to the ending of white rule.

While Mungazi's central concern is the role of Smith and de Klerk in the transition from white to black rule, his focus on the importance of education (as a vehicle for keeping Africans subordinate; yet, conversely, serving as a potential force and major vehicle for democratization) clearly constitutes a second theme of his analysis. What also emerges, especially in his concluding chapter, is a third theme: his concern for the need of African leaders in contemporary Zimbabwe and South Africa to reshape their educational systems so that they serve as liberating and democratizing forces for society, his proposals reminiscent of the visions and pronouncements of the American educator, John Dewey, concerning the close connection between education and democracy, and the Brazilian, Paulo Freire, especially in his *Pedagogy of the Oppressed* (1974). Viewing education and politics elsewhere in contemporary Africa, and apprehensive that a similar path could be taken in Zimbabwe and South Africa, Mungazi warns that the black leadership must institute major reforms in their education systems, ones aimed at democratizing the people for national development; if not, Zimbabwe, and South Africa, too, could turn into authoritarian, one-party states, where the people are ignored and an emergent black elite utilizes government for their own power and privilege, curtailing the freedom and democratic rights of the people. Here his warnings closely parallel those of Frantz Fanon, who in the *Wretched of the Earth* (1968), criticized postcolonial African leaders because their policies of decolonization led not to freedom and democracy but to the establishment of authoritarian governments and dictatorships. For Mungazi, education plays a critical and fundamental role in training and educating people for democracy. His analysis of this period, as a consequence, merits close attention and thought.

Donald G. Baker
Professor of Politics and History
Southampton College
Long Island University

# Preface

## THE PURPOSE OF THE STUDY

In the region of southern Africa, that part of Africa south of the Equator, two of the last colonial governments were led by Ian D. Smith in Zimbabwe and F. W. de Klerk in South Africa. Smith served as prime minister from 1964 to 1979 and de Klerk served as president from 1989 to 1994. The purpose of this book is to furnish the evidence that substantiates the following conclusions: Smith and de Klerk each felt called upon to sustain white governments for many years to come. Neither man saw the need to involve Africans in the political process until the Africans forced them to do so.

Both Smith and de Klerk had to experience a bitter civil war to relinquish political power. In 1992 de Klerk decided to negotiate with the African National Congress (ANC) to turn over political power to Africans. In 1979 Smith was forced to do so; he had no choice. The irony of the political behavior of these last two defenders of the laager is that Robert Mugabe, the man Smith sent to political prison for eleven years, succeeded him in 1980, and Nelson Mandela, the man the system of apartheid sent to political prison for twenty-seven years, succeeded de Klerk in 1994. The last laager was therefore eliminated, and the restoration of Africans became complete.

The thrust for national development in southern Africa as a region could not be undertaken without seeking the elimination of the colonial conditions that existed in both South Africa and Zimbabwe since the

nineteenth century, when the laager was established. Political development in both countries could not be effected without determination on
the part of Africans to end the colonial systems that both de Klerk and
Smith represented. National development is defined as the advancement
of the individual in terms of social development, economic security, and
political freedom. This freedom allows the individual an opportunity to
set goals and engage in activities that help him realize his own concept
of self.

## QUESTIONS TO BE ANSWERED

In discussing this evidence, this book seeks to answer the following
questions: What conditions prevailed in Zimbabwe and South Africa to
form elements of political leadership that both Smith and de Klerk felt
compelled to sustain? Who are some of the leaders in both countries who
laid the foundation of political behavior that formed the basis of that of
Smith and de Klerk? What factors influenced the need to formulate political policy designed to control Africans? What were some considerations that forced the colonial governments to behave the way they did?
How did political change come about in both Zimbabwe and South Africa? What objectives did Africans set for political change in both countries? What conditions did the new African governments find in both
countries? What problems did they encounter in their efforts to create
democratic systems of government? What have these African governments done to resolve these problems?

## THE EVIDENCE PRESENTED

The focus of this book is to show evidence that Ian D. Smith and
F. W. de Klerk, as the last custodians of the laager in Zimbabwe and
South Africa respectively, felt compelled to sustain the systems that had
been created in the nineteenth century. In trying to do so they seemed
to forget that conditions of the nineteenth century were quite different
from those of the late twentieth century, especially the role of Africans.
The determination of Africans and the determination of these two last
colonial officials created an environment that produced inevitable conflict. But, like elsewhere in southern Africa, such as in Mozambique and
Angola, Africans could not be persuaded to give up their self-
consciousness. The more Smith and de Klerk tried to hold on to colonial
power as their way of defending the laager, the more Africans became
determined to end it.

The confidence that Africans had in seeking the end of colonial conditions translated into a new level of confidence by individuals engaged

in purposeful pursuit. This level of confidence for the present translated into confidence for the future. This could not happen in the climate of colonial conditions that inhibited both the freedom and aspiration of the individual for self-actualization. The evidence used to substantiate the conclusions reached in this book was obtained during study trips to South Africa and Zimbabwe in 1994, 1996, and 1997. This evidence consists of original materials and documents that I was also able to access in the National Archives of Zimbabwe and from the South African embassy in Los Angeles. I was also privileged to have interviews with various individuals in both countries. From these I obtained some useful insights.

## CONCLUSION AND IMPLICATIONS

In discussing this evidence, this book reaches the following conclusion: The thrust for political change in South Africa and Zimbabwe to ensure national development was initiated by Africans undertaken in the context of colonial conditions in existence for many years, and which they could no longer tolerate. These conditions included the denial of equal participation in the political process. By the very nature of their succession to the political leadership of Zimbabwe and South Africa, Smith and de Klerk were unable to recognize the imperative nature of change that had taken place all over the world.

This change demanded nothing less than equality in national endeavor to create the climate needed to produce a new society. Once political change took place, the new African governments were faced with a further challenge, that of educational reform. These governments have recognized that educational reform must combine with social, economic, and political factors to create essential elements of the thrust for national development. South Africa and Zimbabwe, like other countries of southern Africa, are experiencing enormous economic and political problems that can be resolved by introducing change in the political system based on educational reform.

The reality that South Africa and Zimbabwe have not been able to face is that failure to initiate successful educational reform and political change translates into failure to initiate successful national developmental programs. In this kind of environment, the nations of southern Africa continue to endure the scourge of conflict and the agony of underdevelopment. The attitudes that de Klerk and Smith adopted toward Africans have been adopted in similar fashion by many leaders of southern Africa today. The change to dictatorial action to have their own way, the manipulation of elections, the lack of a proper constitutional framework for the government, corruption by government officials, and intolerance of different viewpoints on national issues all combine to create the psychology of the laager. They continue to do this at their own peril, and that of their countries.

# Acknowledgments

In the process of writing a book that discusses the political behavior of the two last colonial leaders of two countries in a highly critical region great care should be exercised in obtaining original materials and documents that enable the interpretation of the events and policies they shaped in an accurate and logical manner. It is for this reason that the author wishes to express his profound gratitude and appreciation to the South African Embassy in Los Angeles for allowing him access to important materials on F. W. de Klerk and the events that began to unfold in 1978 when Pieter W. Botha succeeded John Vorster as prime minister of South Africa. He also wishes to thank the National Archives of Zimbabwe for access to some important materials they hold on Ian D. Smith and the Rhodesia Front government that he led from 1964 to 1979. From these materials the author obtained useful insights into the problems that Zimbabwe and South Africa were experiencing under the leadership of Ian D. Smith and F. W. de Klerk.

The author would also like to record his gratitude to Mr. Ian D. Smith, Bishop Abel Muzorewa of the United Methodist Church, who served as interim prime minister in 1979, Rev. Ndabaningi Sithole, founding member of the ANC and former vice-president of ZANU, for granting interviews in 1983 from which he obtained sharpened insights about the impact of the Rhodesian Front's (RF) policy. The author is also indebted to many other individuals who participated in the interviews in Zimbabwe in 1983, 1989, and 1997, and fully understands their reluctance to be identified. However, a partial listing of these individuals is included in the bibliography.

The author particularly wishes to express his appreciation to the Zimbabwe Ministry of Information and the Ministry of Education and Culture for allowing him access to the original documents and materials needed as part of the data required to research this book. The author wishes to thank Betty Russell, computer specialist at the Center for Excellence in Education at Northern Arizona University, for her assistance in programming the computer so that the manuscript could be produced more efficiently. In a similar fashion, he wishes to thank the faculty at Northern Arizona University for their support and encouragement. Finally, the author wishes to extend his special appreciation to Charlene Wingo, his secretary, and Margo Gay, his assistant, for helping to type part of the manuscript, and to Linda Gregonis, indexer and proofreader.

Finally the author wishes to thank the Office of Regents Professors and the Center for Excellence in Education at Northern Arizona University for encouragement and financial support to make it possible to travel to southern Africa in 1995 and 1996 to collect materials for this book.

# Abbreviations

| | |
|---|---|
| ANC | African National Congress |
| ASB | Afrikaanse Studente Bond |
| COSATU | Congress of South African Trade Unions |
| DP | Dominion Party |
| IPF | Inkatha Freedom Party |
| NAACP | National Association for the Advancement of Colored People |
| NCC | National Coordination Council |
| NDP | National Democratic Party |
| OAU | Organization of African Unity |
| PAC | Pan African Congress |
| PFP | Progressive Federal Party |
| POLSTU | Politicke Studente |
| RF | Rhodesia Front |
| SADCC | Southern African Development Coordination Conference |
| TRC | Truth and Reconciliation Commission |
| UATS | Unitied African Teaching Service |
| UDI | Unilateral Declaration of Independence |

| UFP     | United Federal Party                                      |
|---------|----------------------------------------------------------|
| ZANU    | Zimbabwe African National Union                          |
| ZANU-PT | Zimbabwe African National Union-Patriotic Front          |
| ZAPU    | Zimbabwe African Peoples' Union                          |
| ZUM     | Zimbabwe Unity Movement                                  |

# Introduction

## DE KLERK AND SMITH IN A HISTORICAL PERSPECTIVE

The purpose of this book is to discuss the political behavior of two of the last colonial leaders in southern Africa. These are Frederik W. de Klerk, who served as president of South Africa from 1989 to 1994, and Ian D. Smith, who served as prime minister of colonial Zimbabwe from 1964 to 1979. The first two chapters present some individuals who provided political leadership in both colonial Zimbabwe beginning in 1890 and in South Africa beginning in 1910. It is the legacy of this leadership that both men felt called upon to uphold at all costs. In doing so they seemed to forget that the conditions under which they served were totally different from those of their predecessors.

The word *laager* in Afrikaans means a circle of wagons. In 1836, under the leadership of Piet Retief, the Boers who had settled at the Cape in 1652 began to move north to escape British rule. In 1838 they came into contact with the Zulus under the leadership of their powerful king, Dingaan. Retief and many of his followers were killed in the fighting that ensued. In December 1838 nearly 500 Boers formed a circle of sixty wagons to defend themselves. During a crucial battle on December 16, the Boers killed nearly 3,000 Zulus. The spears the Zulus used as weapons proved no match for the guns in the possession of the Boers. Thus, the Boers won the war and took possession of the land. For years the Afrikaners observed December 16 as a public holiday called Dingaan's Day.

The Boers attributed their victory over the Zulus to their defense of the laager. Over the years, the laager became a metaphorical symbol of the determination of Afrikaners to face and overcome adversity, especially opposition from or confrontation with the Africans. Over the years, the concept of the laager became an inspiration, a moving force that fortified the will power of the Afrikaners to operate by the principles they believed in as a select group destined to rule over Africans for centuries to come. The policy of apartheid was conceived under this belief. This is the meaning that is used in this book.

There are striking differences that one sees in discussing the political behavior of these two men. Smith was born in Zimbabwe in 1919. His father had emigrated from Scotland in search of a better life for himself and his family. The conditions that caused World War I also created in him a determination to overcome adversity. At that time, Europeans had a very low opinion of Africans using this idea to improve their own conditions. They believed that the only function Africans could fulfill in society was to serve as laborers. Smith grew up within this environment and accepted these attitudes toward Africans early in his life. As a result he never developed a good relationship with Africans apart from the notion of servant-master relationships so common among Europeans of that time.

By the time Smith was elected to the colonial parliament in Zimbabwe in 1946 he was fully convinced that Africans were inferior. For him there was nothing to suggest that they could overcome the genetic inferiority, to which he believed nature sentenced them, to become more fully human. Smith's heroes were Cecil John Rhodes, Leander Starr Jameson, John Milton, Godfrey Huggins, and Roy Welensky. All these men held extremely low opinions of Africans. Smith adopted their attitude and believed that if these earlier colonial leaders were able to control Africans, he, too, would be able to do so. He would be disappointed. As a fighter pilot in the British Royal Air Force in World War II, Smith learned the cruelty of war and gained an ability to survive under hostile conditions. For years Smith was an active member of the Dominion Party, which rapidly adopted a hostile and negative attitude toward Africans, especially during the Federation of Rhodesia and Nyasaland from 1953 to 1963.

At the end of the war in 1945 the Liberal Party, which was led by Roy Stockil, had adopted a set of policies that were compatible with those of the British Labour Party, led at that time by Clement Attlee. During the ill-fated Federation, Smith appeared to support the policy of the ruling United Federal Party led by Godfrey Huggins. But he became disillusioned with the policy of partnership between Africans and the whites even though Huggins defined that policy as the kind of relationship that exists between a horse (Africans) and its rider (whites). Smith then became active in supporting the Dominion Party and took advantage of the membership of Isaac Samuriwo, a conservative African, to claim that Africans supported the policy of the Dominion Party.

At the end of the Federation, the Dominion Party became active again until it was defeated in the elections of 1958. Smith played a major role in founding the Rhodesia Front (RF), which won elections in 1962 under the leadership of Winston J. Field. Thus, a stage was set for the RF and Africans to engage in a battle of wills unparalleled in the history of Zimbabwe. In 1964 Smith led a political coup that removed Field from the office of prime minister because he was considered too moderate in his views of Africans and because he wanted to operate under British requirements for the advancement of Africans. As soon as Smith assumed the office of prime minister he led colonial Zimbabwe into one of the most bitter conflicts in Africa resulting in his own political demise, the end of the colonial period, and the beginning of the African government that he had pledged would never come in his lifetime.

F. W. de Klerk was born in Johannesburg in March 1936 into a prominent Afrikaner political family. His father, Jon de Klerk, thoroughly groomed his son in the dynamics of politics in South Africa. For the entire period of white rule in South Africa, beginning with Jan Van Riebeeck in 1652 to the end of F. W. De Klerk's term of office in 1994, the major focus of politics was race relationships. Jon de Klerk served in several cabinet positions including that of Minister of Education, the same cabinet position that Frederik held in the administration of Pieter W. Botha beginning in 1978. His uncle, J. G. Strijdom, served as prime minister of South Africa from 1952 until his sudden death in 1958. De Klerk's older brother, Willem de Klerk, served as editor of *Die Burger*, the influential Afrikaans daily newspaper based in Johannesburg.

With a law degree from the prestigious Potchfstroom University (cum laude), de Klerk was first elected to the South African parliament in 1972. There he quickly developed a reputation as an articulate speaker who based his argument in debates on complete knowledge of the issues. In that year Smith and John Vorster, both of whom de Klerk greatly admired, were at the height of their power and consulted each other frequently about the rising conflict in both Zimbabwe and South Africa caused by Africans' reaction to their respective policies. In 1988 de Klerk led a political coup that removed Pieter W. Botha from the office of president, just as Smith had done in removing Field from the office of prime minister in 1964.

As soon as he assumed the office of president, de Klerk was faced with some hard realities that no previous leader in South Africa had ever faced. As the third generation member of the Nationalist Party from his family, de Klerk became the Saul of Tarsus leading the forces of persecution under the notorious policy of apartheid against the political aspirations of Africans. Both Smith and de Klerk felt that the destiny of their respective countries rested on their shoulders. Smith operated with the view he inherited from his predecessors that it would take Africans at least a thousand years to acquire the elements of European civilization he believed they needed to make a transition from their primitive culture. De Klerk did not set a time limit, but he believed that Africans were incapable of running a government by democratic means. But as soon as he assumed the office of president of South Africa in 1989, de Klerk encountered the Damascus Road experience, which helped him see himself, his country, and Africans in an entirely different manner from what he had in the past. He became the St. Paul of South Africa preaching the gospel of social justice and equality as the only means to future security of the Afrikaners.

Smith so believed in African inferiority that his political behavior, combined with the policy he designed, resulted in a devastating civil war that finally led to his political fall and the end of the colonial system that he represented. The war lasted from 1966 to 1979. In December 1979 Smith, unlike de Klerk, was still angry when Britain convened a conference to work out a constitution that would end the colonial system. De Klerk spared South Africa the agony of the kind of conflict that Zimbabwe experienced under Smith by deciding to negotiate the transfer of power to the African majority. This was accomplished in the elections that were held in April 1994 from which Nelson Mandela, the man apartheid considered dangerous and kept in prison for twenty-seven years, emerged as the new president. Indeed, de Klerk, unlike Smith, had learned some hard lessons about the determination of Africans to bring the colonial system to an end.

## THE CONCEPT OF NATIONAL DEVELOPMENT

This book presents the effect of the political behavior of Ian D. Smith, the last colonial leader in Zimbabwe and F. W. de Klerk, the last white leader in South Africa. Although South Africa gained political independence in 1910, its government had been considered colonial because all the elements of the colonial system were present, such as the denial of participation in the political process, discrimination and segregation, and the lack of an adequate standard of living for the African population. The political behavior of Ian D. Smith and F. W. de Klerk was quite typical of the behavior of colonial enthusiasts everywhere in Africa.

Two questions are critical to this book. The first question is: On what considerations did Smith and de Klerk base their political philosophy and behavior? The second question is: How did Africans react to that behavior? The answers to these questions lie in the character of southern

Africa itself. Before discussing that character, the expression *political development* must be defined.

Flowery as it sounds, this expression is not fully understood by the leaders of the nations of southern Africa. However, *political development* carries the definitive meaning of embracing a political program of action designed to improve the essential features of national institutions. This meaning includes efforts to ensure fundamental political freedoms of the people, such as self-expression, the right to participate in national politics, to earn a decent income, and freedom of social association. A nation that denies its citizens these basic freedoms cannot be regarded as progressive, and under these circumstances any thrust for its own definition of national development is void of any real meaning.

In the context of contemporary terminology, national development means affording all the citizens basic freedoms to pursue goals and objectives that are consistent with their interests and purposes. These include the right to pursue careers without restrictions, to participate in the political process, to run for public office, to exercise freedom of self-expression, to own property, to exercise choices, to criticize the government without any reprisals, to belong to a political party of one's choice, to earn a decent living, and to live where one wishes.

In short, national development means the ability and freedom of individuals to set goals that, when pursued, improve their living conditions so that they are better off than they were in the past. This freedom allows citizens to identify with national purposes. These are the elements that combine to create a national social climate that brings happiness and security to citizens. National development has its basis in this climate. It will be seen that conditions in existence under Smith in Zimbabwe and de Klerk in South Africa did not permit Africans to exercise these freedoms. Africans in both countries were faced with a painful choice: to accept the conditions imposed by the colonial systems and deny themselves an opportunity for development, or to struggle for change and face the reprisal of the governments. Recognizing the dangers involved in their decisions and actions, Africans were ready to face those dangers. The struggle was on.

## RESISTANCE TO POLITICAL CHANGE IN SOUTH AFRICA

Now, an answer to the first question, on what considerations did Smith and de Klerk base their political philosophy and behavior, must be provided. Since 1962, when Tanzania gained political independence, the character of southern Africa itself was altered by the demand Africans made to the colonial governments to initiate fundamental change in the political process as a viable way to solve the problems of national development. Since Ghana gained political independence in 1957, Africans were in a restive mood. They were no longer willing to accept political activity that exclusively belonged to whites. But the more Africans demanded change, the more colonial officials resisted. This situation created a major conflict between Africans and colonial governments. This would suggest that Smith and de Klerk based their political philosophy and behavior on what their predecessors had done.

The release of Nelson Mandela on February 10, 1990, from life imprisonment, following his conviction in 1964 on charges of attempting to overthrow the government of South Africa, was a dramatic turn of tragic events that began to unfold with the victory of the Nationalist Party led by Daniel Malan in the elections of 1948. Can one define Mandela's release as an element of national development without making an effort to dismantle apartheid? The answer is no because apartheid did not allow the components of basic human freedoms to combine and operate in the manner that would translate subsequent events into a thrust for national development. This, then, provides the answer to the second question: How did Africans react? Given the conditions arising out of 1964, the year that Smith assumed power and Mandela went to prison, Africans could no longer accept political domination by the colonial government. This refusal set the stage for the unprecedented conflict to emerge between Africans and the colonial governments that Smith and de Klerk represented.

The enactment of the infamous Bantu Education Act in South Africa in 1953 was an event that set South Africa on a deadly course of national conflict. When Malan retired from active politics in 1958, he was succeeded by de Klerk's uncle, J. G. Strijdom. Strijdom was succeeded by Hendrik Verwoerd, a man of uncompromising belief in the supremacy of apartheid, the superiority of the Afrikaners, and the assumed inferiority of Africans. As the director of Bantu Administration in the Malan government, Verwoerd became the principal architect of apartheid as he systematically formulated new elements and then applied them to reduce Africans to the level of bare existence. To accomplish this objective, Verwoerd used provisions of the Bantu Education Act to elevate the Afrikaners to the pedestal of absolute political supremacy enshrined in their invincibility and infallibility. Under Verwoerd the meaning of the laager reached a new level of significance.

Verwoerd's assassination in 1966 brought John Vorster to the seat of power from where he directed apartheid and fortified the laager to unprecedented heights. The decision of his government to enforce new provisions of the Bantu Education Act created a national climate that led to the explosion that was heard around the world from Soweto in June 1976. The confession made on January 28, 1997, by five former police officers that they killed Steve Biko in September 1977 added a painful episode to the activities of those who were prepared to go to any length to defend the laager. In 1978, facing a barrage of outcries and criticism from the international community, Vorster decided to resign on grounds of poor health, rather than face the reality that apartheid was setting South Africa on a course of self-destruction. Indeed, apartheid was rolling and roaring with a vengeance. Although the laager showed cracks in its wall, Vorster felt he had no choice but to defend it at all cost.

Vorster's successor, Pieter Botha, approached the problems created by apartheid in southern Africa, not just in South Africa, with a new determination to ignore the protest from the international community and to make apartheid the sacred shrine that both Afrikaners and Africans must worship with total supplication. The intensification of the armed struggle, spearheaded by the African National Congress (ANC)—along with a series of bomb explosions throughout South Africa that killed many and injured even more—created a dangerous situation raising questions as to whether Botha was able to defend the laager in the manner that previous defenders had done.

The imposition of economic sanctions combined with internal conflict to force Botha to urge his fellow diehard Afrikaners to *adopt or die*. Cracks in the laager began to show more signs that it was a matter of time before it would fall. However, Botha did not have the courage to face up to the reality that apartheid had gone too far. Instead, he warned the world, "Don't push us too far." When Frederik W. de Klerk succeeded Botha in 1989, he recognized that South Africa had become a cruel victim of apartheid and that the laager could no longer be defended in the manner it had been defended in the past. Africans were shooting too many arrows into the cracks. This is why he decided to take the initiative to hold dialogue with the ANC.

It is not surprising that Mandela's response to de Klerk's call was his own call to initiate change in the political system on the basis of nothing less than dismantling apartheid in order to transform the character of South African society. This was his own call to give up the defense of the laager. De Klerk and his fellow Afrikaners were forced to realize that while maintaining a political status quo could not be done forever, it was an equally elusive task to initiate change in the social structure without accepting the challenge of political transformation. Therefore, the immediate challenge to de Klerk was to respond to the call from the ANC to end apartheid in order to change the political system so that a thrust for national development could be made free from efforts to continue to defend the laager.

This approach was the only way solutions to the problems of national development in South Africa could be found. This is the reason Africans demanded an end to apartheid as a prior condition of that development.

This initiate would bring the people of South Africa, both black and white, closer to understanding each other for the benefit of their country. This is what Mandela saw when he said on February 13, 1990, that education under apartheid was a crime against humanity. The recognition of this truth constituted a critical prerequisite of the challenge of the new political transformation of South Africa.

That for years Africans did not have the right to vote in national elections, that they were not allowed to run for national public office because they were not regarded as citizens of South Africa, were, indeed, forms of the ultimate crime against humanity that apartheid instituted for many years. Indeed, the first order of business for de Klerk and his government should have been to dismantle the Bantu Education Act to convince Africans that its leaders meant well. That they did not do this raised some serious doubt about their sincerity to bring about genuine political change. The action taken by the South African parliament on June 5, 1991, to repeal provisions of the apartheid law did not constitute the final act to remove the last vestiges of an oppressive system because the black people were still second-class citizens and foreigners in the land of their birth. Although apartheid was falling, the laager was still in place.

## RESISTANCE TO POLITICAL CHANGE
## IN ZIMBABWE

In Smith's Zimbabwe the saga of conflict acquired historical dimensions. The war of independence, which placed Zimbabwe in the pages of international news headlines from 1966 to 1979, was a national tragedy that might have been avoided if the parties to the conflict that preceded it had agreed on some basic principles. But to appreciate why such an agreement was not possible to reach, one needs to understand what was at the center of the conflict that cast Zimbabwe in the international spotlight. Since the inception of the colonial government in September 1890, Zimbabwe was subjected to the political behavior of the white men who were so obsessed with sustaining political power—the laager—that nothing else mattered.

In a unilateral declaration of independence on November 11, 1965, Ian D. Smith, unaware that he would be the last colonial leader to defend the laager, claimed that his government took this action—to sustain Western civilization in what he called a primitive country—because the mantle of the colonial pioneers had fallen on his shoulders. It did not occur to him and his associates in government that that mantle had, in effect, fallen from their shoulders. The laager could not be defended in the way it had been defended in the past. The attitude and the policies of the political party that Smith helped form in 1962, the Rhodesia Front (RF), demonstrate the tragic nature of its political behavior—their efforts to defend the laager.

This leads to the conclusion that, in their own way, Smith and the RF became the Don Quixote of the new era. They thought they were tilting the giant windmills of rising African nationalism. Instead they were setting in motion events that resulted in the fall of the laager, as well as an ensuing major conflict that would permanently alter conditions. In the process, Smith and the RF became the Pied Piper of the old political system leading their white followers, not from the cave of their dreaded fear of their inability to defend the laager and the advent of an African government, but to the cave of political oblivion due to the conflict that emerged as a result and led to their inevitable end. How this happened is also the subject of this book.

The book will explore the nature of race relationships that emerged as a result of Smith's seeking to fulfill his political agenda and objectives. Smith, in this search, created a new explosive situation that had not existed before. The conflict that emerged between the RF government and Africans was rare in its bitterness. The RF government was led by a group of white men who espoused policies and a political philosophy that were considered extreme. The African nationalists were led by men of absolute determination to realize their political aspirations. The confrontation that emerged between the two sides added a new twist and pathos to this drama. The two sides seemed unwilling to compromise any of their own principles and objectives, adding to a tragic outcome.

Failure to see this perilous situation from the other's point of view could have only one consequence—confrontation. It would appear that each side was ready for such a showdown, and there was no way of avoiding it in the context of the climate that existed at the time. In South Africa, de Klerk avoided this level of conflict by a timely action. While this book furnishes evidence to show that the policies of the RF government led to the conflict, one must see the causes of the war from a broader context. The quest for better socioeconomic opportunity and the demand for political rights were among the major factors that transformed the African world in a way that led to conflict with the existing system of government. It is this transformation that compelled church leaders to see their role of supporting the African cause in relation to RF government policy.

One must not, therefore, conclude that this conflict was a racial war, because it was not. The conflict was between the vestiges of the colonial establishment, who were trying to defend the laager, and the rising tide of African nationalism fighting for a just cause. This is what Robert Mugabe meant when he said in 1981 that the war of independence could not be avoided because Africans had a cause to fight for and the colonial system had its own cause to defend. In this context race only became an incidental factor when the RF government, by its own admission, made it so. But what is important to remember is the extreme positions that the combatants took suggests the critical role of the forces behind it and the explosive nature of the conflict. On the one hand is Ian D. Smith, the last colonial political leader of Zimbabwe and the Pied Piper of the old era of colonial political objectives.

On the other hand, Smith was a man whose political philosophy manifested a behavior that upheld and reflected the views Cecil John Rhodes expressed at the height of his political power in 1897. It was Rhodes' absolute belief that the white man in Africa must retain political power for at least a thousand years. Rhodes had concluded that Africans would take that length of time to acquire the elements of Western culture, without which, he argued, they would remain primitive and unable to run a government efficiently. Throughout their careers both Smith and de Klerk based their philosophy and political behavior on Rhodes' line of thinking. However, because he served later than Smith, de Klerk was more readily able to recognize that the laager could no longer be defended. It was only after the laager had fallen that Smith admitted to me in 1983 that, indeed, the days of successfully defending it were over.

Smith's absolute belief in Rhodes' views became an obsession in his action to formulate political objectives and policies of his own administration. He believed that he had a duty to launch a *kamikaze* assault on the rising tide of African nationalism unmindful of the consequences of his action. He failed to realize that this action would turn out to be an ill-conceived strategy that would mean his ultimate self-deception in the calm before the storm. On the other hand, the African nationalists believed that they had a solemn responsibility to liberate their people and to rescue their country from what they regarded as colonial usurpers who were exploiting them under the aegis of Victorian principles of the profitability of founding colonies.

There is no question that both Smith and de Klerk fully operated under the influence of these Victorian principles. This belief fortified their will power to defend the laager. But inadvertently this belief also inspired the determination of Africans to fight for their cause. It is this kind of setting that produced an environment ripe for a major conflict in both countries. One must now ask the question: What were the real causes of the war of independence in Zimbabwe? The answer depends on whom one asks. Smith told the author in July 1983 that it was caused by the African nationalists who, he argued, were seeking to replace what he claimed was a democratic government with a Marxist dictatorship. In South Africa de Klerk was operating under a similar belief. But recognizing that he could not convince the international community that he, like Smith, was fighting against a possible Communist takeover, he knew he had to change his strategy to suit new demands. Whatever both men did, they knew their ability to defend the laager was eroding rapidly.

In Zimbabwe, the African nationalists argued that the conflict was caused by the RF's oppressive policies, especially the denial of equal opportunity to participate in the political process. In South Africa, the ANC argued that conflict was caused by the application of the policy of apartheid as the ultimate defense of the laager. Assuming the reasons advanced by both sides were plausible, one must seek a more reliable basis of determining the actual causes. This author believes there are three basic reasons why war could not be avoided. These are: historical precedence, the rise of African nationalism, and the policies of the RF and the Nationalist party government themselves. Let us take one at a time and discuss briefly how each contributed to the causes of war.

## HISTORICAL PRECEDENCE: COMPARISON OF DE KLERK AND SMITH

In Zimbabwe, as soon as the British South Africa Company established a colony in September 1890, Leander Starr Jameson, the first administrator who served from September 10, 1890, to April 1, 1896, operated under the Victorian principle that Africans must be trained to fulfill the labor needs of the country. For the next six years, a philosophy steadily developed that embraced the belief that practical training and manual labor should form the major component of the curriculum in African schools. Therefore, from the beginning of the colonial government policy for Africans, this became an integral part of its political agenda. Until the end of the RF government in 1979, the political process acquired dimensions far beyond the level of ordinary policy. In South Africa, beginning with the end of the Boer war in 1901, the Afrikaners approached the formulation of policy with religious dedication to subject Africans to a position from which they could not rise. The formation of the Union of South Africa in 1910 gave them the power they believed they needed to control the African population.

In Zimbabwe, during the period that Earl Grey served as administrator from April 2, 1896, to December 4, 1898, this practice had become an official government policy. Indeed, in 1898, during a debate on the first education bill that became law in 1899, Grey argued that the best way of promoting the advancement of Africans was not through the introduction of the Christian values the missionaries were trying to promote, but rather through training them to function as cheap laborers. The church-state crisis, which became part of the history of Zimbabwe, began to form with Grey's views and the reaction of the church leaders to them.

The cooperation that had existed between the missionaries and the European entrepreneurs, and which David Livingstone so eloquently advocated in 1864 as the best means of advancing British commercial interests in Africa, suffered a severe setback as a result of Grey's attitude and the policies of his administration. In South Africa the Dutch Reformed Church fully supported the apartheid policy of the government until 1978 when world opinion had turned against apartheid. Within this context, a triangle of badly strained relationships began to form at the conclusion of the war of occupation in Zimbabwe in 1897. There the church took the side of Africans. In South Africa it took the side of the government, especially in 1948.

However, in Zimbabwe it was the administration of Godfrey Huggins from September 12, 1933, to September 6, 1953, which established a strong precedence that the RF government effectively used in designing its own set of policies, making the road to conflict a truly perilous one. Huggins' definition of the policy of partnership between Africans and the whites, "that kind of relationship which exists between the horse and the rider," is what the RF government used as the basis of its own policies and political action. Not only did Smith admire Huggins and accept him as his mentor, he also adopted all of his policies, programs, and philosophies. In South Africa it was the government of Daniel Malan that began, in 1948, to lay the foundations of apartheid that de Klerk later utilized with impunity. Defense of the laager was thus ensured, but not for a millennium as Cecil John Rhodes had predicted in 1896. When Smith proclaimed loud and clear in 1964 that he did not believe in a black government ever, not in a thousand years, he was showing total confidence in his ability to defend the laager. All it took was fifteen years to prove him wrong.

Arguing that there was nothing wrong with the policies of his administration beyond the reaction of misinformed individuals, Smith told the author in 1983 that they were part of the history of policy in Zimbabwe, and that to expect his government to change history was unrealistic. He preferred to neglect the reality that, because conditions from Jameson to Huggins were different from those of his own time, there was a need to change both attitudes and policies to suit these new conditions. The reason why Smith and the RF government did not think much of the policies of the administration of Garfield Todd from September 7, 1953, to February 16, 1958, and that of Edgar Whitehead from February 17, 1958, to December 16, 1962, is that both tried to reverse the policies that Huggins had pursued for many years.

Smith and his RF government so admired Huggins and the policies of his administration that they used them as a model of their policies, neglecting the fact that new conditions demanded a fresh appraisal. In South Africa both Vorster and Botha were operating under similar considerations. Failure to understand this basic and simple fact constituted the elements of the tragedy of both the RF and the Nationalist Party in South Africa. Both Smith and de Klerk strengthened the policy of their immediate predecessors. This added a fateful twist in the drama of conflict they encountered with Africans in their efforts to defend the laager.

## THE RISE OF AFRICAN NATIONALISM

The second reason why a major conflict could not be avoided in both South Africa and Zimbabwe is the rise of African nationalism. World War II had a profound effect upon Africans in ways that neither they nor the colonial governments could have foreseen. The campaign by the colonial governments to recruit Africans as volunteers for military action against the Axis powers gave them an opportunity to see conditions of human life in major countries of Europe—something they could not have learned about in any other way. Tragic as World War II was, it gave Africans an entirely new view of themselves in relation to the character of the colonial society and the governments that controlled them.

Indeed, the colonial governments all over Africa asked Africans to fight against possible Nazi oppression, yet they returned home to endure old forms of colonial oppression. They had been asked to fight for the freedom and rights of all people, yet Africans returned home to experience a lack of freedom and a continual denial of equal rights. They had been asked to fight to end racism, yet Africans returned home to face new colonial racism. That Africans grasped the effect of this contradiction on their lives suggests how the war had aroused a new level of consciousness for them.

The reality of this awareness had its basis in the conference that African leaders held in London at the conclusion of the war in 1945. Not only did they assess their contribution to the war efforts of the Allies, but they also made an evaluation of themselves as a people in light of the colonial conditions. From that moment, out of Africans' understanding of what it meant to be human, African nationalism was born. The return of Kwame Nkrumah to Ghana in 1947, following the completion of his educational *safari* in Europe and the United States, gave new meaning to the momentum that was building rapidly. When Nkrumah was elected prime minister of Ghana in 1950, he began to work toward its independence as a prelude to the struggle for the liberation of the African continent as a whole. To that end, at the inauguration of the independence of Ghana, Nkrumah made a solemn pledge to launch a continental campaign to rid Africa of colonialism. He argued that independence was meaningless for Ghana unless it was dedicated to the liberation of the African continent.

The attainment of independence for Ghana in 1957 altered the political landscape in all of Africa. Suddenly Ghana and Nkrumah became the twin symbols of a new era of consciousness in Africa, the beacon lighthouse giving direction to African political boats sailing in the troubled waters of colonial high waves. The British imperial ship sailing in the equally troubled waters on the Dark Continent had hit an iceberg and was now beginning to sink. Nkrumah's role in the founding of the Organization of African Unity on May 25, 1963, ushered in a new level of African nationalism and offered the British an opportunity to make a political SOS call. It really is not surprising that the very first target of the African nationalists was the political system under colonial control. The assault on the laager was on.

The inauguration of the African National Congress in Zimbabwe in 1957 (the year Ghana achieved independence and Martin Luther King Jr. and Rosa Parks were making news headlines in the struggle of black Americans for civil rights) was an event destined to alter the course of political events in the country. When Edgar Whitehead outlawed the ANC in February 1958, the relationship between Africans and the colonial government entered a new phase. The formation of the National Democratic Party (NDP) in 1959, its banning, again by Whitehead, in 1960, and the formation of ZAPU (Zimbabwe African People's Union) and ZANU (Zimbabwe African National Union), also in 1960, were developments that suggest the colonial governments failed to accept African nationalism as a major factor shaping the political development of the country.

The RF's failure to accept this reality would have dire consequences for the future. When two powerful forces—the rising tide of African nationalism and the RF determination to preserve white political institutions—clashed, the outcome was devastating. In South Africa, the banning of the African nationalist organizations and the arrest of hundreds of individuals opposed to apartheid signaled the beginning of a new level of conflict between Strijdom and Africans.

At the time of his death in 1958 ,Strijdom thought that he had found a solution to the problems apartheid had created. De Klerk, then 22 years old, was busy learning from both his father and his uncle the dynamics of defending the laager. Verwoerd, Strijdom's successor, believed that the Afrikaner mission of sustaining apartheid fell on his shoulders. He felt that he had a mission to defend the laager for future generations of Afrikaners. He would not stop to review the situation and design a new set of policies to reflect the new reality in South Africa. Conflict between Africans and the colonial governments in both countries was cast in this kind of environment.

## THE POLICIES OF THE RF AND NATIONALIST GOVERNMENT

The third reason why a major conflict could not be avoided in both countries concern the policies of the RF and the Nationalist governments themselves. When Ian D. Smith told the author in 1983 that because the policies of his administration were part of the history of government policy in Zimbabwe, he justified them on that basis alone. He felt that easing them would weaken his resolve to defend the laager and would lead to the formation of an African government, the prospect of which he detested completely. This is the reason why the RF declined to consider changing those policies. But neither Smith nor his RF government were aware that, in remaining rigid about the influence of past policies on those of their own, they were inadvertently accelerating the fall of the laager and the advent of an African government itself. When, in response to a letter from the author, de Klerk indicated that it was unfair to blame the conflict between his government and the ANC on apartheid, he justified it and saw nothing wrong with the policy that had been condemned around the world. Even though he knew that the laager was going to fall, he felt that it had to be defended.

When a black government became a reality in Zimbabwe on April 18, 1980, well short of the thousand years that Smith and Rhodes had predicted it would take for Africans to acquire the essential elements of Western culture, Smith was stunned by a turn of events that he could not control. When a black government became a reality in South Africa on May 9, 1994, de Klerk was equally stunned by the pace of events that he could not control. In Zimbabwe Robert Mugabe, and in South Africa Nelson Mandela, the African leaders who successfully led the charge against the laager, proved to be more than a match for Smith and de Klerk. Where did Cecil John Rhodes, Earl Grey, Godfrey Huggins, Paul Kruger, Daniel Malan, Hendrik Verwoerd, and John Vorster go wrong in their prediction that the colonial laager would last at least a millennium because Africans would be unable to storm it and bring it down? It is clear that the historical significance that the Nationalist government in South Africa and the RF in Zimbabwe used as a basis for their own policies had a profound effect on the relationships between themselves and Africans. The more the colonial systems tried to defend the laager, the more Africans became determined to bring it down.

In Zimbabwe the storming of the laager began with the announcement of a new educational policy and the enactment of the infamous Land Tenure Act, both put into force in 1969. This shows how the RF government's policy was at the center of this triangle of badly strained institutional relationships. In South Africa the storming of the laager began with the announcement of a new educational policy in 1974. Two years later the situation exploded in Soweto. This book addresses the conflict that emerged between the church and the RF in Zimbabwe as each wanted to exercise dominant influence on the development of Africans. But the effect of that conflict readily translated into conflict between the RF and Africans. Why Vorster in South Africa and Smith in Zimbabwe failed to realize that the educational policy in both countries acquired political dimensions of major proportions is hard to explain.

In reacting to the church's support of Africans' demands for better educational opportunity, the RF once more proved that its policies were influenced by Zimbabwe's history. In expressing appreciation of the Dutch Reformed Church's support of apartheid, the Nationalist government also proved that such support was a product of South African history. Both countries could not afford to extend that opportunity to Africans without putting the political interests of the whites in jeopardy. The RF and the Nationalist governments could not remain unmoved without igniting a new crisis. How were the two governments going to resolve this dilemma? In the context of already badly strained relationships that emerged between Africans, the church, and the RF government, the action of the church leaders manifested the behavior of an institution that recognized the imperative nature of change and the need to preserve its own position in the future. The RF's educational policy of a 5 percent cut in salary grants, announced in 1969 for African primary teachers, only served the purpose of aggravating an already bad situation.

There is another factor that influenced the deterioration of the relationships between the RF and Nationalist governments and the church leaders. In Zimbabwe, on the one hand, the church leaders believed that they had a responsibility to identify themselves with the aspiration of Africans. On the other hand, the RF government believed that there was nothing wrong with its policies even though it was fully aware, as Smith told the author, that Africans were unhappy with them. In South Africa the Anglican Church, led by Archbishop Desmond Tutu, raised similar concerns. But these were muted by the support of the Dutch Reformed Church. What actually led to the conflict in both countries was a combination of three critical factors.

These factors are the influence of history, the rise of African nationalism, and the policies of the Nationalist and RF governments themselves. The crisis between the church and these governments resulted from the interaction of these factors. Both the Nationalist and the RF governments faced a dilemma of choice: to recognize these factors and move accordingly to resolve the conflict they created by recognizing African aspiration, or to resist change and accentuate the conflict. Smith chose the latter course of action and de Klerk chose the former course, both of which led to their demise. Neither man could defend the laager any longer. Their defense forces had been depleted.

Finally, both Smith and de Klerk were different from their predecessors in two critical respects. The first is that their obsession with the white control of the government stood in the way of any effort to design a policy that would help solve the problems that both South Africa and Zimbabwe were facing. When this obsession collided with the rise of African nationalism, the inevitable outcome was a confrontation of major proportions. In both countries the conflict turned into outright struggle. The second difference is that Smith's and de Klerk's administrations made them the first governments to reverse the educational development of Africans to ensure that the government remained in what it called responsible—meaning white—hands.

In Zimbabwe Ian D. Smith, Lance Smith, Arthur Smith, A. J. Smith, Andrew Skeen, Charles S. Davies, M. G. Mills, and David Stewart all became spokesmen of a policy that was designed to control and limit the political development of Africans as the most effective means of defending the laager—preserving white political control. In South Africa the same conditions prevailed. Frederik de Klerk, Pieter Botha, Roelf Botha, Kruger Malan, and Garrit Viljoen became the spokesmen of a policy that was recognized across the world as an oppressive system. In the end, the mantle of the pioneers—to sustain European civilization—which these men thought fell on their shoulders, actually fell from their hands as the African governments that they had dreaded so much and that they had dedicated their lives to stop from becoming a reality, became their nightmare. This was the final act of defending the laager. How this happened is the subject of this book.

There is one thing that can be learned from the conflict in both South Africa and Zimbabwe during the government of de Klerk and Smith: No government can long endure when it tries to preserve a system to serve the political, economic, and social interests of the minority at the expense of the majority. There is no doubt that de Klerk and Smith were so committed to the policies of past administrations that they were not able to envision themselves as playing a dynamic role in the development of national policy that would respond affirmatively to the conditions of the times. There is also a lesson for the new governments of Zimbabwe led by Robert Mugabe and of South Africa led by Nelson Mandela in these tragic events.

It must be understood that democracy demands that the people be involved at every phase of developing a national policy. Many countries of Africa have yet to learn this truth, which is the reason why African nations have experienced enormous problems, worse than those in existence during the colonial period. It is imperative that African nations come together in an effort to find new solutions to old problems. The problems are many and complex. They include the rising population, economic decay, and political disintegration to name only a few. These problems can be resolved, not by using old methods, but by designing strategies to suit the conditions of the times. The introduction of a new constitution to South Africa on December 10, 1996, seems to mark the beginning of a new era of hope.

## POLITICAL CONDITIONS IN OTHER COUNTRIES IN SOUTHERN AFRICA

The character of other countries in southern Africa also shows that political policy is critical to reshaping their societies. In Mozambique, a country with a literacy rate of 17 percent in 1997, and Angola, with a literacy rate of 32 percent in 1997, brutal civil wars have left the people without hope for the future and without purpose or direction. The plundering and brutality with which Afonzo Dhlamini's Renamo in Mozambique and Jonas Savimbi in Angola waged the struggle for their respective causes leads to the conclusion that a new approach would help the warring parties to understand the destructive nature of their conflict. These two former Portuguese colonies have endured discord since they gained independence in 1975. Conventional wisdom would suggest that investing in education would make it possible for Mozambique and Angola to recognize the critical nature of national unity. Once people are educated sufficiently, they understand the need to restructure national programs to ensure the happiness and security of all. This cannot be done in the context of existing conditions. Without adequate education it is not possible to recognize this reality.

Instead of directing their resources toward the destruction of each other, the people of these countries could direct them toward the development of dynamic societies with a potential for greatness. Observers have concluded that the economic, physical, and psychological damage that people of both countries have endured will take years to repair. If there is a need to make a new thrust for educational innovation anywhere in Africa, that need is greater in these two countries than anywhere else on the continent.

The granting of independence to Malawi and Zambia in October 1964 was an occasion that raised hope for a brighter future among the Africans of these countries. But, when Hastings Kamuzu Banda of Malawi and Kenneth Kaunda of Zambia converted their countries into a one-party government system, the euphoria of a brighter future turned into an abyss of despair. The efforts that these two countries made in changing the system of education to reflect the needs of the people as a basis for a brighter future fell into the background while every activity by their national leaders focused on strengthening the notion of one-party rule. Both Banda and Kaunda had been in power since that time, but were not willing to admit that they had become the major problems of their respective countries. By 1990 Malawi had a literacy rate of 25 percent and Zambia of 54 percent.[1] Indeed, both countries have endured the agony of underdevelopment as a result of the action of their leaders.

This pattern of one-party government has been prevalent in southern Africa. When Mobutu Sese Seko (1930–1997) staged a military coup in Zaire on November 25, 1965, it was the beginning of the road to a military dictatorship that has entrenched itself even deeper than in 1965. Mobutu himself has shown no mercy toward those who hold different political views from his own or have differing opinions about the direction that Zaire must take. Over the years Mobutu has been reported to have a personal fortune estimated in the billions of dollars while the people have endured grinding poverty. Instead of directing his efforts toward the development of the people through educational innovation, Mobutu designed a strategy to keep himself in office for life, just like Banda and Kaunda. Zaire's literacy rate of 55 percent in 1989 could have been higher if national resources had been directed toward the educational development of the people. The civil war that was raging in Zaire in an earlier year was a result of the brutality that Mobutu had imposed on his people since 1965.

In 1990, Botswana was the only country in southern Africa whose government and people seemed to understand and appreciate the importance of casting the educational process in the national framework of democratic principles. Although its literacy rate of 35 percent, out of a total population of 1.2 million in 1990, was comparatively low, its people were among the happiest in all of southern Africa because they enjoyed all the fundamental freedoms that are essential to national endeavors as defined in this book. While this author was there in 1983 and 1989, he was pleased to see that a multiparty democracy was alive and well. There was no government control of the media, no restrictions on the people's right to belong to political parties of their choice, and no massive nationalization of major industries. The National Commission on Education of 1977 seemed to understand the importance of accepting the challenge of initiating educational innovation to sustain these democratic values and practices. This book discusses its findings and the implications of its recommendations.

Since Botswana achieved independence from Britain on September 30, 1966, under the leadership of Seretse Khama, it has never wavered in its commitment to democracy. When Quett Masire assumed the office of president on July 13, 1980, following Khama's death, there was no fear that the democratic principles established at the inception of independ-

ence would be in danger. The people and their government fully coop-
erated in a new endeavor to ensure national development based upon a
new drive for educational innovation. Botswana's efforts in this effort
are also discussed in this book as an example of what nations of southern
Africa can do to promote national development through educational innovation.

The problems that these examples highlight are the reasons why
nations of southern Africa, more than other countries of the Dark Continent, with possible exception of the Horn of Africa, must initiate educational innovation. Conventional wisdom seems to suggest that
problems of national development cannot be resolved in isolation from
those of education. Because change in education is necessary to initiate
change in society, the concept of innovation becomes an imperative to
acquiring the ability to face other problems.

## CONCLUSION AND IMPLICATIONS

The real tragedy of the conflict that emerged in South Africa and Zimbabwe lay in the inability and unwillingness of the Nationalists and the
RF to see things from the perspective of conditions in 1966, not those in
1896, when Cecil John Rhodes, Leander Starr Jameson, Earl Grey, and
William Milton were at the height of their political power. Indeed, in
viewing the Great Industrial Revolution as the ultimate white man's
technological superiority over Africans, these men created a political and
socioeconomic environment that would later have an adverse effect on
human relations in Africa. Zimbabwe and South Africa took the full
impact of it by 1966 and 1990, respectively. This is why the Nationalists
and the RF governments were the ultimate victims of a system that had
long served the political purpose of the white man. This was a major
contributing cause of the conflict in both countries. Finally, it would be
misleading to suggest that Smith's and de Klerk's policies were the sole
cause of the conflict. One must regard those policies in the context of
other major factors that were at the center of the conflict.

These factors include the general political turmoil that characterized
political events in Africa following the granting of independence to
Ghana in 1957; the break-up of the Federation of Rhodesia and Nyasaland in 1963, with its severe implications for political conflict; the mass
arrests and the formulation of the Freedom Charter in South Africa, both
in 1955; and the events that led to the unilateral declaration of independence in Zimbabwe in 1965. But when these events combined with
what Africans considered a lack of equal opportunity, the political process itself became a far more important factor than any other issue because
it became the ultimate, and thus the most important, cause of conflict.

When one considers how opportunity was crucial to socioeconomic and political opportunity, one can readily see that the educational process became a major factor that contributed to the unhappiness of Africans. The more Africans expressed that unhappiness, the more the Nationalist and RF governments suppressed them, and the more these governments suppressed them, the more Africans resisted. This is how a major conflict gathered momentum between the two sides.

Nations of southern Africa must remember that, as critically important as it is, national development and independence must be initiated within the environment of fundamental change that must take place in the political system. This means that the political system has to change to embrace the general concept of change itself. The elections held in Namibia in November 1989 to pave the way for independence scheduled for March 21, 1990, the change of socioeconomic system in Mozambique announced by President Joaquim Chissano in August 1989, the efforts made toward a negotiated settlement between the warring parties in Angola, and de Klerk's peace overtures toward the ANC and other formerly outlawed political parties all combine to create a climate of regional peace so desperately needed to place southern Africa on the road to a new society and prosperity.

It must be understood that the conditions that prevailed in southern Africa in 1966 are quite analogous to the psychology of the laager that handicapped both de Klerk and Smith from discharging their proper responsibility to all the people. Resistance to meaningful political change to accommodate the wishes and aspirations of the people, a general state of social and economic decay, corruption by government officials, and manipulation of elections all combined to create a national climate of the psychology of the laager. To overcome this psychology, nations of southern Africa need to initiate real and meaningful political change.

This task is an enormous undertaking. But it is a task that must be accomplished. While the risk of failure is there, the consequences of not trying are devastating. The relationship between social change and national development are two pillars of stability the nations of southern Africa need to ensure the success of national programs. For that cooperation to come about, South Africa had to first recognize that apartheid had to be dissolved so that a new nonracial society could be created. Smith's and de Klerk's defense of the laager must provide lessons for the governments of Africa. This is now the challenge before southern Africa as a region.

## NOTE

1. *The World Almanac and Book of Facts*, 1990.

*The mantle of the pioneers has fallen on our shoulders to sustain civilization in a primitive country.*

Ian D. Smith, November 11, 1965

*It is only when justice is done to all sectors of our population that a lasting peace will come.*

F. W. de Klerk, March 23, 1990

# Beginnings of the Laager: F. W de Klerk in the Context of Political Leadership in South Africa

The history of South Africa is a history of the clash between the imposed government and the true leaders of the people.

Ntotho Motlana, 1990

## THE SETTING

This book examines the political behavior of Ian D. Smith, who served as the last prime minister of colonial Zimbabwe from 1964 to 1979, and F. W. de Klerk, who served as president of South Africa from 1989 to 1994. Smith was succeeded by Robert Mugabe, whom Smith sent to prison for eleven years for opposing the colonial government. De Klerk was succeeded by Nelson Mandela, whom the government of South Africa, led by Hendrik Verwoerd, sent to prison for twenty-seven years. In their respective behavior to defend the political systems they found in place, both Smith and de Klerk were defending the laager.[1] The succession to the government by both Mugabe and Mandela symbolizes the storming and the fall of the laager.

The action taken by the British Parliament in 1909 in passing the South Africa Act, which created South Africa as an independent country effective May 31, 1910, set the stage for one of Africa's most bitter conflicts. On that date the formation of the Union of South Africa, made up of the Cape Province, Natal, the Orange Free State, and the Transvaal, proved to be the ultimate conspiracy against the African population. The Union

Constitution did not even make a reference to the place of Africans in the country.

It can be seen that the denial of political rights to black South Africans was deliberately intended in the constitution because it produced a totalitarian system of government that excluded Africans for over eighty-three years. The British government later regretted its action when it saw that the denial of equal rights to Africans went far beyond the extent of conditions imposed by the colonial system. Britain, knowing the racial philosophy of the Boers, did not ensure that the future of Africans would be secure under the domination by Afrikaners. Under the terms of the Treaty of Vereeniging of 1908 bringing the Boer war to an end, the question of the place of Africans in society was not even raised. From the inception of the independent nation of South Africa, political leadership was exercised for a single reason: to ensure the domination of Africans by Afrikaners. The Africans had no recourse except to hope that the new government would treat them humanely. They hoped against hope.

## THE NATURE OF POLITICAL LEADERSHIP

The first independent government of South Africa was formed in 1910 by General Louis Botha as prime minister following his victory in the national elections. Botha served until 1919. Out of a number of parties that contested the elections, the South African Party, of which Botha was leader, emerged with a majority of seats in Parliament. Botha adopted immediately a policy of reconciliation with the British, whom he felt had demonstrated goodwill and understanding toward the Boers. But the policy was bitterly opposed by Afrikaners in the Transvaal and the Orange Free State. The leader of Transvaal–Orange Free State opposition forces was J. Hertzog, who served as prime minister from 1924 to 1939. The elements of the political leadership of the future were slowly forming. In 1912, Hertzog had formed the Nationalist Party, which was destined to lead the country toward a disastrous racial policy of apartheid until its end in 1994.

Hertzog immediately attracted considerable support from Afrikaners, whose sense of nationalism and purpose called for the total elimination of Africans from the political process in the country. At that time the Boers believed that the British decision to grant them independence was a result of their ability to elevate themselves to a position of absolute political power sanctioned by the belief of their superiority. From its inception, the Nationalist Party envisaged South Africa as governed by Afrikaners without sharing political power with either English-speaking people or Africans. Africans were to be carefully trained to accept and fulfill their role as laborers. The Nationalist Party was committed to this end without any reservation. It remained committed until 1991 when F.

W. de Klerk, who became its leader in 1989, recognized the disastrous direction that apartheid was leading the country.

The outbreak of the war in 1914 placed Botha and Hertzog on opposite sides of the conflict. Botha announced in Parliament, one month after the outbreak of the war, that South Africa, as a part of the British Empire, was automatically at war with Germany. In 1915 Botha's forces invaded Namibia, a German colony, while J. C. Smuts (1870–1950) invaded Tanganyika, another German colony, in an effort to check the advance of the German forces in the African subcontinent. But Hertzog strongly opposed Botha's policy and the Botha-Smuts military activities against the Germans. Hertzog called on Afrikaners to join him in staging protests throughout the country against Botha's policy.[2] In the subsequent engagement, three generals were killed, making them the first Afrikaner martyrs since independence. This greatly boosted the political fortunes of the Nationalist Party and considerably improved the political ambitions and image of Hertzog himself.

The war was having serious political implications for Botha and his South African Party. People were divided throughout the country, and Afrikaner hostility toward the English-speaking community was increasing rapidly. Confidence in Botha's policies and in the future was sagging. Botha was clearly worried by the growing popularity and strength of the Nationalist Party, though Hertzog himself was known to be a man without charisma or ability to provide the effective leadership needed during this time of national crisis. Botha decided to call new elections in 1915. There were a number of important issues that had to be resolved such as the place of Africans in South Africa and the side South Africa should take in the war. Also, the economy was declining rapidly. The personality and leadership of these men became two major election campaign issues as each man accused the other of leading South Africa on a disastrous course.

The political differences between the two men reached a level of intense bitterness previously unknown to South Africa. Botha was totally surprised to learn that the Nationalist Party had received 77,000 votes out of a total of 95,000 ballots cast. However, Botha's South African Party won fifty-four seats in Parliament and so had the largest number of seats, but they failed to gain an absolute majority. Botha then negotiated with the Unionist Party, which had won forty seats, to form a coalition government, but he was forced to make concessions that in fact eroded the principles of his party, especially its efforts to develop friendlier relationships with Britain and to improve the status of the African people. Africans indeed became the victims of Afrikaner political grandstanding.

Meanwhile, Africans were alarmed by what was happening. In 1912, the same year that Hertzog formed the Nationalist Party, African leaders and rank and file met in Bloemfontein and founded the African National Congress (ANC), which was destined to confront and challenge the Afrikaner philosophy of racial superiority.[3] Until it was outlawed in 1960, the ANC represented African interests in an extremely oppressive society, as Afrikaners vowed that Africans would never be part of the political process. The ANC articulated the concerns and the aspirations of Africans in clearer terms than they had done in the past. The ANC also formulated an impressive list of goals and objectives, among them, to end oppression by the denial of equal opportunity in employment, education, and housing.

Other African organizations began to emerge during the first decade of South African independence, showing how critical the national climate was becoming with increasing hostility toward the developmental interests of Africans. For example, the African Workers Union was formed in 1919 to protect the economic interests of African workers who were exposed to physical hazards in the industrial plants where they were employed. Its leader, Clement Kadalie (1896–1951), originally from Malawi, demonstrated the brilliance of Africans by articulating positions intended to protect the interests of Africans. Kadalie was also an intelligent and courageous leader, an orator who swayed his audiences with the sharpness of his mind and wit and the logic of his speeches.

Kadalie warned Africans that harder times lay ahead for them because Afrikaners were going to deprive them systematically of any rights they might have, including the universal right to peaceful assembly. When Kadalie urged Africans to unite and fight for their rights, the Afrikaner government was considerably alarmed by his leadership abilities and so it placed him under constant surveillance, intimidating him with threats of arrest if he became too critical of government policies. Kadalie would have suddenly and quickly disappeared without the South African government having to explain what happened to him were it not for the concern expressed by organizations based outside South Africa.

The political fortunes of the South African Party and of Botha himself were steadily declining following the elections held in 1915. The coalition government had been totally unable to move forward and implement policies that would enable the country to move forward. This created an impression in the minds of the people that the coalition government was, in fact, incompetent to discharge its leadership duties. Between 1915 and 1919 Hertzog and J. C. Smuts generated a new Afrikaner hatred of Africans in the guise of politically responsible opposition. Thus, in its extreme political philosophy and policies, the Nationalist Party sowed the seeds of the politics of racial conflict that intensified with the passage of time.

That Africans were not allowed to participate in the electoral process added a tragic twist to an already deteriorating situation. Botha, unable to provide effective leadership and frustrated by the Hertzog-Smuts tactics, was bitterly disappointed to see the direction that his nation was taking. His declining political fortunes, combined with his declining health, reduced the South African Party to its lowest level of popularity among Afrikaner voters. Botha died in that same year, 1919, a bitterly disappointed man. For several months nobody seemed to emerge to exert leadership influence within the ranks of the South African Party. The only way to resolve the problem was to call new elections.

The major election issues of 1920 were South Africa's relationship with Britain and the place of Africans, just as these were major issues in the election of 1915. Botha had been unable to resolve these questions, and a new effort had to be made. Afrikaners wanted to see these issues resolved once and for all because they had paramount importance for the future of the country. Botha's inability to formulate a national policy intended to bring Africans into the mainstream of political activity invariably created a dangerous situation, a conflict of major proportions. The question of political leadership was leading South Africa toward a major national crisis.

## THE NATIONALIST PARTY, APARTHEID, AND POLITICAL LEADERSHIP

Botha's death did not simply translate into political gains by the Nationalist Party. To the surprise of everyone in South Africa, the election results of 1920 were almost the same as those of 1915. The South African Party won forty-one seats and the Nationalist Party won forty-four seats. Although Smuts became prime minister, his party was unable to form a government because it did not have an absolute majority. Smuts did not want to form a coalition government because he did not want to experience the same political difficulties that disabled Botha. So, another election was held in 1921 following a vigorous campaign which, surprisingly, was not marked by racial overtones or attacks on the relationship between South Africa and Britain. In that election the Nationalist Party won forty-five seats, but the South African Party gained twenty-two more seats than it had in the elections of 1915. Smuts was able to form a government without a coalition but had fewer seats than he would have liked.

The political instability that characterized South African development during its formative years continued until 1948. Between 1921 and 1948 there were developments, both local and international, that had a profound impact on South Africa itself. For example, in 1924 Hertzog and Smuts formed a coalition government with Hertzog as prime minister. Hertzog served as prime minister until 1939, when he was succeeded by

Smuts.[4] Smuts had serious difficulties in carrying out his programs; he was as disabled as Botha had been by political dissension. However, Smuts felt that a new leader might break the vicious political circle that Afrikaners had created for the country.

Once in the seat of power, Hertzog recognized the seriousness of the problems that the country was facing. He then began to move in the direction of closer and friendlier relationships with the English-speaking community in the country. The move displeased the vast majority of the Nationalist Party, and Hertzog was accused of selling party principles down the river. Some demanded his resignation. As a result of the confusion and wide differences of opinion that prevailed within the Nationalist Party, there was a split. The leader of the rebel group was Daniel F. Malan (1874–1959), an ordained minister in the Dutch Reformed Church[5] and an Afrikaner whose dedication to party principles and belief in Afrikaner providence as a select race were total and absolute.

Malan was a man deeply committed to the total separation of the races and who had little time for humor and no tolerance for those who held views different from his own. On Malan's shoulders rested the fate and the destiny of Afrikaners. Malan was visibly worried by the prospect of Africans demanding to be treated equally with white men. The conference of African leaders held in London in 1945 raised troubling questions for Malan as to the nature of racial relationships in the future. In 1939, war once again placed Afrikaners on opposite sides of the conflict. The Hertzog-Smuts coalition was broken. As soon as war broke out, Hertzog argued against South Africa supporting Britain. He further argued that Hitler was only reacting to the oppression of the Versailles Peace Treaty of 1919.

Seeing an opportunity to make the most political gains, Malan was quickly drawn into the controversy, taking Hertzog's side by arguing that Hitler was acting in self-defense. But Smuts saw Hitler's activities differently. He maintained that the Germans and Hitler were motivated by a desire to dominate the world. A crucial debate ensued in Parliament, with members divided on the question of South African involvement in that bloody world conflict. When Parliament voted 80–67 to support Britain in the war, Hertzog resigned in protest, frustrated by events and a set of circumstances beyond his control. However, Malan, though humiliated and defeated, would not take such a step, but this was not the last time that he would make his views known.

Hertzog's resignation created a leadership gap that would not be filled easily. Hendrik F. Verwoerd (1901–1966), prime minister of South Africa from 1958 to 1966, and a brilliant editor of *Die Transvaaler*, launched a vicious propaganda campaign in support of Hitler and the Nazi Party.[6] Smuts assumed the position of prime minister as soon as Hertzog resigned, but during that time the political controversy, coupled with economic and social problems, paralyzed his efforts to attend to pressing national problems. Because Afrikaners did not want to bring instability to South Africa during the war years, Smuts managed to stay in office until the end of the war, but his administration was unable to accomplish anything important.

On receiving the news of the death President Franklin D. Roosevelt (1882–1945) on April 12, 1945, Smuts introduced a motion in Parliament to send condolences to President Harry S. Truman (1884–1972). Malan and his Nationalist Party refused to support the motion because they argued that the action might establish a precedent and some day they would be asked to send condolences for Joseph Stalin (1879–1953), the Russian dictator from 1928 to 1953. It became increasingly evident that Malan was, indeed, the man to watch in the political utopia that Afrikaners were searching for.

The political feud between the Nationalist Party and the South African Party continued throughout the war years and into 1945. Neither party had been able to formulate a racial policy that could work. Both parties ruled out the possibility of allowing Africans to play a role in the political process of the country, although the South African Party was more sympathetic toward them. That was as far as it could go. At the end of the war, J. C. Smuts, prime minister from 1939 to 1948, represented South Africa at the U.N. conference in San Francisco, making him one of the few people who had also attended the Versailles Peace Conference following the end of World War I. Between 1939 and 1948, Smuts had not been able to provide the leadership that was needed to resolve the more pressing problems of the country. The war years appear to have had a profound effect on his racial views. He felt that South Africa could not advance politically, socially, and economically without Africans participating in a meaningful way in the affairs of the country.

Smuts was limited by political realities that, in fact, controlled his programs. Meanwhile the Malan-Verwoerd alliance was steadily becoming a powerful political factor. In 1948 South Africans once more went to the polls to elect a new parliament and government. The issues that had dominated the politics of the country were debated more intensely this time. Racial overtones had taken on a new and powerful dimension. Smuts and Malan held clearly differing views on the race issue. Smuts advocated better racial cooperation based on mutual respect. Malan held the exact opposite view. In this setting, a vicious election campaign ensued with each party accusing the other of pursuing dangerous policies.

When the election results were announced, the country and world were stunned to learn that the Nationalist Party had won, and that Daniel F. Malan, the rebel leader who opposed Hertzog's appointment of Smuts as deputy prime minister in the coalition government of 1939, had, indeed, become the new prime minister. The Nationalist Party remained in office until April 1994 when F. W. De Klerk was replaced by Nelson Mandela. Following the election results of 1948 the Nationalist Party and the Afrikaner Party, led by M. C. Havenga, formed a powerful coalition and announced that the racial policies pursued by the South African Party would be discontinued. Havenga and Verwoerd became the spokesmen for the new policy. Indeed, the Malan-Havenga political coalition exploited the political stalemate that had existed in the country since 1910 and promised that the Nationalists would be more aggressive in seeking to establish the supremacy of Afrikaners.

For the next forty-six years the Nationalist Party fortified itself as the only party that could ensure the supremacy of Afrikaners. The party was not aware that it represented a tragic dimension of the political system of South Africa under the Afrikaner philosophy. Even in the drama of party conflict in which de Klerk and members of ANC were engaged in 1990, Afrikaners hoped to pull a fast one. Until 1994 the Nationalist Party formulated and implemented its philosophy and policies designed solely to enshrine the majesty of Afrikaners and the myth of their racial superiority and the inferiority of Africans. Indeed, for Afrikaners the happy days of Paul Kruger were here again. The application of these policies created a level of racial bitterness rarely known in the world. Racial relationships were destroyed as Afrikaners saw Africans only in their assumed inferior position and Africans saw Afrikaners as perpetrators of unprecedented social injustice. The rancor and enmity that characterized human relationships in South Africa at that time can only be compared to those that exist in the Middle East, Northern Ireland, and in the southern United States during the height of the civil rights movement.

## THE SUPREMACY OF APARTHEID AS A FORM OF POLITICAL LEADERSHIP

The term "apartheid" (pronounced "apart-hate") is an Afrikaner word that means "separateness" or "apartness." But the Nationalist Party preferred to characterize the policy of apartheid as "separate development," so that it would acquire a positive overtone in the eyes of the outside world. But while they held the reins of power, Afrikaners and the Nationalist Party made no pretense of hiding the real intent of the policy. The first reference to apartheid as the racial policy of the future appeared on March 26, 1943, in Die Burger, a radical Nationalist Party newspaper. "Dawie," a pseudonym for an Afrikaner writer, strongly urged the South African government to formulate a policy that would keep the races completely apart. On January 25, 1944, Malan described his view of the future of South Africa by saying that a government policy must "ensure the safety of the white race by the honest maintenance of the principles of apartheid."[7] Indeed, in this manner Malan was putting together the pillars of the laager.

The Nationalist Party formulating its policy of apartheid appears to have been guided by the report of a commission that was appointed by Smuts in 1947, just before the general elections that resulted in his humiliating defeat in 1948. The Fagan Report, named after its chairman, Mr. Justice Fagan, had recommended that the influx of Africans into the urban areas must be curbed, that African labor must be regarded as migratory so that African workers would not qualify for any benefits or claim to possess any skills that would make them compete with white workers on an equal terms.[8] The Fagan Report also recommended that Africans who lived in urban areas be given limited rights because their permanent living quarters would be in areas called "Native Reserves."

This is the reason why in 1947 the Nationalist Party published a pamphlet that stated, "The policy of our country should encourage total apartheid as the ultimate goal of a natural process. It is the primary task and calling of the State to promote the happiness and well being of its citizens, realizing that such a task can best be accomplished by preserving and safeguarding the white race as the fundamental guiding principle of its policy."[9] To give effect to its principles and beliefs, the Nationalist Party began to enact a series of laws that made apartheid the cornerstone of the South African system of justice and political social order. For example, the Prohibition of Mixed Marriages Act of 1949 made it illegal for people of different racial groups to marry.

The Group Areas Act of 1950 prohibited Africans and so-called Coloreds from living in areas designated for whites. The Suppression of Communism Act of the same year empowered the government to arrest and detain indefinitely anyone suspected of activities promoting communism. The Natives Passes Act of 1952 required Africans to carry passes on their person at all times. The Bantu Education Act of 1953 established an education that prepared Africans for only menial services.

The Nationalist Party was so pleased with the success of the application of its apartheid policies that in 1951 Malan appointed the Tomlinson Commission, named after Professor F. R. Tomlinson, to investigate and recommend new ways of making apartheid even more effective.[10] The Tomlinson Commission published its report in 1954 and recommended extending apartheid policies beyond its present scope. Among other major recommendations of the Tomlinson report was that: 87 percent of the land should be reserved for exclusive occupation by whites and the remaining 13 percent for exclusive occupation by blacks. Africans in the so-called white areas must be moved to areas to be called Bantustan or Homeland areas scattered across the country. In white areas, blacks must regard themselves as laborers and servants who do not have any rights whatsoever.[11]

The Afrikaners and members of the Nationalist Party were far more pleased with the recommendations of the Tomlinson Commission than they were with those of the Fagan Commission. This is the reason why the Nationalist Party pushed through Parliament a series of legislative acts that was designed to implement those recommendations. Parliament amended the Bantu Authorities Act of 1951, repealed the Natives Representative Council Act of 1936, and created, instead, the new Bantu Authorities Act, which, in 1959, further strengthened the application of apartheid. Under these new laws the closing of the African world had become complete. Now, Afrikaners hoped, Africans would function and operate like robots, mechanical and artificial with no sense of purpose or direction. The Nationalist Party would be disappointed.

By the time that Malan retired from active politics in 1954, he could do so in complete and total confidence in the ability of Afrikaners to maintain their assumed superiority. Afrikaners also worked hard and tirelessly to fulfill their vision of themselves as undertaking a pilgrimage to eliminate Africans, whom they regarded as condemned heathens, from any role in the affairs of the country. Malan was succeeded by another hard-core Afrikaner segregationist, J. G. Strijdom, who served as prime minister from 1954 until his unexpected death in 1958. Soon after taking office Strijdom reassured Afrikaners that his administration would be guided by the principles and the philosophy that had shaped the character of the Malan administration. Said Strijdom, "Our policy is that the Europeans must remain boss. If the franchise is extended to non-Europeans, and if the non-Europeans are given representation and the vote and are developed on the same basis as the Europeans, how can the European remain the boss. Our view is that in every sphere of national life the European must retain the right to rule the country and keep it a white man's country."[12] Strijdom was strengthening the laager so that future leaders would find it possible to defend.

It became evident that Afrikaners had now begun to believe that the Nationalist Party had at last found a racial policy that would keep Africans in a perpetual condition of oppression. Hendrik Verwoerd, who succeeded Strijdom as prime minister and served from 1958 until his assassination in 1966, restated his dedication to the supremacy of apartheid when he said on January 25, 1963, "We want to keep South Africa white. If the white man should be able to continue to protect himself and retain white domination, we say that it can be achieved by apartheid."[13] During an election campaign speech on March 13, 1970, John B. Vorster (1915–1983), who served as prime minister from 1966 to 1978, was widely cheered when he said, "The South Africa is for whites only. That is how I see it, that is how you see it, and that is how you will see it for the future."[14] It is evident that Vorster remembered well what had been said nearly a century earlier in the Cape legislature during the height of Cecil John Rhodes' political power. Rhodes said with confidence, "The Native is to be treated as a child and denied the franchise. We must adopt the system of despotism in our relations with the barbarians of South Africa. These are my policies and these are the policies of South Africa."[15] Vorster even boasted that there was nothing in the past, and there would be nothing in the present and future, to prevent the Nationalist Party from assuming total control and leadership of not only South Africa and Namibia,[16] but also of the entire subcontinent of southern Africa itself in every sphere of life.

With the passage of time, members of the international community fully recognized that apartheid entrenched itself as the fearsome monster that increasingly threatened world peace and ruthlessly oppressed Africans. In 1967 Kenneth Kaunda, president of Zambia from 1964 to 1994, observed, "Apartheid is on the offensive. The old commando spirit in South Africa is being implemented to extend the boundaries of the influence of apartheid. The Boer trek is still on and is now instrumental to the wider concepts of neocolonialism, the pillars on which the minority regimes find their livelihood and derive their confidence."[17] Africans recognized that the laager was indeed strong. Was there anything they could do to storm it?

Together, the Nationalist Party and Afrikaners regarded apartheid as an obsession, a religion that guided their total and absolute domination and cruel imposition of slave conditions on Africans. For the African masses there was no break, no rest, no release from the grip of the timeless and brutal shackles that created what Charles Dickens called "the other way" and engulfed their existence, their whole being. Since its imposition, unofficially in 1652 and officially in 1910 and 1948, apartheid sought a systematic destruction of the fiber of African consciousness and the laying waste of the vital human resources that provide the human spirit with the will to survive.

Indeed, from sunrise to sunset, from the cradle to the grave, Africans were constantly reminded that they were a conquered and enslaved people. Every moment of their existence they must remember that they committed a serious crime when questioning the power of the white man. Paul Kruger (1925–1904), an uneducated but an uncompromising believer in the Boer myth of racial superiority, while he was at the height of his power as the popular and revered president of the Transvaal republic, constantly argued that the black people everywhere must be trained to fulfill tasks appropriate to their assumed inferior mind and social position. Kruger then stated his own political philosophy for Africans, saying, "The black man must be taught that he has an inferior mind and that he belonged to the inferior class which must obey and learn."[18]

Kruger's views provided the foundation on which Afrikaners later built the formidable prison house that apartheid became for Africans. Although they were bitter political enemies, Cecil John Rhodes and Paul Kruger had one philosophical belief in common, their dedication to treat Africans with despotism and absolute severity. Therefore, one is led to the conclusion that the foundations of apartheid were laid solidly years before the Nationalists came to power in 1948. But it is equally true that it was the Nationalists who built the fortress prison that apartheid became from 1948 to 1994. This is the reason why, in 1990, de Klerk was facing a serious national problem he did not seem to know how to resolve.

Louise Stack and Don Morton aptly described the extent of suffering black people were forced to endure everyday of their lives: "Africans suffer daily disaster, from homicide to humiliation, from land expropriation to grinding poverty, from brutal torture and imprisonment to relentless persecution. Family life is shattered, careers wrecked, education withheld, and life is a round-the-clock struggle for survival."[19] One wonders how Africans managed to maintain their sense of identity at all. In 1976 Stack and Morton also made an impressive list of specific examples of how apartheid was designed to seek systematic oppression of Africans. The following examples illustrate this fact. An inquest revealed that a young African man who died in police custody in September 1977, Steven Biko, had been tied up by his hands and feet and had been dropped on a hard floor and kicked in the stomach.[20] Nicodemus Shezi, a 25-year-old high ranking official of the Black People's Convention, told his mother just before he died that a white man had pushed him under a fast moving train. In the Orange Free State, a white farmer assaulted a colored entertainer because he failed to tell the difference between the terms "boss" and "sir." The entertainer had stopped to offer assistance to the white man in repairing a flat tire and had addressed him as "sir" instead of "boss."[21]

These examples show that apartheid indeed carried a lethal and venomous bite so deadly that no antidote, as Professor A. K. Matthews, a brilliant black ANC leader stated in 1952, except Africans themselves, was able to save the lives of its victims. To equate the Nationalists with venom is simply to understate the gravity and the magnitude of the effect of apartheid itself. For example, in the general elections held in April 1881, the Nationalist Party won 131 of the 165 seats in Parliament. Could one realistically expect Afrikaners to question the right of the Nationalist Party to rule the country as it saw fit? But in their collective deception, both the Nationalist Party and Afrikaners were leading themselves not to the promised land, but to the cave of their own political demise.

The election results of 1981 were the worst political setback the Nationalist Party had experienced since 1948. The reason for this setback was that then–prime minister, P. W. Botha (born in 1916), a life-long Nationalist Party member and Afrikaner, appeared to indicate a desire, motivated by what he perceived as dangers created by the rise of African political consciousness, to consider a policy of "adopt or die," which gave the appearance of a country facing increasing and dangerous opposition from both Africans themselves and the international community. By August 1981 Botha must have been aware that the interests of the Nationalist Party came before those of South Africa because he began to reassert the familiar Afrikaner philosophy that completely rejected the view that 20 million Africans, who constituted 72 percent of the population of South Africa, must be allowed to vote in elections. It is, therefore, a tragic fact that the Nationalist Party and Afrikaners inadvertently became the victims of the venomous serpent they had been breeding since 1948. Botha could not dare to infuriate the majesty of apartheid, indeed, the Dr. Jekyll and Mr. Hyde of South Africa. Was he suggesting that the laager was vulnerable to attack?

In August 1981, while Botha was reminding everyone of his "own ideas and pattern for leading South Africa"[22] under Afrikaner racial philosophy, apartheid once more delivered its deadly bite to Africans. As hundreds were huddled in a freezing slum after they were arbitrarily evicted from their decaying shanty homes in areas designated for whites near Cape Town, the police moved in and destroyed everything they possessed. The Africans were ordered to move into one of the ten so-called Bantustan homelands where grinding poverty and deprivation were the lot of the African masses who were crowded there.

The homelands constituted no more than 13 percent of the land in South Africa, yet they were expected to contain 20 million Africans. Many Africans moved to the crowded Bantustan homelands, but others refused to move and were immediately arrested and sent to detention camps where they joined hundreds of other Africans who dared to question the supremacy of apartheid. Botha also lashed out his anger at those he called "white liberals" who criticized apartheid as an evil enslavement of African masses. He also argued that such a criticism generated a sense of fear among the whites. Said Botha about the "liberals," "They are Satans walking about in white garb."[23]

That is the reaction one would expect from a fanatical leader who—all of his life—regarded apartheid as a religion. Botha was not likely to consider the Satans that swelled the ranks of the Nationalist Party since 1910 in their determination not to ease in the slightest the subjection of Africans. Any suggestion that questioned the absolute power of apartheid was immediately regarded as evil. What a tragic situation! When de Klerk succeeded Botha in 1987, there was dissension and disagreement within the ranks of the Nationalist Party over the question of how to make apartheid more effective. Like Mikhail Gorbachev, who tried to introduce glasnost and perestroika in the former Soviet Union from 1984 to 1992, de Klerk's efforts to strengthen apartheid led, not to its supremacy, but to its demise in 1994. This book traces the major events that led to the end of apartheid under de Klerk.

## AFRICANS RESPOND TO APARTHEID: PROVIDING AN ALTERNATIVE FORM OF POLITICAL LEADERSHIP

As soon as South Africa became independent, Africans began to organize an effective resistance. On January 8, 1912, African peasants, tribesmen, chiefs, farm and factory laborers, professionals, the affluent and the destitute, all assembled in Bloemfontein from all parts of the country to inaugurate the formation of the African National Congress, the oldest black political organization and liberation movement in all of Africa. This sudden development took place only three years after the formation in 1909 of the National Association for the Advancement of Colored People (NAACP) in the United States. The formation of the ANC was an ominous event for the Afrikaner-African relationships and an indication of things to come.

In 1913, one year after the formation of the ANC, the South African Parliament passed the Land Act, which stripped Africans of 87 percent of their land and placed it under white ownership. At that time Britain still claimed to retain the constitutional authority and power over any legislation that, in the opinion of the British government officials, violated the rights of Africans. Although Britain recognized that the new law violated the rights of Africans, it failed to take any action to protect or restore those rights. The ANC sent a high-level delegation to Britain in 1915 to petition British protection against the laws that violated the rights of Africans.

The ANC delegation requested that the British government, led by Herbert H. Asquith (1852–1928), prime minister from 1908 to 1916, intervene on behalf of Africans. The inaction of the British government greatly boosted the determination of Afrikaners to deprive Africans of any land and other forms of rights. Afrikaners saw the refusal as a license to do as they pleased. But the delegation returned to South Africa more aware of themselves as a people and more determined to do something for themselves to ease their oppression. Immediately, Africans organized massive demonstrations that led to serious confrontations with the police. Many Africans were injured and many more were sent to prison. But this was not the last time that Afrikaners clashed with Africans.

In 1919, recognizing the brutality of the South African regime, the ANC strongly protested at the Versailles Peace Conference against the League of Nations' decision to allow South Africa to administer Namibia as a mandatory territory. The ANC tried in vain to convince the League that South Africa had no intention of honoring its "sacred trust of civilization" both in Namibia and South Africa, and that, instead, it sought to annex Namibia as its fifth province. Unfortunately it took the world community seventy years to recognize that fact. More tragic still, in 1946 the U.N. did not listen to the protests and views expressed by Africans regarding the real motives that pushed South Africa to behave the way that it did with respect to the position of Africans.

In 1926 the South African Parliament passed the Color Bar Act, which made it illegal for Africans to perform skilled jobs in the mining industry. This law was the result of the Mines and Works Act of 1911, which gave the government power to control the number of Africans applying for certificates of competency to perform some skilled jobs that were the exclusive right of the whites. But when the government tried to enforce the law in 1923, the courts ruled it unconstitutional, forcing the government to amend it in 1926. Africans once more organized mass demonstrations against the application of that law, which they believed stripped them of their livelihood. But the government responded with more suppressive force by amending the Color Bar Act in 1956 to give itself absolute power to deny Africans an opportunity to engage in meaningful employment.

In 1943 the ANC designed a new strategy in their steadily increasing confrontation with apartheid. It formed the Youth League, which immediately adopted a set of resolutions stating that conferences, petitions, and delegations were methods of the past. The Youth League also called on African masses to initiate extensive programs of strikes, boycotts, and civil disobedience. This resolution was approved and accepted in December 1949 by the ANC itself as part of its new program of action. The new policy was to be implemented in May 1950 following a massive campaign to educate African masses about their oppression under the supremacy of apartheid. At the beginning of the strike, more than 60 percent of African workers stayed away from their work. But the police went on a rampage of terror, killing some, injuring many more and arresting hundreds. The ANC proclaimed June 26, 1950, as a day of mourning, but the struggle between Africans and apartheid intensified with the passage of time.

Two years later, on June 26, 1952, Africans inaugurated another resistance strategy known as the Defiance of Unjust Laws Campaign. ANC officials and leading Africans went into many areas that apartheid reserved for whites as part of that defiance campaign. The South African regime issued a ban prohibiting Africans from organizing public meetings to protest against apartheid. When Africans ignored the ban, the police arrested thousands of them. During the disturbances the police opened fire indiscriminately on groups of African demonstrators and began a thorough search of suspected leaders. Homes, churches, and streets all became a hunting ground for the police. There was no sanctuary; there was no place to hide; the deadly tentacles of the vicious octopus of apartheid reached every place where Africans were. Apartheid was on a rampage of terror grabbing and destroying everything in its path.

The most serious confrontation at that point in the struggle between Africans and apartheid came in February 1955. Nearly 60,000 African parents kept their children home from school in protest against the Bantu Education Act of 1953. African parents had recognized that under that law African students were being provided with an education that only prepared them for servitude. Thousands of policemen moved in with weapons and forced the parents to let their children go to school. According to the provisions of the Bantu Education Act, African students were to be taught the vernaculars. Their curriculum was quite different from the one provided to the white students. Funds for African schools had been drastically cut so that there was very little equipment in the schools.

Because African parents refused to let their children go to school under these provisions, a serious confrontation ensued and the police killed many and arrested hundreds. On June 26, 1955, Africans from all parts of South Africa assembled at Klipton and adopted the famous Freedom Charter,[24] whose preamble, "We, the People,"[25] resembles that of the U.S. Declaration of Independence. The Freedom Charter was one of the best documents that Africans of South Africa ever produced. It was a scholarly, well-articulated document that demonstrated an incredibly high level of intellectual capacity. The Charter stated that South Africa belonged to all people, not just whites. It also called for an immediate end to the racism and despotism that were embraced by the Nationalist government. The Charter called for equal rights in the political and socio-economic development of the country and demanded that the people be allowed to govern as was the case in democratic societies. The Charter demanded that the land be shared equally among all people and that all people be equal before the law.

The Charter ended by warning that the African people would fight and put their lives on the line until these fundamental freedoms were achieved by all people of South Africa. It is evident that Strijdom and his administration were alarmed by the determination of Africans to fight against apartheid, and they took extremely oppressive measures to ensure that there was no outbreak of violence as a result of the Klipton conference and the excitement that came with the Freedom Charter. The arrest of the people who were charged in 1956 with high treason was in part the regime's reaction to the Freedom Charter. Within a few days, police reinforcements were quickly dispatched to centers that were regarded as possible areas where political violence would easily break out. With this action the government created one of the worst police states in the world in order to sustain apartheid. But there was a heavy price to be paid.

The brutality with which the South African government suppressed Africans was now a matter of serious concern, not only among Africans themselves, but among South Africans of all races. Moderate whites began to question the legitimacy of the government and the supremacy of apartheid. People from various ethnic backgrounds came together in an effort to express their unhappiness with both the apartheid laws and the methods of suppression that were being used against Africans. Because Strijdom believed that a conspiracy of major proportions was about to take place against his government, on the night of December 4, 1956, without warning, the South African regime began a mass arrest of people of all races, both men and women, professionals and laborers, all over the country. These 156 people were charged with high treason, which was punishable by death. The arrested people included medical doctors, university professors, journalists, lawyers, teachers, clergymen, and politicians.

On February 3, 1960, Harold Macmillan (1894–1986), the British prime minister from 1957 to 1963, made a speech in the South African Parliament while on an extensive tour of Africa. Macmillan said that the winds of change were blowing over all of Africa and that national policies must take African nationalism into account. Macmillan warned the colonial regimes in Africa that unless they made changes to accommodate African aspirations, there would be serious confrontation between the colonial forces and the African masses. The South African regime, now led by Hendrik Verwoerd, angrily accused Macmillan of indirectly supporting African insurrection. A little over one month after Macmillan's speech, South Africa created a black page in its history. On March 21, 1960, a large crowd of Africans gathered at Sharpeville to demonstrate against apartheid in general and the *passbook* (a form of identity Africans must carry on their persons) in particular. Believing that the demonstrators were about to attack the laager, Verwoerd ordered the police to prevent it. They opened fire, killing nearly seventy people and wounding many more. Most of the victims were shot in the back, many of them women and children. The Sharpeville massacre triggered a wave of protests from all over the world, but the South African regime demonstrated that it did not care and ignored the protests.

The government even went a step further. Two days after the massacre, it proclaimed a state of emergency and arrested over 20,000 Africans and banned the ANC and the Pan African Congress (PAC),[26] both of which had provided the leadership that Africans needed for an effective opposition to apartheid. Thousands of protesters demonstrated across the country, but the regime adopted even more ruthless methods of suppressing Africans. For now the laager was safe. On September 6, 1966, many ANC leaders decided either to go underground or leave the country to organize full-scale guerrilla warfare against the government.

The struggle between Africans and the forces of apartheid, therefore, took on a new and dangerous dimension, but Africans felt they had no choice. The relationships between South Africa and members of the British Commonwealth were deteriorating rapidly. Increasing pressure was being placed on Verwoerd to change the apartheid policy, but Verwoerd, like any other hard-core Afrikaner segregationist, was unwilling to tamper with an absolute supreme institution that he worshipped with the devotion of a saint. On March 31, 1961, Verwoerd, instead of giving way to international pressure to end apartheid, pulled South Africa from the Commonwealth and proclaimed it an Afrikaner republic, just as Paul Kruger had done nearly eighty years earlier. This was his way of defending the laager.

But, as if to prove Macmillan right, in April 1960, a white farmer shot Verwoerd in the head. Somehow Verwoerd recovered, reinforcing his deep religious conviction in the supremacy of apartheid. However, on September 6, 1966, while he was preparing to deliver a speech in Parliament following the Nationalist's resounding victory in the elections of that year, Verwoerd was assassinated by Demitrio Tsafendas, a white Parliamentary messenger of Greek origin who was disillusioned with Nationalist Party policies. The laager was under attack. Verwoerd was succeeded by another hard-core supremacist and segregationist, John B. Vorster. Vorster, a life-long Nationalist, was regarded by many as far more extreme in his views of Africans than Verwoerd. The election of Vorster as the Nationalist Party leader signaled a new twist in the struggle between Africans and apartheid. Vorster wielded a high hand as soon as he took office until he resigned in 1978 disgraced by a serious scandal involving his close aides. His successor, the emotional Pieter W. Botha who appeared to behave like Roy Welensky in the Federation of Rhodesia and Nyasaland, faired no better in seeking solutions to the problems apartheid had created for South Africa.

The most serious confrontation between Africans and Vorster's administration came in June 1976, ten years after the death of Verwoerd. In 1974 the South African regime ordered 256 black schools with a total enrollment of 200,000 students to teach those students in Afrikaans. It would appear that the regime had changed at will its own law, such as the Bantu Education Act of 1953, which stipulated that African students must learn only in the medium of the vernaculars. In 1974, African parents and the students were strongly opposed to the new government demand for students to study in Afrikaans because they saw Afrikaans as the most visible symbol of their oppression and an instrument of fortifying the laager. In addition to this, Afrikaans was a local dialect and Africans felt that learning it would seriously handicap their ability to communicate with the rest of the world.

During the next two years, Africans organized a massive resistance to the new policy and mass demonstrations against apartheid itself became commonplace throughout the country. While the new education policy was the major target of these demonstrations, they were ultimately aimed at the pillars of apartheid themselves. The South African government appeared to panic over these demonstrations and tension between the two sides rose rapidly. Suddenly in June 1976, the worst violence South Africa had ever seen exploded all over the country. Over a thousand Africans lost their lives in the pandemonium that followed, and many more were wounded. Thousands more were arrested. But that was not the end of the struggle. Soweto, a sprawling and decaying black ghetto outside Johannesburg, was the worst hit.

Schools were closed, and gangs of black youth went on a rampage of uncontrollable anger destroying anything in sight and attacking any white motorists who drove through the ghetto. Cars were set on fire with their occupants inside; buildings and other forms of property were subjected to uncontrollable violence. For days violence converted Soweto into a towering inferno. From sunrise to sunset, throughout the night, Soweto had indeed become hell with Lucifer commanding his forces to lay waste to everything that was in their path. The innocent, the guilty, the old, the young, men and women—all became victims of a carnage that seemed to have no end. For days the burning, the looting, the destruction, and the smoke descended upon Soweto with a brutal vengeance and wrath comparable only to the destruction of Hiroshima and Nagasaki. The black youth matched the senseless brutality of apartheid and created a turmoil rarely known in the course of human relationships. Indeed, Soweto had become the international symbol of human decay, and apartheid had done it all. However, it also became the fountain of inspiration that Africans needed to fortify their willpower to storm the laager.

In August 1981, an African in Soweto, where the bitterness and physical and psychological scars have permanently remained the order of things, reflected on the violence that destroyed his ghetto in 1976. He spoke with determination when he said Africans would fight on to end all forms of oppression. Said the man, "It is a matter of time before we get organized. We talk about it together every day. Revolution is in the making in South Africa."[27] On February 18, 1983, a bomb exploded in a provincial government office building in Bloemfontein, injuring seventy-six people, eighteen of them very seriously. All of them were black. How long would the laager withstand this attack?

Many people in South Africa suspected the South African government itself in the Bloemfontein explosion. During the next four years no part of South Africa was safe as bomb explosions became as routine as the midafternoon cup of tea. During the day, during the night, both black and white were subject to instant death. The home, the street, the office, the bus, the train, the movie house—all became targets of the ire of a scorned people. Ordinary national business was slowly grinding to a halt. Travel anywhere in the country was becoming increasingly dangerous. No place, rural or city, was safe from a surprise attack. The economic activity of the country, crippled by the economic sanctions imposed by the international community, was declining rapidly. As South Africa was traveling on a dead-end street, a political sunset, the cracks that appeared on the laager became wider. This is the situation that forced de Klerk to call a truce and decide to hold negotiations with the ANC in an effort to resolve the problems apartheid created over many years. It was the eleventh hour for Afrikaners and the dawn of a new era for Africans.

## THE EFFECT OF APARTHEID: TRAINING AFRICANS FOR MENIAL POSITIONS

By the time South Africa achieved independence in 1910 apartheid had been well established. From 1910 to 1922, the provinces financed the education of Africans and designed and implemented their own policies without regard to the national government. But provincial control of education was not destined to last indefinitely because the central government soon decided that it wanted to control African education itself. In 1922 the South African government suddenly ended the provincial responsibility for education and assumed it directly.

The central government saw financial resources as the major weapon with which it would strike a blow at African political development. The government also gave itself unlimited power to design educational policies for Africans that were consistent with its philosophy of Afrikaner political superiority and intellectual inferiority of the African mind. Although the policies of the South African Party—led by J. C. Smuts from 1919 to 1924 and from 1939 to 1948—were less oppressive than those adopted by the Nationalist Party, the adoption of a policy of limited educational opportunity for Africans by the Smuts government laid a solid foundation for the perfection of policies that stripped Africans of a viable education under the Nationalists and the supremacy of apartheid. From all dimensions the laager was strengthening itself.

In 1922 the central government set aside some R680,000 (about 340,000 pounds sterling) for the support of African education. This figure was to become a fixed annual amount and was not to exceed 10 percent of the amount set aside for white education. This figure was so small that it did not enable African education to develop at a reasonable rate of speed. Africans desperately needed better and more education. By limiting the financial support of African education to this small percentage, the stagnation of African education became a reality. This is exactly what the South African government wanted. By 1925, only three years after the government assumed direct control of education for Africans, there was such a staggering stagnation and deterioration that the government decided to increase the proportion of the poll tax paid by Africans in order to save face in its deliberate policy of reducing educational opportunity for Africans.

In 1945, again under Smuts,[28] the government decided to introduce a new clause to its disabling policy toward African education. Recognizing that Africans were making great sacrifices to pay the tax to secure an education for their children, the central government announced that the financial support it gave to African education would no longer depend on the proportion that Africans paid, but on funds drawn from the general revenue. This meant that the government was at liberty to further cut the funds it allocated for the education of African students. The Smuts administration took political realities into consideration in formulating this latest policy.

There was an increasing fear among Africans that the government regarded their education as a threat to its political supremacy because education would place in the African mind "ideas beyond their station"[29] and make them unfit for manual labor. The condition of servitude and the performing of manual labor was the only role education was expected to enable Africans to play. There was no doubt that the government wanted to see education prepare Africans for just that role. Hilda Bernstein observed, education for Africans was designed "to create bondage out of racial setting."[30] Indeed, education for Africans was "the only education system in the world designed to restrict the productivity of its pupils to lowly and subservient tasks and to fix them to a tribal world."[31]

The universal objective of education as a channel to full human development and to utilize resources for the benefit of all, the fulfillment of fundamental human freedoms, the enrichment of cultural refinements, and the development of professional skills and competencies, coupled with civic and social responsibility, were totally incompatible with the narrow educational philosophy espoused by Afrikaners. This is the reason why, in 1953, Hendrik Verwoerd, then minister of Bantu Affairs, which was responsible for African education, was quite candid in explaining the policy of his government toward the education of Africans, stating, "Native education should be controlled in such a way that it should be in accord with the policy of the state. If the native is being taught to expect that he will have his adult life under a policy of equal rights, he is making a big mistake. The native who attends school will know that he is the laborer in the country."[32] Verwoerd believed that this policy was one of the most effective means of defending the laager. However he was not aware that it could not be defended forever.

The results of implementing this policy were tragic for South Africa. By 1971, two of every three African students had less than five years of education. For fiscal year 1969–1970 the government spent R3,900,000 on African education. This figure was less than 0.4 percent of the GNP of that year. In the same year the government spent 4.1 percent of the GNP for white education in spite of the fact that the number of white students constituted less than 25 percent of the total student population. In the final analysis, the intended purpose of limiting the development of the African mind heavily impeded the ability of the country to do what other societies have tried to do: generate a pool of sufficiently educated human resources and be placed at the disposal of the country. It was not Africans who paid the ultimate price, but Afrikaners themselves.

The Nationalist administrations, from that of Luis Botha to that of Pieter Botha, have persistently denied Africans equal educational opportunity in many other ways. For example, under the terms of the Bantu Education Act, evening classes were prohibited. Adults, workers, laborers, and domestic servants eager for education were denied an opportunity to secure the education they had missed earlier in life through the stress of circumstances. In 1959, a retired African teacher gathered a number of African students and brought them into his house and taught them the skills they needed to survive in South African society. Neither the teacher nor his students knew the full implication of their action in seeking education outside the control of the Nationalist government. The teacher was arrested, tried, convicted and fined R150 with a suspended prison sentence. The white magistrate stated, "You are a learned and respected man in the community, yet you keep defying the law."[33]

The three months from June to August 1967, may very well go down as the darkest period in South Africa's history since the Sharpeville massacre of 1960. During that period, thousands of black students boycotted classes and clashed with police. The students were protesting the limited educational opportunity that was available to them. As usual the police opened fire, killing many and wounding more. Hundreds were arrested and banned from any education process for the rest of their lives. In 1974 the government again announced changes in its educational policy with the overall effect of reducing the educational opportunity for Africans.

Among the changes that were announced was the requirement to teach African students in Afrikaans and to use textbooks that were produced by the order of the government stating, "The practice of the government is to continue to deny fundamental human rights to blacks. In so doing it has dealt a severe blow to the philosophy of non-violence as a viable formula for change."[34] When the South African regime declined these proposals, violence once more broke out and quickly spread to other centers. In 1978 the damage to property was estimated at $8 million, but the damage to human life was incalculable. In 1978 one black student observed, "No one is now pretending that our complaint is only against the teaching of Afrikaans in our schools, as it was in 1976. Our complaint is against the whole system."[35] In 1980 Adam Small, writing for *Time*, seemed to agree when he stated, "People are in limbo, they don't care anymore. Their children are bitter and ready for violence. Like the sand of the Cape flats, apartheid lies beneath it all."[36] For now the laager was safe.

The racial bitterness and hatred that has characterized the relationships between Afrikaners and Africans was simmering with the power of a nuclear force. The vengeance and rancor that became the major motivating factors were once more resurfacing with forceful power. In November 1980 the South African regime, recognizing the error of its ways, but never admitting it, suddenly announced a new education policy for Africans. Beginning with the new academic year in 1981, some form of compulsory education would be introduced for the black students in six black townships. Ferdinand Hartzenberg, the Minister of Education, did not address the painful issues that had for years caused racial bitterness and hatred in South Africa.

Hartzenberg neglected to give details of the plan and how it would be implemented. He also neglected to mention that in 1980 the government spent $800 to educate a white student and less than $100 to educate a black student. Further, since the Soweto riots of 1976 and 1978, the government closed eighty black schools, banning hundreds of black students from ever attending school again. In the same year it was estimated that 65 percent of the black workers lacked formal education and that they were paid starvation wages for their labor.[37] This is exactly what the Nationalist Party wanted, educating Africans for perpetual servitude. It is evident that the compulsory education introduced in 1981 was intended to promote that objective. Where South Africa would find the financial resources to make compulsory education work well was not clear. Africans, therefore, dismissed Hartzenberg's announcement as a political hoax. Instead, everything pointed to a prolonged racial struggle.

## SUMMARY AND CONCLUSION

There is no doubt that the racial confrontation that apartheid had created over many years was destined to intensify with the passage of time. This situation actually led to one thing—a major racial war such as the one that occurred in Zimbabwe from 1966 to 1979. Apartheid was a cancer that destroyed the delicate tissue of the South African vitality, human resources without which no nation can prosper. Even Brian Nel, a Herstige Nationale Party organizer, seemed to agree when he said ironically in 1980, "The cancer is spreading and is going to follow you wherever you go."[38] In the determination of the Afrikaner to sustain apartheid at all costs and in the determination of the oppressed Africans to rise and envisage the restoration of their rights, lay the seeds of the destruction and the tragedy of the South African system. The world community exercised its moral duty to help Afrikaners see the tragic course they had charted for the country. Because apartheid extended beyond the boundaries of South Africa, it must therefore be viewed from a global perspective. In apartheid's oppression of the black masses of South Africa, humanity as a whole is inescapably enslaved.

This is the reason, speaking on October 14, 1981, at the University of the Witwatersrand in Johannesburg, Alan Pifer, president of the Carnegie Foundation, attempted to put the South African situation into global perspective when he said, "With the advent of the Carter administration in 1976, representatives of non government groups achieved powerful positions in government, and the official policy of our government toward [South Africa] became distinctly hostile. The sustained protests by faculty and students on [United States] college and university campuses against institutional investment in American corporations doing business in South Africa [were] presented at annual shareholder meetings."[39]

In January 1982, nearly 50 percent of the black students who took their high school examinations at the end of 1981 were told that they had failed. Even those who had passed the examination had done so with such poor grades that they were told they could not qualify for college entrance. By contrast, more than 90 percent of the white students in the Johannesburg area were told that they had passed the examinations so well that they were assured of a place in the college of their choice. *The Sowetan*, the only daily newspaper for blacks, stated angrily in an editorial, "We are disgusted about the whole business. Our frustration is slowly turning to livid anger at the damage the education system is doing to our children."[40]

Africans all over South Africa recognized that the oppression to which apartheid subjected them had no limits. Thomas Manthata, a former teacher reacted, "The idea is to frustrate the black students and the black nation."[41] In 1982, the South African government planned to spend about $1,075 per white student and only $114 per black student. Because the government continuously harassed black teachers, many of them left teaching—as if to suggest that their conditions of employment elsewhere would be better—and so deprived the schools of nearly 85 percent of the trained teachers needed; the government could not care less.

Apartheid forced black teachers and students to lose morale, for there is incredible futility in providing black students with an education that is designed to make them more effective slaves within the South African system. The view is that education for blacks in South Africa is being perverted to create absolute conditions for servitude. This is the condition that has invoked in the African mind a call to action to restore itself. There is no question that South Africa was in a state of decay under apartheid. Blacks will continue their struggle for freedom, and their search for education will also continue. On March 18, 1980, Bishop Desmond Tutu delivered a speech at Witwatersrand University inviting white students to join blacks in the struggle to save South Africa from a disastrous course. Bishop Tutu said, "You will never be free until we blacks are free. So, join the liberation struggle. Work for a better South Africa, for yourselves, and for our children."[42]

The discussion in this chapter leads to a simple conclusion, and that is, from its inception, apartheid presented a choice before white South Africa: to accept Tutu's invitation or continue to allow Afrikaners to manipulate and mislead them, and thus, drag the country toward a national disaster in which the consequences would affect the country in profound ways for generations to come. The tragedy of apartheid is that it betrayed and inflicted damage to Africans in two ways. The first way was the blunt manner in which it systematically robbed them of their legitimate rights. The second way was the senseless conflict and killing that took place between the supporters of the ANC and those of Inkatha Freedom Party since 1990. In 1991 it was disclosed that de Klerk and his administration made secret payments to Inkatha to wage a campaign of violence against the ANC and its supporters. Where did de Klerk think this action would lead South Africa? Would that make the laager safe for the future? This book examines the dynamics of human relationships that emerged in South Africa under de Klerk's leadership.

## NOTES

1. The laager is an Afrikaans name that means a circle of wagons. In 1838 Afrikaners were in a migration known as the trek to escape British rule at the Cape. As they moved north they intruded into the land of the hostile Zulu. The Afrikaners formed the laager to defend themselves. The laager came to symbolize the Afrikaner determination to withstand adversity. The term acquired metaphorical meaning over the years. This is the meaning used in this book.

2. *The New Republic*, May 2, 1981, p. 17.

3. Nelson R. Mandela, *Long Walk to Freedom: The Autobiography of Nelson Mandela* (Boston: Little, Brown and Company, 1994), p. 148.

4. Smuts served twice as prime minister, from 1919 to 1924, and from 1939 to 1948. Other leaders of South Africa were: D. F. Malan, 1948–1954; J. G. Strijdom, 1954–1958; Hendrik Verwoerd, 1958–1966; John B. Vorster, 1966–1978;

P. W. Botha, 1978–1989; and F. W. de Klerk, 1989–1994. De Klerk was succeeded by Nelson Mandela.

5. Mandela, *Long Walk to Freedom*, p. 96.

6. *The New Republic*, May 2, 1981, p. 18. During an interview in March, 1981, President Ronald Reagan rhetorically asked, "Can we abandon the country (South Africa) that has stood beside us in every war we have fought?" It was not clear whether the president was basing his apparent support of South Africa on actual historical fact or whether he was merely attempting to justify the policy of his administration toward the policy of apartheid.

7. Brian Bunting, "Origins of Apartheid," in *Apartheid: A Collection of Writings on South African Racism by South Africans*, ed. Alex La Guma (New York: International Publishers, 1971), p. 24.

8. Leo Marquard, *The Peoples and Policies of South Africa*. (London: Oxford University Press, 1969), p. 161.

9. Bunting, "Origins of Apartheid," p. 25.

10. Marquard, *The People and Polices of South Africa*, p. 37.

11. Ibid., p. 38.

12. Bunting, "Origins of Apartheid," p. 29.

13. Ibid., p. 25.

14. Ibid., p. 30.

15. Bunting quoted in La Guma, *Apartheid*, p. 13.

16. Namibia achieved independence in 1990 after seventy years of control by South Africa.

17. Bunting quoted in La Guma, *Apartheid*, p. 40.

18. Ibid., p. 35.

19. Louise Stack and Donald Morton, *Torment to Triumph in Southern Africa* (New York: Friendship Press, 1976), p. 18.

20. The most celebrated case of police brutality in South Africa was in 1977 when Steve Biko, founder of the Black Consciousness Movement, was murdered by police, raising a storm of protests from the international community. It took the leaders of South Africa another thirteen years to recognize the tragedy of their racial policy.

21. Stack and Morton, *Torment to Triumph in Southern Africa*, p. 50.

22. *Time*, August 17, 1981, p. 45.

23. Ibid.

24. For the full text of The Freedom Charter, see, for example, Dickson A. Mungazi, *The Struggle for Social Change in Southern Africa: Visions of Liberty* (New York: Taylor and Francis, 1989), p. 110.

25. Freedom Charter of South Africa, June 26, 1955.

26. *New York Times*, August 2, 1981, p. 11.

27. Ibid., p. 4.

28. Smuts was Prime Minister of South Africa twice, from 1919 to 1924 and from 1939 to 1948, the year he was defeated by Daniel Malan. During the last two years, Botha assumed the title of state president. This is the title that de Klerk took when he assumed office in 1985. (See note 4 above for a list of other prime ministers.)

29. Marquard, *The Peoples and Policies of South Africa*, p. 201.

30. Hilda Bernstein, "Schools for Servitude," in *Apartheid: A Collection of Writ-*

*ings on South African Racism by South Africans*, ed. Alex La Guma (New York: International Publishers, 1971), p. 43.

31. Ibid., p. 44.

32. Ibid., p. 46.

33. Ibid., p. 75.

34. *Lincoln Evening Journal* (Lincoln, Nebraska), August 23, 1976, p. 1.

35. *Time*, June 30, 1980, p. 31.

36. *New York Times*, December 12, 1980, p. 11.

37. Ibid., p. 31.

38. Ibid., p. 11.

39. Alan Pifer, *South Africa in the American Mind*, Commemoration Day Lecture at the University of Witwatersrand, Johannesburg, October 14, 1981. New York: Carnegie Foundation, p. 6.

40. *Christian Science Monitor*, July 14, 1982.

41. Ibid.

42. Desmond Tutu, *Crying in the Wilderness: The Struggle for Justice in South Africa* (Grand Rapids, MI: William B. Eerdmans Publishing Company, 1982), p. 43.

# 2

# Origins of the Laager:
# Ian D. Smith in the Context
# of Political Leadership in
# Colonial Zimbabwe

> The foundations of all good living are built on man's relationships
> with his fellow men. This requires effective leadership on the part of
> the government.
>
> Reverend Kennedy Grant, 1947

## THE RUDD CONCESSION AND
## THE COLONIZATION OF ZIMBABWE

The myth that began to emerge among Europeans during the Enlighten-
ment that Africans were intellectually inferior provided a justification for
the colonial adventure in Africa in the nineteenth century.[1] British colonization of Zimbabwe was carried out in accordance with the specifications
of the Berlin Conference of 1884–1885. No consideration was given to the
opposition of Africans to the intrusion of their society and culture because,
as William McIntyre concluded, they were considered "incapable of formulating opinions and to define positions consistent with the application
of human logic on important issues."[2] Ability to articulate opinions on issues was considered to require a demonstration of highly developed intellectual skills. This is exactly the reason why, throughout the colonial
period, Africans remained nothing more than what Kenneth Knorr identified as "a commodity or raw materials to be employed in the service of
the white man."[3] The architect of British colonial adventure and policy in
Zimbabwe was none other than Cecil John Rhodes (1853–1902) himself.[4]
The fortification and defense of the laager rested on his shoulders.

Indeed, Rhodes became both a product and an agent of Victorian thinking toward Africans and British objectives in Africa. In the process he became the vehicle by which the British government, including Queen Victoria herself (1837–1901), sought to fulfill their grand objective of bringing British civilization to what they believed to be the heathen and barbaric races of Africa. They believed that they had a mission to build and defend the laager in Africa. Until his death Rhodes exercised political leadership in southern Africa on behalf of the British government in a way that had not been done previously in the British empire. The exploits of Oliver Cromwell (1599–1658) and Horatio Nelson (1758–1805) were no match for those of Rhodes, the most successful of the British entrepreneurs. This was his way of building the British laager in the rapidly expanding empire throughout the world. But in his desire to attain this objective and in his self-appointed mission to salvage Africans from the presumed condemnation of their equally presumed primitive culture, Rhodes launched an invasion of the African society that left a legacy of racial bitterness. This in turn led to the collision of the two cultures much sooner after colonization than he and the British government had anticipated. In his efforts to build the laager that he believed would last a thousand years, Rhodes inadvertently provided the Africans with the weapons they needed to storm it.

The specific occasion which shows Rhodes to be the mastermind of the British objective of establishing a colony in Zimbabwe as the first stage of establishing a colonial empire all over Africa came in 1888 as a result of his own schemes. In that year Rhodes commissioned a party of men, led by Charles Rudd (1844–1916), presumably to negotiate with King Khumalo Lobengula (1836–1894) to allow British fortune hunters to prospect and dig for gold in his land for a limited period of time.[5] In return Rhodes promised to offer Lobengula security and delivery of a thousand rifles which the king needed for defense purposes. Rhodes also promised to pay Lobengula a hundred pounds sterling per month in fees for twelve months. King Lobengula, who had ascended the Ndebele throne in 1870, the year that Rhodes arrived in South Africa and following the death of King Mzilikazi (1792–1868), was extremely suspicious of the white man's ultimate intentions in his land.

Besides Rudd, who was a partner of Rhodes' in the diamond diggings at Kimberly, the party included Rochfort Maguire (1855–1925), a leading proponent of the British Empire in Africa, and Robert Thompson (1857–1927), a one-time secretary to Rhodes. Rev. Charles Helm (1834–1915), who was born in South Africa and who went to Lobengula's country in 1875 in the service of the London Missionary Society, had studied African culture, including language, well enough to be recognized by the whites as an expert on African culture in general. This is the reason why King Lobengula took Helm into his confidence and appointed him official interpreter and adviser on all matters relating to his dealings with the white man. Indeed, King Lobengula thought that Helm was a good and honest Christian gentleman who would not deceive him or allow the white man to take advantage of him in any way.

Lobengula was bitterly disappointed to discover that Helm, the Christian missionary he trusted so much, actually betrayed him. However, because Helm was not an official member of the Rudd team, he enjoyed the trust of both sides. Although Helm seemed genuinely interested in the welfare of Africans, Lobengula did not know that at the same time he was secretly paid by Rhodes to provide information used to facilitate the colonization of Zimbabwe in accordance with the provisions of the Royal Charter that Rhodes received from Queen Victoria in 1889. In their respective ways both the Queen and Helm contributed materials to the building of the British laager.

As the negotiations between the two sides progressed, the Rudd party found Lobengula to be a shrewd leader and politician, a highly intelligent man who understood the implications of the deliberations. His ability to articulate positions and to comprehend the significance of the discussions surprised the Rudd team and created a shocking realization that cast doubt on their assumed knowledge of the intellectual inferiority of Africans. Peter Gibbs described the extent to which Lobengula demonstrated leadership and intellectual skills as a negotiator, saying "Hour after hour, week after week, month after month, the king argued with remarkable success with the Cambridge men. He tore to shreds their thesis on the advantages of granting Rhodes the concession. The pillars of learning made so little headway that Rhodes felt compelled to force the issue."[6] Indeed, Lobengula demonstrated that he had the ability to storm and bring down the laager. However, that mission would be accomplished by his descendants much sooner than Rhodes, Helm, and Queen Victoria thought possible.

Under these circumstances Rhodes instructed Rudd to ensure that, by fair means or foul, Lobengula must be pressured to sign a paper that, in effect, had the appearance of a legal contract.[7] With his patience running out, Rhodes demonstrated an intolerance that was so typical of the behavior of Victorian Europeans toward Africans. Lobengula's ability to think logically to preserve the integrity of his society and culture did not sit well with him. In this way, Rhodes realized that the white man was wrong in holding onto the myth of African intellectual inferiority. However, he did not want to be the first high-level colonial official to admit that he and other Victorian individuals were wrong about their views of Africans.

At this time, Europeans lost a valuable opportunity to build human relationships with Africans on the foundation of mutual cultural respect. Unable to manipulate Lobengula, Rhodes secretly paid Rev. Helm to supply information that he utilized in planning the colonization of Zimbabwe. Lobengula was, thus, betrayed by a Christian man he trusted.[8] Rudd also found Lotshe Hlabangana (?–1989), Lobengula's senior counselor, so capable of exercising reason and logic that he refused to be manipulated. The result was that Rudd and Rhodes felt compelled to use the threat of military force and bribery to have their own wishes prevail, but to no avail.

On October 30, 1888, taking the advice given by Helm into consideration and without the slightest knowledge that the missionary he trusted was, in effect, Rhodes' agent, Lobengula signed a paper known as the Rudd Concession. This pseudolegal document granted Rhodes exclusive rights to dig for minerals for a limited period. But Rhodes took the charter as a blank check to do what he had always wanted to do—colonize Zimbabwe as the first stage of his grand plan to bring all of Africa under British imperial rule. By the time Lobengula knew that he had been misled and cheated, Rhodes had already obtained a Royal Charter from Queen Victoria in 1889 to colonize his land.

The charter gave Rhodes legal authority to form a colonial administration known as the British South Africa Company, which ruled Zimbabwe from 1890 to 1923. This action was the first physical act to build the laager. Everything was in place. Rhodes was so pleased with the terms of the charter that he reacted, "Our concession is so gigantic that it is like giving a man the whole of Australia."[9] Soon after signing the concession and before he knew that he had been a victim of conspiracy, Lobengula remarked to Helm, "Did you ever see a chameleon catch a fly? He gets behind the fly and remains motionless for some time. Then he advances slowly. When well within reach, he darts his tongue and the fly disappears. Britain is the chameleon, and I am the fly."[10] Of course, Helm had no comment because he knew the extent of his role in the betrayal of Lobengula.

## POLITICAL LEADERSHIP AND THE COLONIZATION OF ZIMBABWE

As soon as he knew that he had been cheated, King Lobengula repudiated the agreement and requested Queen Victoria not to honor it because Rhodes, Rudd, and Helm had not been honest with him. He did not know that the queen herself was part of the plan to colonize his land. To make matters worse, Rhodes failed to honor the terms of the agreement. The guns and ammunition he had promised were never delivered. The promise that he had no intention of colonizing Zimbabwe was also not kept. The tragic reality is that Lobengula felt that the trust and confidence he had placed in Helm went down the drain as the white men with whom he had dealt made him a victim of the myth that they cunningly tried to maintain as the only viable means of fulfilling their own objectives.

In September 1890, Rhodes secretly dispatched a squadron of 400 mounted police and troops to protect a column of 200 colonial adventurers who were going to settle in Mashonaland. There they hoisted a Union Jack without Lobengula's knowledge or permission. With this action Rhodes officially colonized Zimbabwe. Leander Starr Jameson (1853–1917), his close associate and partner in the De Beers Mining Company, was appointed the first administrator and served from September 10, 1890, until April 1, 1986. Britain had finally built the laager that Rhodes considered essential to bringing all of Africa under British colonial rule. He dreamed of building a laager big enough to stretch from Egypt to the Cape Province. But this proved to be a task bigger than his ego.

A series of unfortunate events precipitated a deterioration in the relationship between the colonial adventurers and Africans. First, a severe outbreak of foot and mouth disease killed hundreds of cattle. The whites, having taken some precaution to prevent a devastation of their herds, tried to exterminate those of Africans to stop the spread of the disease. But this is not how Africans saw the situation; they simply regarded the white man's action as a callous and brutal strategy to subdue them. Then a severe drought brought a crisis in the food supply. During the next two years, Africans were in a restless state. The whites were able to obtain assistance from South Africa to ease the problems caused by the foot and mouth disease. However, they did nothing to assist Africans in their effort to minimize the effect of the disaster giving the impression that they did not care.

In October 1893, suddenly and without warning, Rhodes ordered the invasion of Lobengula's kingdom. The invaders killed[11] the king, destroyed his royal village, confiscated his livestock, and declared Matebeleland a British colony. The superiority complex that became Rhodes' preoccupation had finally found a target and a channel of expressing itself in accordance with the Victorian belief of African cultural inferiority. Rhodes would no longer allow Lobengula time to learn the tactics of the white man. He had to be eliminated quickly in order to establish Rhodes' own authority to make the British laager safe. To allow him more time to design his defense strategy would greatly embarrass those who believed in African intellectual inferiority. Rhodes was not prepared to endure this agony any longer. Besides, everything pointed to the fact that, indeed, Lobengula had been framed into a situation that left him no options at all.

## COLONIAL POLITICAL LEADERSHIP
## AND CONFLICT

The European belief in the cultural superiority of Europeans did not make it possible for Rhodes, Rudd, Queen Victoria, or Helm to consider

Africans equal partners in building human relationships. If this had happened, an ideal social environment could have emerged, enabling all parties to exercise proper political leadership that would have brought Africans and the British colonial officials together to ensure cooperation for the benefit of all. The manner in which Rhodes and his associates conspired against Lobengula certainly demonstrates a lack of respect for African culture. British colonization of Zimbabwe, and other countries in Africa, constituted what Paulo Freire considers cultural invasion as an act of violence against the colonized.[12] Freire also concludes that a very important feature of cultural invasion is that the invader makes the invaded feel the full weight of his power by designing and implementing a policy detrimental to their developmental interests.[13]

In the diary entry he made on April 24, 1893, Leander Starr Jameson argued that the rising conflict between Africans and the colonial officials was a result of African resistance to what he regarded as a properly constituted and civilized authority.[14] He never saw the behavior of the white man as its major cause. Instead, Jameson blamed the victims of his own administrative policy. In March 1896, after the colonists had destroyed their cattle, Africans concluded that they had gone too far. Fierce fighting between them raged from 1896 to 1897. The British laager was under siege. Nearly 10 percent of the whites were killed[15] and many more were injured. The casualties of the war of 1896 indicate how serious the conflict was. Table 2.1 shows white casualties of that war.

**Table 2.1**
**Casualties of the War of 1896**

| Dead | Volunteers | Imperial Troops | B.S.A.C. Police | Total |
|---|---|---|---|---|
| in action | 47 | 8 | 4 | 59 |
| of wounds | 17 | 3 | 5 | 25 |
| killed by Africans | 262 | 1 | 1 | 264 |
| **Total** | 326 | 12 | 10 | 348 |
| **Wounded** | | | | |
| in action | 121 | 29 | 8 | 158 |
| accidentally | 15 | 1 | - | 16 |
| at start of war | 14 | - | - | 14 |
| **Total** | 150 | 30 | 8 | 188 |

Source: *Reports on Native Disturbance in Southern Rhodesia, 1896–97.* Zimbabwe National Archives.

The British South Africa Company did not keep accurate figures of African casualties for a good reason: to conceal the atrocities it committed in subjecting Africans to colonial rule. It can therefore be assumed that these figures were much higher than those of the whites.

Among the colonial officials who felt compelled to exercise political leadership in the unprecedented debate over the appropriate role of Africans was Earl Grey (1851–1917), who served as administrator from April 12, 1896, to December 4, 1898. With the sense of duty he felt was required by the high office that he held, and highly conscious of the implications of finding an answer to the question of what constituted proper government policy for the development of Africans, Grey argued that the government, not the church, must assume the responsibility of designing the policy because the development of the country was not based on religious values only, but on sound socioeconomic and political policies.

That is why, in 1898, when he introduced the first bill on education, Grey expressed his belief that he was exercising proper political leadership when he said, "I am convinced that the very first step toward civilizing the Natives lies in a course of industrial and practical training which must precede the teaching of [religious] dogma."[16] Grey was, in effect, suggesting that religious instruction, such as the missionaries were promoting as a viable form of educational development for Africans, must come after the policy of industrial training. Grey was quite candid in defining industrial training as being synonymous with manual labor, exactly the kind of education intended by the Education Ordinance of 1899 enacted by the British South Africa Company legislature.

The conclusion that this kind leadership was the reason for the growing institutional controversy about the main objective of African educational development is evinced by the views that Rev. Arthur Bathe expressed in opposition to Grey, saying, "I am sorry that on the part of the whites there is a reluctance to encourage good education among the Natives under the pretext that they will not be useful as cheap laborers when they can read and write."[17] It is evident that, in their respective positions, Grey and Bathe believed that they were articulating an appropriate leadership position consistent with their own objectives regarding what policy should be.

The difference of opinion about policy constituted the beginning of the conflict between the colonial government and the church. This is evident in the events that followed. In 1899, aware that it had an advantage over the church leaders, the colonial government took action to formulate its own policy. The enactment of the first legislation on education[18] in that year was an event that gave the government power to implement its philosophy of education based on its major objective of training Africans to make a contribution to the economic development of the country.

This legislation gave the colonial government power it had not had since its inception in 1890. This is why it moved aggressively to assert its authority by formulating a policy of industrial training for Africans. Although the primary purpose of the Education Ordinance of 1899 was to assist the development of a completely academic education for white students, its impact was felt more profoundly in the government power to formulate an educational policy for Africans. The main provision of this legislation was an additional grant of $4.00 made for each white student who met an academic standard of proficiency in English, Latin, Literature, History, Mathematics, Geography, Science, Music, and Shorthand.[19] This ordinance demonstrated the real intent of the colonial government as it sought to exercise its leadership in seeking to control all aspects of the development of Africans. All the church leaders could do then was hope that their influence on the conduct of the development of Africans would not erode completely.

It was by this intent and design that Section B of this ordinance made provisions for African schools, all under church organizations, to receive grants of 10 shillings ($1.00) per student per academic year for each school that offered no less than two hours per day for practical training and manual labor from a total of four hours per day, and whose average daily attendance was not less than fifty during the preceding school year of two hundred days.[20] This is one way the church leaders hoped to retain some measure of influence on the development of Africans. The British settlers found in the educational process the essential materials they needed to build and defend the laager.

From the Education Ordinance of 1899 two things are clear. The first is that the colonial government placed more restrictions on the education of Africans than it did on that of white students. While it required white students to show evidence of academic performance as a condition for receiving the grants, it specified that African schools must engage in rigorous manual training as a condition for receiving financial aid. The second is that by instituting two systems in the educational process—one for white students, the other for African students—the colonial government had put in place an effective strategy for exercising power in designing inferior educational policies for African students. The effect of this racism is that, while the education of whites steadily improved, that of Africans remained comparatively underdeveloped until the advent of a black majority government in 1980. In this context the colonial government missed the proper function of political leadership.

The colonial government was quite pleased with its action. This is evinced by the response of one high-ranking government official who took it upon himself to write in April 1903 to the editor of *Rhodesia Herald*, a daily newspaper, to say, "The black peril will only become a reality when the results of a misguided system of education have taken root and the veneer of European civilization struggles with the innate savage nature of the African."[21] This seems to reveal a hidden agenda in the colonial government's policy for education of Africans. Among the evidence to substantiate this conclusion is that in 1904, the Chief Native Commissioner for Matebeleland, also a high-ranking colonial official, argued, "The Native in his ignorance almost invariably abuses a purely bookish education, utilizing it only as means of defying authority. A purely literary education for Natives should not be considered for many years to come."[22]

That this opinion was part of the official government policy and strategy is why his counterpart in Mashonaland went even a step further in outlining the principles which he argued must guide the government in formulating an educational policy for Africans in order to control it, saying, "It is cheap labor that we need in this country, and it has yet to be proved that the Native who can read and write turns out [to be] a good laborer. As far as we can determine, the Native who can read and write will not work on farms and in mines. The official policy is to develop the Natives on lines least likely to lead to any risk of clashing with Europeans."[23]

These opinions were the conditions which William Milton (1854–1930), the administrator from 1898 to 1914, took into consideration in naming a seven-man commission under the chairmanship of Marshall Hole, a high-ranking civil commissioner in Bulawayo, to investigate all aspects of education for Africans. Its terms of reference were to "inquire into and reporting upon the laws and system under which education is at present provided and making such recommendations as will improve efficiency in government role."[24]

During his term of office as administrator from 1914 to 1923, Francis P. Chaplin (1866–1933) held regular meetings with African chiefs in order to reduce tension and increase dialogue. While this form of political leadership proved effective, it did not lead to the establishment of confidence among Africans because policy did not change to suit their developmental needs. In effect, Chaplin improved the effectiveness of the system of collecting taxes from Africans in a manner they considered oppressive.

## CHARLES COGHLAN: POLITICAL LEADERSHIP OF A NEW ERA

The election of Charles P. Coghlan (1863–1927) as prime minister, serving from October 1, 1923 to September 1, 1927, was an event that had great significance in the political leadership of colonial Zimbabwe. Coghlan was born in South Africa where he was educated and studied law. He came to colonial Zimbabwe at the beginning of the twentieth century and decided to try his hand in politics. He was first elected to the legislature in 1908 and supported the view that the country should attain the status of responsible government. The term "responsible government" was used by the British to indicate a political status considered to be higher than that of direct rule from White Hall. It had no other significance except for the colonial government to claim that it had the power to determine its own internal affairs with little interference from Britain. In 1965, Ian D. Smith would base his political action on this claim, but to no avail.

Coghlan was part of a delegation to London to negotiate with the British government, led at the time by James Ramsay MacDonald (1866–1937), the great liberal leader of the Labour Party. That both MacDonald and Coghlan shared liberal views about the future of British colonial Africa reflected the conditions of the times. MacDonald served as secretary to the Labour Party for eleven years beginning in 1900. As leader of the Labour Party, MacDonald opposed Britain's entry into World War I. Both MacDonald and Coghlan felt that the government must assume a major leadership responsibility in assisting its citizens in their struggle for development. Coming out of the Victorian era, MacDonald embraced a social creed that compelled him to recognize the social and economic problems that the British masses were facing. For MacDonald and Coghlan, building and defending the laager had a different meaning than that of other leaders of the British colonial empire.

In colonial Zimbabwe Coghlan was trying to ease the economic burden thrust on the people by the exploitive nature of the colonial policy. This is why the two men developed an unusual understanding of the role of government in seeking improvement in the living conditions of the people. Coghlan's sudden death on September 1, 1927, at the age of 64 brought an entirely different political complication that put his successor Howard Unwin Moffat (1869–1951) in an uncomfortable position, not because he was unable to exercise proper political leadership at a critical time, but because Coghlan had such a high reputation as a colonial leader that it was difficult to match. Indeed, Moffat tried to build the same type of laager as McDonald and Coghlan, but the forces of opposition were too strong to permit him to succeed.

Under these political conditions, Moffat was faced with the task of defining policy using Coghlan's political philosophy that the development of the country was dependent on the role the government played in promoting equal opportunity for all people. This was the only viable instrument for promoting the advancement of Africans. Moffat was aware that MacDonald and Coghlan shared the common belief that, while the Industrial Revolution forced European entrepreneurs to exploit the resources in Africa, everything possible must be done to preserve the cultural integrity of Africans. As a grandson of an early missionary, Robert Moffat (1796–1883), Moffat tried to operate under these principles. He also knew that MacDonald and Coghlan were appalled by the report of the Hadfield Commission of 1911 passing judgment on the values of African culture as a strategy of weakening it so that the British laager could be strengthened and defended.

Indeed, the liberal views that MacDonald, Coghlan, and Harold Jowitt (1893–1963), director of African education from 1927 to 1934, shared was not a rush to bring about a rapid transformation of Africans, but a strategy to caution the settlers in Africa that it was necessary to have a view of Africans that would make it possible to bring about better relations between the races in the future. The desire for raw materials, however, did not make it possible to see that future from this perspective. Therefore, the views expressed by these three men became a lonely voice lost in the wilderness. The urge to build and defend the laager was too powerful.

It is important to remember that espousing liberal perspectives on social conditions by national leaders, whether in Africa or in Europe, was considered the mark of statesmanship. This is why some great liberals of that time included Robert Clarkson Tredgold (1899–1979), chief justice of the supreme court in colonial Zimbabwe during the turbulent period of its history. Tredgold and other liberals championed the cause of the oppressed masses who had no means of alleviating the hardships arbitrarily imposed on them by their society. This is why Garfield Todd (born 1908), who served as prime minister of colonial Zimbabwe from 1953 to 1958, championed the cause of the oppressed African masses in their struggle against colonial oppression. These liberal leaders felt that they had a national duty that only they could understand and carry out. They operated under the assumption that their failure to operate by higher standards than the rest of those who were involved in the colonial entrepreneurship would lead to the strengthening the laager and, thus, a national disaster.

The liberal views that these men held and the desire to minimize the effect of the laager is the reason why they came forward to offer their talents in the service of their countries. They included David Lloyd George (1863–1945), who served as British prime minister during World War I, Herbert Henry Asquith (1852–1928), leader of the Liberal Party in Britain and who served as British Prime Minister from 1908 to 1916, and who succeeded George in 1916. Indeed, during Asquith's term of office, the British Parliament passed a number of laws intended to protect the interests of the people. These laws include the Old Pension Act of 1908 and the National Insurance Act of 1911. Even in Britain, defending the laager carried implications for the less fortunate. Although Neville Chamberlain (1869–1940) and Winston Churchill (1874–1965), both members of the Conservative Party, served Britain during a period of great crisis, they are not known for their liberal and humanitarian endeavors.

Although Churchill was a signatory to the Atlantic Charter[25] of August 14, 1941, he refused to honor its terms, arguing that he was not appointed His Majesty's Government to preside over the dissolution of the British empire. In this context Churchill subscribed to the building and defending of the laager in Africa.

Apart from Churchill and Chamberlain, these men were convinced that the salvation of their society lay in their endeavor to salvage positive attributes from European entrepreneurs whose sole motivation was to gain profit in whatever they did in Africa. They tried to temper the imperatives of the Industrial Revolution with the a set of moral and human values which they believed must be preserved to sustain the critical features of the human beings who were being threatened by the search for material wealth. They believed that building and defending the laager must take second place to the promotion of human relationships based on equal opportunity. For them the greatest attribute of the Industrial Revolution was the development of human understanding of the imperative nature of values that would sustain the strength of national institutions so that they would promote equality, justice, and fairness. They also believed that the recognition of this reality would elevate human life to the position of dignity and worth to which they were entitled. That colonial entrepreneurs, as builders and defenders of the laager, did not see things this way created problems for colonial officials like Moffat, whose enthusiasm to accomplish national goals was totally incompatible with those values.

## HAROLD JOWITT: POLITICAL LEADERSHIP IN A NEW ENDEAVOR

Harold Jowitt deserves a brief discussion as one of those great liberal visionaries who made a difference in seeking an improvement in the life of Africans. When the Committee on Native Development of 1925 recommended the establishment of the Department of Native Education separate from the Department of Native Affairs,[26] the colonial government found a temporary solution to the embarrassment it had experienced in the failure of the plan that Herbert Keigwin[27] had outlined in 1920. In December 1927, the Department of Native Education was established and $9,520 was allocated for its installation. Harold Jowitt, a liberal on the level of Coghlan and MacDonald, and far more intellectual than Keigwin, was appointed its first director. Jowitt had 14 years of experience in education for Africans in South Africa. He was assisted by four inspectors.

Jowitt seemed equal to the task of rebuilding the shattered image of the colonial plan that had failed under Keigwin. He was an educator of imposing stature, a dynamic leader of immense popularity, an administrative technocrat, and an innovator willing to risk his reputation in order to try new ideas. His enthusiasm for success was a reasonable substitute for lack of experience with the political conditions that controlled how things were done in Zimbabwe. However, Jowitt's success must not be measured by what he did to minimize the effect of the laager on Africans, but the efforts he made to provide good education as a strategy of helping Africans in reducing its impact on their lives.

A relentless negotiator and a cunning diplomat, Jowitt's approach to his new responsibilities was a breath of fresh air for church leaders, who felt that under Keigwin their influence was slipping. Jowitt seemed to have healthy relationships with the various segments of the communities involved in African education. In his desire to succeed where he thought Keigwin had failed, Jowitt had become a fragile bridge over troubled water. With respect to the education of Africans, he tried to mediate the conflict between political philosophy and the reality of human existence, between past policies and a new idealism. He tried to strike a functional balance between politically expedient programs and realistic philosophy, between African desire for a good academic education as a means of eliminating the old colonial stereotypes and the shackles that bound their minds, and the colonial intent to have them provide cheap labor. He tried to satisfy both Africans' desire for a good education and the expressed wish of the white entrepreneurs to sustain their economic and political power base through cheap labor, which only Africans could provide.

The conditions of the times made Jowitt's task much harder than that of any of his associates in the colonial government. He knew that his options were few, and that he had to play his limited number of cards carefully. There was no room for error, and the stakes were high. Believing that it was possible to strike a working balance between these conflicting positions, Jowitt began his task with a clear understanding of the importance of his mission. In his first annual report submitted in 1928, Jowitt acknowledged the fact that he faced some rather serious and unexpected problems, and went on to discuss some of them, saying, "The non-existence of data and records regarding the work, the thinking that education for Natives is a step-child receiving the crumbs from the dinner table of the accredited educational family, the absence of any qualified officials in Native education, all tend to preclude the development of an adequate system of official records and constitute the fundamental problems in Native education."[28]

It is quite clear that Jowitt was expressing disappointment over the disorganized and haphazard manner in which Keigwin had carried out his responsibility. In saying so, he was suggesting how difficult his own task would be. Jowitt observed that there were "practically no data bearing upon definite conditions in over 90% of the schools, upon the teaching staffs and their qualifications or duties, upon the number of boys and girls, upon the rate of increase in the number of schools."[29] This suggests the extent of Keigwin's obsession with the policy of practical training at the expense of every other consideration of the educational needs of Africans. Jowitt was also disappointed to discover that Keigwin, whom every colonial official credited with solving problems of African education, did not keep accurate records of the work he did in such a critical area of national policy. This means that his leadership in the development of policy was lacking.

Jowitt criticized Keigwin's plan as an attempt to institutionalize African life in a mechanical fashion,[30] and his policy of village industries as "lacking clarity and definition, and so failed to reach a central unifying principle to serve in the development of criteria."[31] He warned of the consequences of continuing the traditional colonial negative attitude that "the security of one race can be ensured by the repression of another."[32] He did not hesitate to express his opinion that Keigwin's plan was nothing less than a repression of Africans, both mentally and politically. There is no doubt that Jowitt disagreed fundamentally with Keigwin's policy and plan. His argument that "The Africans must not be trained by an inferior kind of education to function as better hewers of wood and drawers of water for their white masters" was intended to refute what a high-ranking colonial official had promoted during the debate on the Education Ordinance bill of 1912, a position Keigwin had supported.[33] The building of the laager was being effected in a climate of conflict between the colonial enthusiasts and the liberals like Jowitt.

Jowitt then established his own set of aims for African education. These included "breaking down the separate compartments which have been created by different government departments,"[34] creating affinities between the educational process and efforts to restore the position of detribalized Africans, creating a working balance between academic education and practical education, seeking full cooperation between church organizations and the government in determining proper educational objectives and priorities for Africans, returning the benefits of African labor to improve the school system, training teachers in sufficient numbers and at a sufficient level so that the educational process would be improved, and designing the curriculum so that students would be adequately prepared to relate what they learned to seeking solutions to problems of political and socioeconomic injustice.

There is no doubt that Jowitt knew that the change Africans would accept was the introduction of a good academic education, that they had no objection to practical training as such but recognized that, by itself, it was limited in what it offered them for the future. He also knew that the change his superiors would accept was the strengthening of the policy of practical training. How was he going to reconcile these extremely conflicting positions? He needed the wisdom of Solomon to play the game of colonial political hide-and-seek between colonial entrepreneurs and Africans in order to maintain his perspective. In this context Jowitt was caught between two worlds, that of laager builders and that of Africans. How would he play his cards?

In his annual report for 1930, Jowitt attempted to furnish some answers to the question of how he was going to present his juggling act in the arena of increasing conflicts saying, "It seems fairly evident that progress was made during the year. It may not be so clearly realized that this would not have been possible without taking other factors into consideration. Such factors include missionaries, who continue to spend themselves unreservedly in the cause of Native development. The critics of our work claim that we differ from them in that they alone regard things as they really are. It is our conviction that the best products of this work will gradually add to the dynamic strength of this country."[35]

Regardless of the dilemma that he faced, Jowitt was able to speak with this high degree of confidence to sustain his position because he had gained the support of the missionaries. Unlike the rigid Keigwin, Jowitt was open to new ideas and was sensitive to the educational needs of Africans, which the missionaries claimed to represent. His ability to perceive what was possible in light of what was ideal gave him the balance he needed as he walked this delicate political tightrope. But his inability to convince his superiors that both practical training and academic education had an important place in the education of Africans was the gusty wind that threw him off balance and brought his act to an untimely end only seven years after it had started.

Jowitt, unlike Keigwin, was sensitive to the views of the church leaders about the importance of religious education. This sensitivity gave him an advantage over his associates within the colonial government. This is why, from the very beginning of his term of office, Jowitt enjoyed the trust and confidence of the church organizations, a group whose support he needed to carry out the task of bringing about a much-needed reform in African education. One can conclude that the government took this action to register its disapproval of Jowitt's liberal views on the education of Africans, especially his belief in the importance of good academic education, and what it perceived as his acquiescence to missionary demands for a forceful approach to the problems the educational process was experiencing. One can also see that, early in his term of office, Jowitt did not enjoy the absolute support of his superiors in the way that Keigwin did. Translated into practical realities, this situation put Jowitt in a precarious position because his superiors perceived him as being opposed to the building of the laager.

Not only did Jowitt's superiors disapprove of his innovative ideas and approach to African development, they also thought that he was moving too fast to dismantle a policy, a critical material for the laager, that dated from the enactment of the Education Ordinance in 1899. The truth of the matter was that Jowitt disagreed with his superiors over the fundamental purpose of education for Africans. There is no question that while the core of the colonial government officials believed the essential structure of African education must remain one of practical training, Jowitt felt that this form of education was totally inadequate to meet the needs of the students and to prepare them for the future because it was designed to train Africans "to function as hewers of wood and drawers of water for their white masters."

In 1933, the relationship between Jowitt and his superiors had deteriorated to the point where they could not be mended. To the Chief Native Commissioner, Jowitt's immediate superior, and the one most vocal against his innovative approach to African educational development, Jowitt directed a stinging attack. He could no longer listen to the commissioner urging him not to change a system that they both knew was doing no one any good. Jowitt went on to say, "The problem of education is the problem of a community making the most of it. The problem of the school or of a school system, is merely a chapter in that more inclusive problem. School is important, but the school unrelated and unacquainted with the world in which the students live, is an impertinence."[36]

Concluding that the policy of practical training for Africans was "in the long run, an immoral institution,"[37] Jowitt viewed the problem from its proper educational and intellectual perspective. He argued that, because education must be universal, there was no reason to practice racial discrimination. He called the latter an immoral act coming from an immoral institution. Unfortunately, Jowitt's superiors were unwilling and unable to see things from this perspective. Rather, they saw them from the perspective of political expediency. Thus, there was no common ground between Jowitt and his superiors. This fundamental difference of philosophy and opinion was the major problem that handicapped his ability to discharge his responsibility well.

In November 1934, nearly seven years after he was appointed, Jowitt resigned to accept a similar position in Uganda. It is surprising that Jowitt, considering the liberal views he held, was able to stay in office that long. Franklin Parker, an American researcher and scholar who interviewed Jowitt at his home in Uganda in 1960, told the author in 1988, "Jowitt had a vision of Africa of the future. He could not fit in the system of which he was a part."[38] This view of Jowitt shows that he exercised proper political leadership in an important area of national policy at a critical period. He did this by refusing to subscribe to materials that were needed to build the laager.

## HUGGINS' POLITICAL LEADERSHIP OF A WHITE
## ISLAND IN A SEA OF BLACK

The circumstances that brought Godfrey Huggins, prime minister from September 12, 1933, to September 6, 1953, to power were typical of the conditions which influenced colonial political behavior in the past. A physician who arrived in Zimbabwe in 1911, Huggins was known among his patients as a conservative and orthodox general practitioner who had no time for innovative ideas. Indeed, Huggins practiced medicine not because he wanted to make it his career but because he wanted to establish a political base. The national debate in 1923 about the referendum to determine the future of the British South Africa Company administration brought him into the political arena. Instead of talking to his patients about their medical problems, he talked about the political future of the country.

Often skeptical about the British Imperial Government's policy of promoting the advancement of Africans, Huggins threw his support behind Charles Coghlan, a man respected for his moderate views. Huggins did this, not because he shared Coghlan's views, but because he wanted to establish credibility as a politician who understood the nature of national responsibility. But Huggins's influence on the outcome of the referendum was quite minimal. When Coghlan died suddenly in 1927, he was succeeded by Howard Moffat. At the time of Coghlan's death, Howard Moffat was deputy premier and former Minister of Mines. He was considered a man of integrity because of his missionary background, but was believed to detest the character of colonial politics because of the anti-African rhetoric that became a popular theme and standard political campaign strategy among white political aspirants. Political extremists, including Huggins, exploited his moderation to portray him as a weak leader who lacked the forcefulness and the leadership they believed were required during a time of great economic difficulties and political turbulence.

Recognizing an opportunity for assuming the reins of power in a political vacuum, Huggins withdrew his support of Moffat and formed the Rhodesia Reform Party, drawing his support mainly from the dissident elements of Moffat's Rhodesia Party.[39] During the election campaign of 1928, Huggins attracted national attention with his strong anti-African rhetoric. Such rhetoric had been an important part of colonial politics since Cecil John Rhodes used it successfully to come to power in the Cape Parliament in 1895. Any person who sought political power used anti-African rhetoric to climb the colonial political ladder. It was the only viable route to national prominence, and Huggins was only being true to a colonial tradition that had paid heavy political dividends in the past.

But because Huggins was a relative newcomer to the political leadership of the country, the voters preferred to return Moffat to power. However, in 1930, when Moffat opposed the Land Apportionment Act of 1929 in favor of moderation in the government's approach to African advancement, his popularity among whites began to decline. Moffat had lost the leadership that he once exercised effectively. Also, the action that his government took in 1930 to protect the economy shattered by the Great Depression, and the purchase of mineral rights from the defunct British South Africa Company for $4 million when many thought they should have been acquired free of charge, brought sharp criticism from Huggins. Hence Huggins's image among the whites was suddenly elevated as someone to whom they could entrust their future by exercising this kind of new leadership.

Unable to weather the political storm he had not caused and could not control, and with his government greatly weakened by poor public opinion, Moffat resigned on July 4, 1933, in favor of George Mitchell (1867–1937), another moderate of the Coghlan-MacDonald school of thought, in an effort to restore the confidence of whites in the government. In many ways Howard Moffat was the Herbert Hoover of colonial Zimbabwe: he was a victim of the Great Depression and the prevailing difficult economic conditions. In the struggle for influence between the liberals and the conservatives the scale was tipped in favor of the latter because they proved to the colonial entrepreneurs that Africa was there for them to exploit for their own benefit. The building and defending of the laager came out of this line of thinking.

Deciding that he needed a new mandate from the voters, Mitchell dissolved Parliament in August 1933, less than two months after he had succeeded Moffat, and called for new elections. Huggins had the chance of a lifetime. Extreme members of the Rhodesia Party abandoned Mitchell and joined the ranks of the Rhodesia Reform Party. The election campaign was marked by a lack of clearly articulated issues, except for the continuation of anti-African rhetoric and the problem of finding ways to minimize the effects of the Depression. When the election results were known in September, Huggins had won with a slim majority. Mitchell, like his mentor Moffat, went into the cave of political oblivion. Huggins became prime minister on September 12 and remained in office until he retired in 1952.

But, with a slim majority in Parliament, Huggins faced a new crisis he had not anticipated. The effects of the Depression were more devastating than in 1929. Transport and essential services had come to a halt. When he tried to introduce a new railway bill, there was so much opposition that Huggins not only withdrew it but also dissolved the Rhodesia Reform Party and reactivated the Rhodesia Party, hoping to restore its reputation to what it had been during the leadership of the charismatic Charles Coghlan.

While he was working on his political strategy to win the new elections, Huggins was having secret discussions with George Stark, Jowitt's successor, about formulating an educational policy for Africans that the white business community would support. The reason for secrecy was that neither man wanted to subject the major features of that policy to public scrutiny while it was being developed. That Huggins used it as a major political strategy to win the elections of 1934 with a comfortable majority shows how cruel colonial politics was. What appealed to the voters[40] was what Huggins called parallel development for the two racial groups.

Huggins's underlying philosophy was that each race should be allowed to develop under its own conditions—whites according to their Western cultural traditions and Africans according to their tribal traditions. As Huggins and Stark saw it, the two races had nothing in common except in a master-servant relationship. Without any political leverage through the electoral process, Africans were at the mercy of Huggins and Stark. It was not by coincidence that the introduction of compulsory education for white students in 1935, which whites hoped would protect them from the threat of Africans, occurred in the same year that Stark was confirmed as Director of Native Education. In 1938, when Stark felt secure in his position, Huggins decided that it was time to state clearly the policy of his government concerning the place of Africans in society.

After consulting with Stark, Huggins spoke in Parliament in a way that surprised only a few, "The Europeans in this country can be likened to an island in a sea of black, with the artisan and tradesman forming the shore and the professional class the highland in the center. Is the Native to be allowed to invade the shores and gradually attack the highland? To permit this would mean that the haven of civilization would be removed from the country and the Native would revert to a barbarism worse than before."[41] There is no question that this line of thinking was intended to strengthen and defend the laager. Huggins' position was exactly the same position Stark had taken as inspector of schools in 1930. Huggins went on to say, "While there is still time, the country must be developed between white areas and Native areas to protect both the shores and the island."[42] To accomplish this objective, Huggins and Stark decided that the educational policy for Africans must be developed from the perspective of its intended objectives, which had always been the primary concern among whites.

At that time, education had become a more sensitive political issue in which leadership was needed more than in all other national issues combined. In 1938 the impact of the Great Depression was no longer as devastating as it had been in 1930. The renewed confidence in the future had increased substantially because Britain, under the arrangements made at the time of the introduction of "responsible government" in 1924, was slowly giving up its constitutional responsibility to protect Africans from exploitation by colonial entrepreneurs.

Huggins could not have been happier. These were the circumstances which he took into consideration in outlining the essential elements of the new educational policy of his government in order to convince the voters that academic education for Africans would not be considered then or for the future. He argued that providing academic education for Africans would pose a threat to the political power and influence whites had enjoyed in the past. Both he and Stark knew that this position was the kind of leadership needed to formulate policy that white voters would support. Adding that good academic education was critically important for white students, Huggins stated, "This is essential if all our children are to be given equal opportunity for progress and to keep their position of influence and power. It will prevent the creation of a poor white class. Constant adjustment will take place and the result should be a system of education Rhodesian in character, and especially suited to our own requirements."[43] To Huggins this was one of the best means of building and defending that laager.

There is no question that Huggins and Stark entered a political alliance that had severe implications for the development of African education. That Huggins began to put his philosophy into practice as soon as he felt secure in 1936 shows how carefully he designed his strategy. This is evident in his introduction of a bill into the all-white Parliament in 1937. Entitled The Native Registration Bill, this legislation became law only after a brief and uneventful period of debate. He argued that requiring Africans to carry pass books at all times would help reduce "offenses resulting from the impact of an uncivilized people interacting with our civilization."[44] Huggins was, in effect, suggesting that Africans must constantly be reminded of their presumed uncivilized position in the colonial society, and that the educational process must be such that the differences from education for whites were sustained, not eliminated. This is why, in the same year, he threatened "to deport the so-called educated Natives who are complaining about what they claim to be a lack of equal educational opportunity."[45] Indeed, Huggins saw Africans as inferior to whites regardless of the level of their education and that no one must attempt to change this position.

Huggins' belief that education must condition Africans to tribal life found expression during a debate on a bill to ban Africans from becoming permanent residents of the urban areas. He rhetorically asked the members of Parliament and the white community in general "whether our municipal areas should be polyglotted with a mixture of black and

white or whether we should proceed with the policy of segregation envisaged in the Land Apportionment Act and keep our towns as white
as possible? The Native is a visitor in our towns for the sole purpose of
serving the whites."[46] This position clearly shows that the educational
policy Huggins and Stark pursued was a major problem that Africans
faced in their struggle for advancement. This kind of political leadership
left much to be desired.

That this problem was compounded by Stark's lack of knowledge of
Africans' real educational needs is evident in what he failed to do in
exercising proper leadership. He willingly surrendered to the racist political game that Huggins was playing with so much success. He allowed
the creation of the all-white Native Affairs Department, which Huggins
charged with the responsibility of monitoring the purported development of Africans but which, in reality, retarded it. He compromised
sound educational principles in order to please Huggins and thus ensure
the continuation of his own career.

The inevitable outcome of this action was that the education of Africans was at the mercy of colonial politicians who created problems to
ensure their own political survival. Until he resigned in 1952, Huggins
operated by this kind of thinking. Faced with the reality that the end
was near, Huggins came out swinging as he vigorously defended his
policy, saying in 1952, "You can call me an imperialist of the old school.
I detest the attitude of the people who condemn imperialism. True imperialism entails paternalism. It would be outrageous to give the Native
a so-called political partnership and equal educational opportunity when
he is likely to ruin himself as a result."[47]

On September 6, 1953, Huggins resigned to become prime minister of
the ill-fated Federation of Rhodesia and Nyasaland. The lack of confidence of the people forced him to resign after only three years. This
action set the stage for Africans to struggle for a majority government.
In 1954 Stark resigned for reasons of poor health. The partnership that
had been forced to exist between the horse and the rider had come to
an end. Now Africans wanted to be the rider.

That the Huggins-Stark cooperation was the major problem African
education encountered is evident in more ways than the implementation
of a policy which reduced Africans to the status of cheap laborers and
confined them to tribal life. Not only did Huggins and Stark deny Africans equal opportunity for academic education at the primary level,
but they were totally opposed to secondary education. In 1949, for example, when the Methodist Church applied for government permission
to start a secondary school for Africans at Old Mutare, Charles S. Davies,
senior inspector in the province, acting on Stark's instructions, furnished
the following reasons why the school should not be opened, saying,
"This will require two classrooms and necessary boarding accommoda-

tion for the thirty students. In addition, there is the major question of staff. Secondary teaching is very different from primary teaching. It is a very capable person who can teach English, Latin, Physics, Chemistry, Mathematics, and Biology at the secondary level."[48] The desire to build and defend the laager would not permit or accommodate this kind of development among Africans.

## TODD AND A NEW PURPOSE OF POLITICAL LEADERSHIP

New attitudes influencing the emergence of a new style of leadership began to appear with the man who succeeded Huggins as prime minister in 1953, Garfield Todd (born 1908), a former missionary from New Zealand. This is the reason Todd became sensitive to the church leaders' concerns over policy. On February 9, 1946, the Methodist Church called for new a church-state initiative to improve African education saying, "We affirm that education is the dual responsibility of both the Church and the State, each having its own sphere of duty."[49] The Methodist Church was, in effect, suggesting that Huggins reevaluate the policy of his government toward the educational development of Africans in light of the change in thinking that was taking place. But while it was sincere in making this suggestion, was the Methodist Church realistic in expecting Huggins and Stark to accept ideas moving toward church-state involvement in the conduct of African education?

Four months after the Methodist Church made its call, Garfield Todd, who later served as prime minister from September 7, 1953, to February 16, 1958, and was a senior member of Huggins' administration, surprised the country and angered Huggins by publicly criticizing the educational policy of the government of which he was a part. In characterizing a policy that allocated an expenditure of $0.40 per African student and $20.00 per white student as a national disgrace, Todd underscored the urgent need to redesign educational policy so that it would result in equal opportunity for students of both races. This was his way of attacking the laager.

Todd had been principal of Dadaya School for Africans for some years before he entered active politics in 1946. The problems African students encountered due to inadequate colonial policy was the main reason he decided to enter politics. He believed he could use his missionary background and awareness of the problems to make a difference. When he recognized Huggins' unwillingness to move toward providing equal educational opportunity to all students, Todd decided to launch a national campaign to force the issue.

Speaking before the Bulawayo National Affairs Association in February 1947, Todd exercised proper leadership in calling for a commission of inquiry into African education and warned Huggins about the consequences of continuing his existing policy, saying, "The Africans are aware that educated people can be governed, but they cannot be enslaved forever. They are no longer willing to be controlled in the manner in which they have been controlled in the past. There is a spirit of urgency. Guide it, give it assistance, and there will develop a people who will be a credit to this country. Disregard that spirit of urgency or hinder or cripple it in any way, an adverse effect will result racially."[50]

That Todd's views were shared by Africans is the reason why, in an editorial one week after Todd's speech, *The African Weekly* addressed this critical question saying, "The African view is that since education is the complete formation of the whole man, what reason is there to classify the educational process into black education and white education? To Africans the term "Native Education" carries with it such labels as little finances, inferior equipment, few qualified teachers. The product of this is a man ill-fitted for the economic, social, and political life in the colony. We favor a system of education based on total equality and which shapes all people so that they come into a world which gives them a hope for the future, not despair and bitterness, as Africans are now experiencing."[51] Like Todd and the Methodist Church, the *African Weekly* concluded by calling for a commission of inquiry into African education with the purpose of removing all inequalities that handicapped the education of Africans and enabling them to adjust to new political and socioeconomic conditions.

The wave of continuing criticism against the Huggins' educational policy aroused the indignation of many individuals who supported Todd's call for a commission of inquiry. This was the line of thinking of Reverend Kennedy Grant, a leading priest in the Anglican Church, when he argued in September 1947 saying, "The aim of education should be to train our pupils in the art of living together. Education is a continuous process of developing a personality which is essential to human relationship. The foundations of all good living are built on man's relationship with his own fellow man. This requires effective leadership on the part of the government."[52]

## SUMMARY AND CONCLUSION

It is quite evident that, in urging Huggins and Stark to name a commission to study ways of ending educational inequality, Reverend Grant was joining the chorus warning them that the consequence of attempting to sustain the existing educational policy would be a rapid deterioration in human relationships. Therefore, these individuals were exercising what they regarded as proper leadership in the formulation of policy. In his response that his administration had a policy of encouraging human relationships, the horse and rider style Huggins demonstrated failed in exercising that leadership. To appreciate why there was an outcry against the educational policy pursued by Huggins and Stark, one needs to understand what African education was going through. In 1949 male certificated teachers earned an annual income of $168.00, compared with $111.98 for certificated female teachers. These were 60 percent less than salaries paid in industry. This was a major reason why, by 1950, 45 percent of all teachers resigned to take jobs elsewhere.

In 1951, only 30 percent of the teachers were certificated. In the same year 66.9 percent of the Grade I (known as Substandard A) pupils were able to go on to second grade. The emphasis on practical training produced less than 15 percent literacy among Africans. In the same year, the government spent 96.5 percent of the national education budget of $32,361,140 for white education and the remainder of $1,178,524 on African education.[53] There were fears that continuing the policy of practical training, as implemented by Huggins and Stark, would lead to an illiterate population within a decade, and that this must be changed immediately. The rigidity that characterized Huggins' leadership would find greater utilization under Ian D. Smith. What effect that leadership had on efforts to defend the laager and the future of the country is the subject of our discussion in this book.

## NOTES

1. Dickson A. Mungazi, *The Mind of Black Africa* (Westport, CT: Praeger, 1996), p. 22.

2. W. McIntyre, *Colonies into Commonwealth* (New York: Walker and Company, 1966), p. 106.

3. Kenneth Knorr, *British Colonial Theories* (Toronto, Canada: University of Toronto Press, 1944), p. 378.

4. In his will Rhodes provided for annual scholarships, which began in 1902, for white students to study at Oxford University, his alma mater. The number of scholarships was specified in the will as follows: Canada=11, South Africa=9, Australia=6, the United States=32, Rhodesia=2, New Zealand=2. In 1976 one happy American recipient remarked that she was accepting the scholarship "to rectify some of the problems he created" (*The Lincoln Evening Journal*, Lincoln, NE, December 20, 1976). Did she really believe that she could do that, or was she simply expressing excitement about receiving the prestigious scholarship?

5. The Rudd Concession, October 30, 1888. Zimbabwe National Archives. For the complete text of The Rudd Concession, see Dickson A. Mungazi, *The Struggle for Social Change in Southern Africa: Visions of Liberty* (New York: Taylor and Francis, 1989), p. 115.

6. Peter Gibbs, *Flag for the Matebele: An Entertainment in African History* (New York: The Vanguard Press, 1956), p. 31.

7. J. S. Green, *Rhodes Goes North* (London: Bell and Sons, 1936), p. 95.

8. Upon learning of Helm's behavior, Lobengula reacted, "The white man is indeed the father of lies." Zimbabwe National Archives.

9. British South Africa Company Records, No. 369/2468–60. Zimbabwe National Archives.

10. British South Africa Company Records, March 1889, No. 369/24639–68. Zimbabwe National Archives.

11. The exact cause of Lobengula's death is not clearly known. Some say that he died while trying to escape. Others argue that he was killed by the colonial military forces. I share the latter opinion.

12. Paulo Freire, *Pedagogy of the Oppressed* (New York: Continuum, 1983), p. 21.

13. Ibid., p. 23.

14. British South Africa Company Records, The Diary of Leander Starr Jameson, Folio 1/11–109/111. Zimbabwe National Archives.

15. British South Africa Company Records, Reports of Native Disturbances in Rhodesia, 1896–97. Harare: Zimbabwe National Archives.

16. British South Africa Company Records, Earl Grey, Ref., EG: 1/1/11: Folio 547–48. Zimbabwe National Archives.

17. Robert John Challiss, "The Educational Policy of the British South Africa Company in Southern Rhodesia, 1899–1904," Masters thesis. University of Cape Town, 1968, p. 43.

18. Ordinance Number 18: The Appointment of the Director of Education, 1899. This ordinance is also known as the Education Ordinance of 1899.

19. Ibid.

20. Ibid., Section B.

21. *Rhodesia Herald*, April 4, 1903.

22. Southern Rhodesia, Annual Report of the Chief Native Commissioner for Matebelaland, 1904. Zimbabwe National Archives.

23. Southern Rhodesia, Annual Report of the Chief Native Commissioner for Mashonaland, 1905. Zimbabwe National Archives.

24. William Milton, announcing the naming of Marshall Hole, Chairman of Commission of Inquiry, 1907. Zimbabwe National Archives.

25. For a discussion of the Atlantic Charter see Dickson A. Mungazi, *Educational Policy and National Character: Africa, Japan, the United States, and the Soviet Union* (Westport, CT: Praeger Publishers, 1993), p. 4.

26. Southern Rhodesia, Committee on Native Education, 1925, p. 58.

27. For a detailed discussion see Dickson A. Mungazi, *Colonial Education for Africans: George Stark's Policy in Zimbabwe* (Westport, CT: Praeger Publishers, 1991), p. 15.

28. *Rhodesia Herald*, Report of the Director of Native Education, 1928, p. 1. Zimbabwe National Archives.

29. Ibid., p. 6.

30. Ibid., p. 7.

31. Ibid., p. 6.

32. Ibid., p. 41.

33. Ibid., p. 7. See also a letter written June 28, 1912, to the editor of the

*Rhodesia Herald* by a colonial official suggesting that Africans must be trained to function as "hewers of wood and drawers of water for their white masters."

34. Ibid., p. 9.

35. *Rhodesia Herald*, Annual Report of the Director of Native Education, 1930, p. 47.

36. *Rhodesia Herald*, Annual Report of the Director of Native Education, 1933, p. 23.

37. Ibid., 25.

38. Franklin Parker during a conversation with the author in Flagstaff, Arizona, August 31, 1988. Parker published *Education and African Development in Southern Rhodesia* (Columbus, OH: Kappa Delta Pi, 1960) which discusses Jowitt's work in colonial Zimbabwe.

39. The influence of this event on future developments cannot be ignored. In 1962, when Huggins' United Federal Party was weakened by circumstances he could not control, Ian D. Smith and Winston Field broke away to form the Rhodesia Front and drew their support from dissident members of the UFP.

40. At that time Africans did not have the vote. The Bantu Voters Association concerned itself with township elections. Africans were not allowed to claim the right to vote until the introduction of the constitution of 1961. Even then, voting was by race until the elections of 1980. This is why the colonial politicians ignored Africans.

41. Godfrey Huggins, during a debate in Parliament, in *Southern Rhodesia: Legislative Debates*, 1938, p. 21.

42. Ibid., p. 22.

43. Godfrey Huggins, "Education in Southern Rhodesia: Notes on Certain Features," 1930. Zimbabwe National Archives.

44. Godfrey Huggins, debate in the Legislature in *Southern Rhodesia: Legislative Debates*, April 2, 1937.

45. Ibid.

46. Ibid.

47. Godfrey Huggins, Political campaign speech, 1952. Zimbabwe National Archives.

48. Charles S. Davies, senior inspector of schools in Mutare, letter dated September 8, 1949, addressed to the superintendent of schools at Old Mutare Methodist Center. Old Mutare Methodist Archives.

49. The Methodist Church, "The Waddilove Manifesto: The Educational Policy of the Methodist Church," February 9, 1946. Old Mutare Methodist Archives.

50. Garfield Todd, "African Education in Southern Rhodesia: The Need for a Commission of Inquiry," an address to the Bulawayo National Affairs Association, February 18, 1947. Zimbabwe National Archives.

51. *African Weekly* 3, no. 38 (February 26, 1947).

52. Rev. Kennedy Grant, "Teach the Children the Art of Living Together," an address to the conference of African Teachers, September 10, 1947. Zimbabwe National Archives.

53. Southern Rhodesia, Commission of Inquiry into Native Education, Alexander Kerr, chairman, 1952, p. 9.

# 3

# Cracks in the Laager: The Fall of Pieter W. Botha and the Rise of F. W. de Klerk

> We face the extremely complex social, political and economic prob-
> lems in southern Africa, so complex that this can result in conflict.
> Pieter W. Botha, March 16, 1984

## BOTHA, APARTHEID, AND THE DILEMMA OF CHOICE

When John Vorster (1915–1983) resigned from the office of prime minister[1] in September 1978, he was succeeded by Pieter W. Botha (born
1916). At that time the people of South Africa, black and white, were
hoping that the new leader would be able to find ways of easing the
increasing difficulties that the application of the policy of apartheid was
causing. In that year the international community expressed increasing
concern about the effect apartheid was having on all the people of South
Africa.

Also at that time the African National Congress (ANC)[2] was slowly
but steadily intensifying its armed struggle, arousing the conscience of
people and organizations around the world about the need to end apartheid. The more the Nationalist government tried to strengthen the policy
of apartheid, the more it was recognized as a major cause of conflict. In
1975 the World Council of Churches concluded that it was necessary for
it, and for Christians all over the world, to support efforts to end apartheid because its continuation constituted a crime against humanity.[3]

Five years earlier, the Zimbabwe chapter of the British Council of Missionary Society took a similar action with regard to the racial policy that was being pursued by the Rhodesia Front government led by Ian D. Smith. The Rhodesia Front, an extreme political party, had been ruling Zimbabwe since December 1962. The British Council of Missionary Society issued a statement in October 1970 saying, "In spite of the great moral difficulties, fighting for a just cause has been generally accepted for a Christian conscience as justifiable. Those who are themselves in comfortable position and security cannot urge armed rebellion on others who would thereby face death or suffering they do not have to bear."[4]

In April 1975 the World Council of Churches voted to donate $479,000 toward assisting the African nationalist organizations that were struggling for freedom in all of southern Africa. Both John Vorster and Ian D. Smith were appalled by the action of a Christian organization in supporting the struggle to end conditions of human oppression in both countries. Although the two leaders tried to argue that conditions in Africa in 1975 in general were less than adequate due to the inaction of national leaders, the international community felt obligated to do everything in its power to end the system that Vorster and Smith represented. With both Mozambique and Angola gaining political independence in 1975, Smith and Vorster found themselves increasingly isolated from the international community. Their unwillingness to renounce the discriminatory policy they were pursuing accentuated the demands to bring their terms of office to an end.

These developments suggest that Botha assumed the office of prime minister at a time of great national and regional crisis. Vorster resigned under a cloud of controversy caused by the scandal that came out of his administration.[5] Apartheid was becoming a growing cause of embarrassment to the government of South Africa and a motivating factor to Africans to intensify their struggle against an oppressive system. Apartheid placed Botha, its ultimate victim, in a situation that rendered him ineffective as a national leader. Botha did not know that apartheid had forced South Africa to become an international outcast, not the supreme being that Nationalist leaders worshipped with total devotion.

Botha did not know that apartheid had become an instrument of oppressing Afrikaners themselves, not a weapon to subject Africans to perpetual domination. He did not know that apartheid was doomed to fail much sooner than he anticipated, even in his lifetime forcing him to recognize Africans as his equals under the law and living under an African government led by an African the Nationalist government kept in prison for twenty-seven years. He did not realize that apartheid had become the object of total contempt throughout the world, not the sacred shrine of reverence and devotion that its creators intended it to be. Where did this situation lead Botha and the Nationalist Party? The sad part of this is that Botha did not have the slightest idea that his own term of office would come to an end forced by the action of one of the members of the inner circle of the Nationalist Party.

In their determination to hold onto the past, Botha and the Nationalist Party believed that the Afrikaners they represented relished the glories of the past and wanted to ensure that it provided the motivation that would shape a greater future for them than they dared dream of. It turned out that the past was not a highway to the heaven of the future they thought they were working toward. In this conflicting situation, Botha faced a dilemma of choice: to hold onto the past in defending the laager and face increasing opposition, or to give way to pressure from the international community, paving the way for the end of apartheid, and thus beginning to storm the laager that had engulfed South Africa since 1948. What course of action was he going to pursue to resolve this dilemma?

## THE NKOMATI ACCORD: BOTHA'S EFFORTS TO DEFEND THE LAAGER

Recognizing that he was facing enormous pressure to end apartheid, Botha decided to do something that he believed would give the confidence he needed to face an uncertain future. What actually happened is that his action in this line of national purpose gave him the illusion that he would be able to sustain apartheid. Shortly after assuming the office of prime minister in 1978, Botha created what became known as government councils in townships. The main responsibility of the councils was to coordinate the implementation of the entire policy of apartheid. In 1966 John Vorster had removed 4 million Africans from urban areas and forced them to move into the homelands that he created under apartheid laws. Vorster also deprived all Africans of their South African citizenship.

Vorster's action in depriving Africans of their citizenship is one aspect of the policy of apartheid that Botha sought to strengthen. However, opposition to both the formation of councils to enforce the policy and the policy itself began to intensify immediately, allowing Botha little time to assess the situation and make necessary adjustments. In 1983 the United Democratic Front was formed by Africans and liberal whites to oppose Botha's agenda. In that same year Botha proclaimed a new constitution that offered limited representation in the legislature for Coloreds and Indians, but not for Africans.[6] This development is the reason why, in 1984, Africans marched in protest against Botha's arbitrary action. As usual, Africans were met with violence. Thousands were arrested and sent into detention camps where some were kept for years without trial. As a result, Botha was riding a wave of popularity among

Afrikaners, totally unaware that he had placed the country on the edge of a volcano. In May 1984, the Congress of South African Trade Unions (COSATU) organized sixteen strikes by June of that year. Two years later, in 1986, Botha declared a state of emergency and arrested 20,000 Africans.[7]

Realizing that the application of apartheid was having a highly negative impact on his ability to be an effective leader, Botha turned his attention to the deteriorating relationships which existed between his administration and other countries in southern Africa. In 1984 the relationship between the government of Mozambique and South Africa was reaching a breaking point. Since 1979, as a result of the support given by the World Council of Churches, the outlawed ANC was intensifying its struggle against the apartheid system. At that time, the government of Mozambique was providing operational bases to ANC nationalist guerrillas to launch raids into South Africa because of the decision that front-line states[8] made in 1969 that all independent nations under African rule would provide operational bases to African nationalist guerrillas fighting against colonial systems in southern Africa. Since 1964, Tanzania provided operational bases to the nationalist guerrillas fighting to bring the colonial government in Mozambique to an end. Soon after it achieved political independence in 1975, the government of Mozambique felt it had an obligation to provide ANC guerrillas operational bases to fight against the apartheid system.

In 1981 the raids that ANC guerrillas were launching into South Africa were having a paralyzing effect on daily activities. In all his enthusiasm and dedication to sustain apartheid, Botha was unable to control this rapidly developing situation. His only viable response was to launch military attacks on Mozambique. In this manner the people of Mozambique were subjected to a new kind of colonial violence meted out by the champions of apartheid under a plan to bring all of southern Africa under their control by using what Colin Legum calls Pax Pretoriana.[9] In order to create a degree of confidence among Afrikaners, Botha tried to convince them that the raids into Mozambique in search of ANC guerrillas would give him the support he desperately needed to show that he was the only leader Afrikaners could support.

As aggression and violence perpetrated by South Africa mounted, the government and people of Mozambique were faced with a painful choice: to remain loyal to the principle, enunciated by the OAU and the front-line states, that African nations must not negotiate with the apartheid government, or to agree to negotiate with South Africa and derail the OAU plan. If the people and the government of Mozambique decided to negotiate with the apartheid system, they would foil the efforts of the ANC in its struggle to end apartheid. If they refused to negotiate, they would continue to endure the violence that South Africa meted out in the form of raids launched against them in pursuit of the ANC guerrillas. The apartheid system would use the excuse of its pursuit of ANC guerrillas to destroy national institutions and kill innocent people in Mozambique.

Such was the cruelty of the dilemma that the government and the people of Mozambique faced. In the end, the need to survive as a nation became the main consideration that Mozambique utilized in deciding to hold negotiations with South Africa. It was a painful choice which Botha exploited to the fullest extent. Samora Machel, head of the government of Mozambique, saw the purpose of negotiations as seeking to end the violence that was coming from South Africa as a result of the application of apartheid. But Botha saw the purpose of negotiations as a recognition of South Africa as a major military power in the region. How realistic would the negotiations be under these circumstances, with a climate of conflict and contradiction in their purpose? Would the outcome of the negotiations be satisfactory to either party? How would the rest of southern Africa be affected by the outcome of the negotiations? How would the ANC fit into the situation that the negotiations would create?

Since it gained political independence from Portugal in 1975, Mozambique endured the agony of political conflict and disintegration beyond what was considered normal. The Mozambique Resistance Movement (Renamo), led by Afonzo Dhlamini, waged a relentless campaign of destruction beyond anything Africans had ever known. The toll that this social and political malaise took was compounded by the relentless attacks by South Africa in its claimed pursuit of the ANC guerrillas who were operating from bases in Mozambique. In order to minimize the effect that the ANC guerrillas were having on South Africa, Botha felt compelled to support Renamo in his determination to assert the role that he defined for South Africa—claiming its position as the most powerful country in southern Africa. Colin Legum suggests that for several years South Africa occupied large areas of southern Angola and supported Renamo and expanded its field of operation to destabilize functional structures and paralyze national operations.[10]

The hardships that South Africa was imposing on Mozambique were compounded in 1982 by the worst drought Mozambique had ever experienced. The combination of the drought and the action by South Africa forced 100,000 peasants in Mozambique to seek refuge in Zimbabwe. In the process 300,000 lives were lost. It was these developments that the government of Mozambique recognized as providing the needed conditions to hold discussions with South Africa in order to ensure the survival of the nation. At that time South Africa was the strongest nation in southern Africa because it received economic support from European nations through investments which it turned into political capital gains. South Africa also used the investments to strengthen its military forces used to control the region as a whole. In October 1983, Samora Machel undertook a tour of Europe to solicit the economic aid Mozambique needed to improve the situation. Machel also hoped that European nations would persuade South Africa to refrain from its activities in Mozambique, and that instead of pursuing ANC guerrillas, it should seek to protect its borders.

With criticism from front-line states, and a lack of encouragement or support from European nations, Machel had few options. He, therefore, gave in to Botha's pressure to meet at the town of Khomatipoort, on the border between the two countries on the banks of the Khomati River. The meeting included four items that were considered crucial to the security of both Mozambique and South Africa. These were: (1) finding ways of eliminating all forms of aggression; (2) discussion to improve transportation and communication between the two countries; (3) designing ways to enhance the tourist industry between the two countries; and (4) establishing the best possible ways of exploiting hydroelectric power generated by the Cabora Bassa Dam.[11] Botha claimed that meeting these objectives would benefit Mozambique more than South Africa.[12] There is no doubt, however, that Botha knew that fulfilling these objectives would strengthen his efforts to defend the laager.

Preparation for the meeting was initiated in 1975, soon after Mozambique gained political independence. John Vorster believed what the Portuguese colonial government told him in 1970 when the Cabora Bassa project was being considered: that they would never allow Africans to come to power, not in a thousand years, as the expression went. As part of Vorster's administration, Botha was operating under this grand colonial illusion. But when Africans assumed the reins of power in 1975, Vorster was at a loss to understand how the Portuguese colonial officials could miss the mark by as much as they did. Vorster's major concern was not that the new African government of Mozambique would assist the ANC guerrillas, but that it would not maintain the dam in sufficient condition to continue to supply South Africa with electricity. That is why, in 1975, he initiated contact with the government of Mozambique. But the initiative was far less than successful.

In 1984 Botha, having made little progress in his efforts to have the government of Mozambique assure him that the flow of electricity to South Africa from Cabora Bassa would not cease, decided to change tactics. Aware that apartheid was costing his government dearly, he utilized both a diplomatic approach and the threat of military force to secure concessions from Mozambique. He wanted the world to believe that he could reach an agreement with any other country in southern Africa on critical regional issues without eliminating apartheid. In doing so he was making new efforts to sustain the laager. The conditions for the Nkomati summit conference were finally put together at a preliminary meeting held in Swaziland on December 20, 1983.[13] Botha was elated; he believed that this would enable him to defend the laager more effectively than he had done in the past. He wanted his fellow Afrikaners to know that he would be the first apartheid leader to do so and hoped that they would come to his aid in defending the laager.

The accord that was signed on March 16, 1984, included the following clauses:

1. The two countries pledged to respect each other's sovereignty and independence. In fulfillment of this pledge they promised to refrain from interfering in the international affairs of the other.

2. The two countries promised to resolve differences and disputes that may arise between them by peaceful means. They would also seek the cooperation of other countries in southern Africa in seeking solutions to problems of relationships with and among them. Where differences seemed irreconcilable, the two countries would resort to arbitration, rather than to military force.

3. The two countries pledged not to allow their respective territories, territorial waters, or air space to be used as bases of any persons or organizations planning to commit acts of violence, terrorism, or aggression against the territorial integrity or political independence of its inhabitants.

4. The two countries promised to take steps, individually and together, to ensure that the boundaries between them be efficiently patrolled and border posts be efficiently administered to prevent illegal crossing from the territory of one to that of the other.

5. The two countries agreed to prohibit acts of propaganda within their territory against the other, and to stop propaganda that may excite aggression, violence, or terrorism.

6. The two countries declared that there was no conflict between the commitments in treaties and international obligations and the commitment undertaken in this agreement. They would also work toward greater harmony between the terms of this agreement and their international obligations.

7. The two countries pledged their commitment to the interpretation of this accord in good faith, and promised to maintain periodic contact to ensure the effective application of what had been agreed upon.

8. The parties stated that there was nothing in this accord that could be construed as detracting from the parties' right to self-defense in the event of an armed attack, as provided for in the U.N. Charter.

9. Each party was expected to appoint high-ranking representatives to serve on a joint security commission to supervise and monitor the implementation and application of this accord. The commission would meet on a regular basis and would convene whenever needed. The commission's responsibilities included: (1) considering allegations of infringements of the provisions of this accord; (2) advising the parties of the conditions that need addressing; (3) making recommendations to the parties to ensure effective application of this

accord; and (4) suggesting ways of settling disputes over infringements, or allegations of infringements.

10. It was agreed that the two countries would make available all facilities necessary for the effective functioning of the commission and would jointly consider its conclusions and recommendations. The commission would also suggest methods of enhancing tourist industry, communications, and better distribution of power from the Cabora Bassa Hydro-electric Dam.[14]

## REACTION TO THE ACCORD: STRATEGY TO CAUSE CRACKS IN THE LAAGER

The accord made no mention of the desirability of ending apartheid. Machel should have known that the conflict South Africa was having with Africans, in South Africa and all over the continent, was caused by apartheid. He should have made the strongest case possible to let Botha know that as long as apartheid remained the policy of South Africa, there was no possibility of reaching any agreement on any issue. The reaction to the Nkomati Accord was immediate. The OAU, the ANC, and the front-line states were stunned that Machel would sign such an agreement at a time when all of black Africa was working toward the elimination of apartheid. The ANC immediately indicated that it would disregard the accord and continue its struggle against the government of South Africa. But Botha himself went into a state of euphoria, as he saw the accord from an entirely opposite perspective, that of enabling him to defend the laager more effectively.

Botha regarded the accord as acceptance of his leadership, not only of South Africa, but of southern Africa as whole. He also saw the accord as his finest hour in his defense of the laager. One wonders if Machel had known this whether he would have signed the accord. Upon learning of Botha's euphoria, Machel seemed to have second thoughts. But there was nothing he could do, he had signed the document. If he pulled out Botha would portray him as a leader without the character or ability to honor international agreements. Clearly, Botha's claim of leadership and the ANC's reaction compounded the problems of regional relationships. Botha must have recognized that an agreement with any country of southern Africa to sustain apartheid would be futile as long as the ANC existed.

Botha should have learned from the so-called internal agreement reached in Zimbabwe in 1979 between Ian D. Smith and three black leaders at the exclusion of ZANU.[15] However, in June 1984, Botha used the accord to tour European capitals in an effort to ward off criticism against apartheid and to drum up support for his policy. It is inconceivable that Botha saw the accord and his role in southern Africa only from the perspective of seeking to strengthen apartheid. He seemed totally unable to view the conflict as an outcome of apartheid. Robert Davis and Dan O'Meara discussed the implications of Botha's tour of Europe, saying, "Botha's controversial visit to Western Europe made it clear that his regime sees the consideration of its regional domination as formalized linkages with neighboring states and as a means through which to break out of South Africa's long-standing international isolation."[16] Success in his defense of the laager depended on the success of the tour. In doing so, he was gambling everything he had with no assurance that the gamble would pay off.

Davis and O'Meara also concluded that the conditions created by the Nkomati Accord brought to the attention of southern Africa and the international community that South Africa under Botha had at its disposal "a wide range of regional policy instruments of tactics,"[17] which Botha could use to sustain both the interests and position of South Africa in the region. This is the reason why Botha was euphoric. This is also why the ANC would not accept the accord, which had opened a new chapter in the conflict between the OAU, the front-line states other than Mozambique and Angola, and the ANC. Botha was totally unaware that he had placed the region in a critical position.

Botha also used the accord to exercise control of the economy of Mozambique. He understood more than any of his predecessors the importance of South African domination of the economy as an added instrument of the political power that he had suddenly acquired in the region. Unfortunately Botha was unaware that, because Mozambique was acting from the position of weakness, the international community and black Africa saw the accord as a new form of domination.[18] Since the accord became the instrument of Botha's domination of southern Africa, it followed that he used it to constitute a new form of oppression, not only of Mozambique and the ANC, but also of the region as a whole. Botha intended the accord to compel Mozambique to stop ANC nationalist guerrillas from continuing their crusade against apartheid. The question was whether the accord could be implemented.

This African treaty of Westphalia[19] posed other serious implications that Botha might not have been aware of. After he succeeded John Vorster in 1978, Botha reorganized his administration to give himself more power and direct access to all functions of the various government departments. Under that reorganization, decision-making responsibilities were directly related to the role the military was expected to play. Because of the shift in emphasis of the military's role in the pursuit of his foreign policy, Botha lost all sensitivity to logic and the concern of the international community in the pursuit of his agenda. In this context he saw the power of apartheid in southern Africa only from the perspective of military power. He viewed the social, economic, and political problems of the region only from the standpoint of the need to use the military in order to sustain apartheid. Indeed, in all his thought processes, Botha was influenced by the question of how to maintain apartheid. In this kind of setting Botha was not aware that he was engaging in an exercise of grand self-deception.

The reaction to the Nkomati Accord in South Africa among Afrikaners was as euphoric as Botha's. *Panorama*, a leading magazine in South Africa, described the accord saying,

A new era of realism has dawned for southern Africa with the signing of a non-aggression pact, the Nkomati Accord. The accord is irrefutable proof that the economic and geographic realities of southern Africa, and a pragmatic approach to the region's problems are of greater importance than widely diverse ideologies and antagonistic rhetoric that exists in the region. By placing their signatures on the accord, Samora Moises Machel and Pieter Willem Botha solemnly pledged to honor the discussions contained in the accord. In the accord South Africa extended the hand of friendship to its neighboring African states.[20]

*Panorama* did not discuss the more serious implications that the accord created, such as Botha's refusal to discuss the need to end apartheid, the determination of the ANC to continue its struggle, the negative reaction from the front-line states, and the continuing doubt among the members of the international community about the role of apartheid in regional relationships. The magazine claimed that Mozambique's failure to convince Botha of the need to end apartheid was a victory for the South African position in the region. Botha did not even acknowledge apartheid as a major problem in the relationships between South Africa and other countries of southern Africa. How could he and *Panorama* fail to recognize this basic truth? This failure is the reason why African countries and the international community refused to recognize the accord as an initiative toward comprehensive peace in the region. Instead, they saw Mozambique as a victim of the latest application of the policy of apartheid.

There is yet another critical factor that played in Botha's favor in the accord. South Africa and Mozambique had not had normal diplomatic relations since the inception of Mozambique independence in 1975 due to the action initiated by the OAU, which prohibited any black African nation from having diplomatic relations with the apartheid government. However, Botha demanded that certain agreements that had been reached between Portuguese colonial government and South Africa be honored even though the government of Mozambique had indicated that it would not honor any such agreements because they were part of a strategy to perpetuate colonial conditions in both countries. Indeed, Botha and Machel knew that the colonial governments in Mozambique and South Africa had reached these agreements as part of their strategy to defend the laager in both countries and that the new black government that Machel led could honor them only at the price of helping Botha defend the laager.

One such agreement had to do with the supply of electricity to South Africa from the Cabora Bassa Hydro-electric Dam. Because South Africa had financed the construction of the dam on the understanding that 80 percent of the electricity generated would be sent to South Africa, Botha demanded that the government of Mozambique honor that pledge. Machel rejected this line of reasoning saying that the Portuguese colonial government had no right to decide the issue for the people of Mozambique because it was motivated by desire to defend the laager. Fearing that the difference of opinion about the supply of electricity to South Africa would derail the conference and weaken his defense of the laager, Botha agreed to a compromise clause stating that the two countries should name a commission whose responsibility would include designing methods of distribution of electricity from the dam. In the end, the commission would never meet to discharge this responsibility because other events engulfed South Africa within a short period of time making it impossible to honor the terms of the Nkomati Accord itself.

There was yet another complication with the accord. Throughout the summit, Botha characterized the ANC's determination to fight for the elimination of apartheid as terrorism. He was unable to recognize the terrorism that apartheid meted out on the region as a whole. This failure is the reason why *Panorama* said, "A banned South African terrorist organization (reference to ANC) had been offered facilities in Mozambique. Terrorist deeds which had been planned in Mozambique were executed on South African territory and had led to retaliatory action by South Africa."[21] The magazine claimed that Botha's ability to force Mozambique to stop the ANC from carrying out raids into South Africa gave him the power and influence he needed to conduct the South African foreign policy more effectively. Therefore, the magazine concluded, the South African domestic policy had suddenly found a way of extending itself beyond its own borders. In this manner the laager would be defended more effectively.

However, Botha's refusal to recognize apartheid as a major cause of conflict between South Africa and other countries of southern Africa did nothing to eliminate the complex problems he was encountering. His refusal to honor Security Council Resolution 385 of 1978 ordering South Africa to withdraw from Namibia, his support of dissident elements in Zimbabwe, and his support of Jonas Savimbi's campaign of terror in Angola all combined to create problems that offset the claimed benefits of the Nkomati Accord. The accord did not suddenly become the vehicle that carried Botha to a position of supreme power where he alone could determine the direction that southern Africa was taking in its struggle for development. It is inconceivable why Botha regarded the accord as a panacea of all problems of southern Africa.

However, at the conclusion of the conference, both Botha and Machel spoke about the importance of the accord and what they believed it was intended to accomplish for both countries. Botha spoke first saying, "We have signaled to the world our belief that states with different social, economic and political systems[22] can work together in the pursuit of common interests. We face extremely complex social, political, and economic problems in southern Africa, so complex that they can result in conflict. It is often difficult to avoid being drawn into the resultant spiral of confrontation and conflict. In these circumstances the real issues are avoided, uncomfortable facts and harsh realities are dusted under the carpet."[23]

Botha went on to claim that both Mozambique and South Africa were countries inhabited by African people whose past and future were firmly entrenched in the southern part of the African continent. Therefore, all people, both white and black were Africans and should have a common future in that part of the continent, and that generations which would follow should find happiness in the land of their birth.[24] Nowhere did Botha recognize the need to end apartheid as a condition of that future happiness. Such was the tragedy of his thinking. By refusing to recognize this reality, Botha was placing that future into jeopardy. It was left to other individuals of a different frame of mind to recognize that, indeed, apartheid had to end if Afrikaners could ever hope to have a future in South Africa. This would not be an easy task, but it had to be undertaken in the interest of all the people of this troubled country.

In response, Machel stated that the signing of the agreement represented non-aggression and good neighborliness at a high point in the history of the relationship between the two countries. It also represented a high point in the history of the region. He argued that the principles he and Botha had enshrined in the accord were universally valid to govern relationships between two sovereign states regardless of their political, economic and social systems. They were principles that opened a new perspective for the improvement of relationships between South Africa and Mozambique, insofar as they were designed to guarantee a solid and lasting peace.

Machel added that what the two leaders had undertaken was a solemn commitment not to launch aggressive action of any kind against one another. He claimed that he and Botha had laid the foundation for a definitive break in the cycle of violence that had been established in the region. Machel concluded, "Let southern Africa emerge as a region of progress whose reason prevails over hate and prejudice where efforts are centralized on the struggle for development and well-being of all the people."[25] For Botha to listen to Machel make these comments was for him to witness the supremacy of the ideology that had been espoused by his predecessors that apartheid must remain the cornerstone of the security of Afrikaners, not only in South Africa, but also in the region of southern Africa as a whole. Clearly, Botha had his sight set on other larger endeavors in seeking the promotion of the dominance of South Africa in the region. He regarded Machel's hope for peace in the region as based on the application of apartheid, his successful defense of the laager. For Botha there was no other perspective from which to view the accord.

It is, however, clear that by using such expressions as "aggressive action," "prejudice," and "breaking the cycle of violence," Machel was using terms that the international community was using to describe the destructive effect of apartheid in all its forms. As much as he tried to use diplomatic language, Machel could not conceal the anger, disappointment, and frustration that he experienced as a signatory to the accord. As an African who had lived under the oppressive system developed by the Portuguese, Machel saw the situation he faced from the perspective of the effect of apartheid. Only he could have such an understanding. Botha had no notion of the extent of the significance of what was happening in the signing of the accord. However, the accord gave Botha his fifteen minutes of fame and a spotlight. His self-confidence suddenly soared to new heights, totally unaware that the accord he was going to use to elevate himself to a new level of popularity among Afrikaners would become the Tower of Babel that would collapse in his face. However, his problems began to emerge sooner than he ever anticipated.

## TROUBLE ON THE HOME FRONT: CRACKS IN THE LAAGER

When Botha succeeded John Vorster in September 1978, he was aware of the problems he was about to face. Vorster had been disgraced by a major scandal involving the misuse of funds that were to be used to minimize the effect of the economic sanctions imposed by the international community to force South Africa to end apartheid. Associates in his administration had diverted those funds to personal bank accounts. When Vorster fell from power as a result, some of these associates jumped bail and escaped to Europe and Australia. By the time of his death in 1983, Vorster had been disgraced beyond repair.

Indeed, John Vorster, the diehard Afrikaner whose belief in the supremacy of apartheid was absolute, had become the Nikita Khrushchev[26] of South Africa. From the time it assumed power in 1948, the Nationalist Party was brought to the test. Botha, aware that he had inherited a serious problem of public trust and confidence, tried something he believed would have the effect and the appearance of restoring confidence among Afrikaners. He named the Schlebusch Commission in July 1979 to study and advise him on the framework of a new constitutional plan he developed as he assumed office. Botha had kept the plan secret because he did not want it subjected to criticism before it was in place. Details of the plan became known only after the Schlebusch Commission released its report.

When the Schlebusch Commission submitted its report in May 1980, Botha immediately submitted it to Parliament for approval. The report recommended the abolition of the senate and the office of prime minister, preferring the appointment of a state president with sweeping powers. The commission also recommended the appointment of a presidential council consisting of sixty members appointed by the president. The advisory council would consist of white, colored, Asian, and Chinese members.[27] Africans would not be represented because they were considered members of the Bantustan homelands and were therefore not citizens of South Africa. Botha had made no provision for participation of Africans either in the composition of the commission or in its recommendations. The decision to have the Chinese representation reflected South Africa's ties with Taiwan. Obviously, Botha's constitutional plan would give him the opportunity to become the first state president of South Africa with powers that no previous national leader had ever exercised. Botha would get his wish in 1983 when the new plan went into effect.

In August 1979, Botha had announced a twelve-point plan that he claimed would address both domestic problems and international relations with South Africa. He argued that Vorster had been aware of the need to address these issues but was unable to do so because he was preoccupied with the scandal. All Botha did was to use the Nkomati Accord as the basis of his claim that conditions in southern Africa had changed and that everyone would benefit. He provided nothing new in the plan. He began to make a concerted effort to convince the international community that the application of apartheid was intended to serve the interests of Africans themselves. Realizing that criticism of apartheid continued to intensify, Botha began in 1980 to make plans to visit western European capitals to promote his agenda and strengthen his own position. The strategy did not work.

Botha was not aware that his constitutional plan led to a major problem because it excluded Africans from the process of national development. Although Botha created a separate advisory council consisting of African representatives, Africans rejected it because it was based entirely on the provisions of apartheid and the council would only function to rubber stamp his decisions. The plan was also criticized by Afrikaners because they saw it as an infringement of Afrikaner political domination.

Botha was unable to resolve the conflict emerging from both sides of the racial line. The cracks in the laager were becoming more visible as Botha was unable to repair them.

At the same time, the Coloured Labour Party concluded that the process of creating the presidential advisory council represented a fragmentation of the political system and threatened to expel from the party Coloured persons who accepted appointment by Botha to serve on the council. This was the same position that Africans took. Botha was left to wallow in the mud of confusion. His grand plan to give himself more power was causing major problems both in South Africa and abroad. Indeed, because Coloureds and Indians declined to serve on the council, its role came to nothing. Everyone concerned knew that he wanted to use the council to argue that he was not acting alone on national issues. Because Botha formed the council in the midst of a national controversy, he was unable to have it operate fully.

Among the items that constituted Botha's agenda was his intent to strive toward what he regarded as "peaceful consultation with states of southern Africa with respect for traditions and ideas expressed for the benefit of each other"[28] for purposes of creating a climate of understanding. What later came out of this perception was that Botha was formulating a new policy to govern his relationships with the leaders of the Bantustan homelands which, during Vorster's administration, were regarded as independent. The implementation of this policy would be initiated in stages beginning with the Transkei, Bophutatswana, Venda, and the Ciskei.

Further application of this policy for the remaining eight Bantustan homelands would depend on Botha's evaluation of the effect on the first four Bantustan homelands. Botha hoped that his policy on these relationships would help him consolidate his national plan to strengthen the policy of apartheid. This is the reason why, speaking to the House of Assembly on June 2, 1980, Botha indicated that urban African communities not directly related to the Bantustan homelands could be related to future council activity yet to be formed under still unspecified conditions. The Africans reacted to the plan with total contempt.

In spite of this setback, Botha managed to convince the white businessmen who met with him in Johannesburg on November 22, 1979, that his plan would produce economic stability and increase profit for them. He also excited their imaginations by trying to convince them that his plan would protect their political interests because economic growth was closely related to political stability. Botha also argued that his plan would help South Africa expand its markets to other countries in southern Africa. Botha saw things exclusively from the need to sustain apartheid. Everything he did was structured around this basic objective. It was not possible for him to see things from a broader perspective in which apartheid was not a factor.

In April 1980, determined to protect their economy from exploitation by South Africa, ten independent countries in southern Africa formed an economic association known as Southern African Development Coordination Conference (SADCC). Botha did not know that, in formulating his plan, he was launching new economic warfare in the region. Africans in South Africa knew that whatever Botha did was motivated by the desire to improve the effectiveness of apartheid to control their lives. They regarded any aspect of his policy as devoid of any real meaning for them. Their response was to consider ways of protecting themselves from the full impact of the implementation of apartheid regulations. This task was not easy because apartheid was implemented by force, not a voluntary response from Africans. In spite of the economic difficulties they would encounter as a result of action by other South African countries, Africans looked to SADCC for help in bringing apartheid to an end.

In 1981, believing that the support he received from the Afrikaner business community represented broadly based national support, Botha decided to seek a new national mandate. He called a general election to be held on April 29, 1981, a full year before it was scheduled. In doing so he was responding to counterpressures coming both from within the Nationalist Party and from various groups and organizations that were now thinking of including Africans on a level much higher than Botha was projecting. For example, some segments of the business community and industry were slowly but steadily recognizing the fact that the African economic segment represented substantial buying power for both the present and the future, and that major changes needed to be made in the application of apartheid to make this buying potential increase. With a rising African population, the business community was going to depend on Africans to remain and continue their business enterprise. Was it possible to expect Botha to understand this dimension of the national economy?

At the same time that South Africa became subjected to new international pressure through economic sanctions, the price of materials, especially gold, was becoming unstable. The business community, other than Afrikaner, recognized that ignoring this basic fact would cost the country very dearly. Many people wanted to know how long South Africa would continue to mislead itself by thinking that everything was fine when, in effect, things were deteriorating rapidly. Botha's refusal to see things from the perspective of the business community compounded the problems the country was facing. But once this groundswell began to form in favor of greater political accommodation of Africans, it would not subside until Botha was removed from office. He had become the major problem. This was the national political and economic climate for the up-coming elections.

There were other considerations that Botha did not take into account in calling for an election in 1981. The education of Africans was becoming a major cause of concern among university officials. In 1980 several universities, including Stellenbosch in the Cape Province and Witwatersrand in Johannesburg, began to admit a limited number of African students in violation of apartheid regulations. They were doing this under their projection that in the near future Africans would help meet a substantial need for a skilled labor force to aid economic growth. Botha never saw the education of Africans from this perspective. The demands of apartheid prohibited him from this level of vision and foresight. He did not know that the growing need for more skilled administrative labor was being dashed by the lack of an effective policy to develop it. In this regard Botha and the universities were on a collision course.

Above all else, the conservative elements of the Nationalist Party— more conservative than Botha—especially those in the Transvaal, began to express opposition to Botha's domination of the party because he came from the Cape Province, which they believed did not represent true Afrikaner ideals. They also resented his constitutional proposals because they thought that implementing them would allow Africans to reach the shores of Afrikaner political power. In addition, they feared the ultimate outcome of the growing influence of the African trade unions, especially COSATU. Botha himself had assured the Nationalist Party members, and Afrikaners in general, that he would never allow Africans to threaten the political power they had exercised over many years. Nevertheless, criticism of Botha's leadership, by both the Nationalist Party and the country, continued to increase the cracks in the laager.

At the same time Africans were more daring in their attack of apartheid. The front-line states were relentless in supporting the ANC struggle. The OAU was intensifying its campaign to discredit Botha and the Nationalist Party. Africans in general were becoming increasingly intolerant of the ways apartheid was oppressing them. Botha was being attacked by the various constituencies of South Africa. His leadership style was causing him problems he never thought he would encounter. He adopted tyrannical methods and refused to discuss policy issues before he implemented them. He was slowly becoming a one-man government. He trusted very few in his administration, and only his associates from the Cape Province had access to him. He became isolated from the people he was there to serve. He was becoming a stranger to Afrikaners.

There were other political problems that Botha did not anticipate. Gwendolen M. Carter discussed some of these problems as follows, "Extreme right wing groups had become increasingly active against what they interpreted as dangerous moves toward racial integration."[29] Although leaders of the newest proponent extremist group, the Wit Commandos were finally arrested in January and February 1981, the bombing of offices of liberal organizations and the homes of prominent individuals like Colin Englin, former leader of PFP (Progressive Federal Party) had been occurring intermittently. This was politically embarrassing to the government and raised disturbing questions about the attitude of defense, security, and civil service."[30]

In calling a general election in April 1981, Botha hoped the results would establish and confirm him as the undisputed leader of Afrikaners and South Africa and as the standard bearer of the Nationalist Party. He hoped that as a result of him winning the election he would have the power to force the acceptance of his constitutional proposals. Botha argued that the alternative would be a disaster for South Africa. It did not matter to him that he was using questionable methods to try to achieve his goals and maintain defense of the laager. All he wanted to do was to accomplish his goals in a manner that would leave his name in the history of South Africa as one of the greatest champions in preserving the supremacy of apartheid.

Although the Nationalist Party won the election in what could be considered an overwhelming victory, with 131 seats out of a total of 165 seats in Parliament, there was only a 70 percent vote turnout. Therefore, Botha could not claim to have the new national mandate he sought and needed to assert his leadership and carry out his agenda. Political observers concluded that the election was a defeat to Botha because of the unprecedented split in the vote among Afrikaners.[31] More humiliating to Botha was the fact that the PFP increased the number of seats in Parliament from 17 to 26 taking away seats from the Nationalist Party, including two cabinet ministers. This was the first time that cabinet ministers had lost an election since the Nationalist Party came to power in 1948. The PFP also received 5 percent of the Afrikaner vote, a major election embarrassment for Botha.

Members of the Nationalist Party and Afrikaners blamed Botha for this humiliating loss of cabinet ministers and the general manner in which he was leading the election campaign. This is why, following the election, disagreement within the ranks of the Nationalist Party began to surface more forcefully. Jaap Marais, an extreme member of the Nationalist Party, reacted, "There can no longer be any talk of political unity in Afrikaner ranks."[32] Marais was joined in the chorus of criticism of Botha by Fanie Botha, Minister of Manpower Utilization, and Andries Trevrnicht, an outspoken conservative known for his anti-African stance. In February 1982, Trevrnicht challenged Botha's leadership of the Nationalist Party arguing that he was leading both the party and the country astray. Botha was slowly but steadily becoming a beleaguered man and troubled leader as the lack of confidence in him increased.

Suddenly the cracks in the laager widened when a meeting of the Nationalist Party was convened in the Transvaal to discuss Botha's leadership and to take any action considered to be in the best interest of Afrikaners and the Nationalist Party. In a surprise move, Botha succeeded in persuading the party to express confidence in his leadership and policy. But there was a price to pay. Trevrnicht and sixteen of his supporters, including Ferdinand Hartzenberg, the notorious Minister of Education, resigned from the Nationalist Party sending a message throughout the country that there was a major crisis in party leadership. Afrikaans students, through their association, Afrikaanse Studente Bond (ASB), joined the chorus of condemnation of Botha's leadership of the Nationalist Party and the country.

The political problems that Botha encountered in quick succession were compounded in 1983 by the action that a liberal Afrikaner student organization, Politicke Studente (Polstu), took to reaffirm its view that apartheid was a sinister policy whose implementation was inflaming every segment of the South African community. Representing 500 students, Polstu called for equal citizenship and social, economic, and political opportunity. This is the position Botha rejected. Harry F. Oppenheimer, the powerful chairman of the equally powerful Anglo-American Corporation, reacted to the saga of Botha's policy by discussing the economic implications that he saw saying, "Economic growth and racial discrimination are in fundamental opposition to each other and economic growth is also an essential element in building a peaceful and just society."[33] Indications to Botha that it was time to dismantle apartheid were coming from all directions, but he refused to acknowledge them.

Two years after the signing of the Nkomati Accord in 1986, Botha was faced with new economic problems. In February 1986, banks, increasingly worried by the rising internal conflict, withheld credit. Nearly 300 international banks began to cancel their loans following Botha's failure to enunciate expected reform during a speech he delivered in Durban in which he told about crossing the Rubican, but made no mention of the need to dismantle apartheid. The banks wanted to see if Botha would offer anything more. When they saw that he was unable, or unwilling, to see the necessity of ending apartheid, the banks decided to do something that would hurt the country but protect their financial interests. Botha had no idea how devastating this would be to the country and to his own political future. Suddenly he was more concerned with his own political survival than with defending the laager.

The political stakes were getting higher with Botha's refusal to confront apartheid. The longer he waited, the harder the problems became. He was unaware that the economic difficulties were rapidly translating into political problems. *Newsweek* observed this reality saying, "The credit squeeze has retarded South Africa's growth, dried up liquidity and sent the rand tumbling. To reverse the slide South Africa needs to strike a deal to end a moratorium on reopening the principal on their $24 billion debt."[34] The central argument made by the banks was that Botha's government was denying 20 million Africans citizenship rights that many nations take for granted. This action created a situation that was slowly leading to a major national conflict. In response, Botha hinted that his government might consider extending citizenship to Africans if certain conditions were met. Although he did not specify those conditions, it was clear that they would include dismantling both apartheid and the Bantustan homelands. These conditions would also mean the end of the forced removal of Africans to the homelands. The banks concluded that Botha was unable to take such action because he was much too engrossed in the philosophy of apartheid.

On September 27, 1987, a group of whites opposed to apartheid convinced a national conference in Johannesburg to express support for a future initiative for a nonracial democracy. There were 800 delegates invited to this unique conference known as Toward Democracy: Whites in a Changing South Africa. Botha was taken by surprise both by the number of whites opposed to his agenda and by the conference decision to invite black guests. However, he was still unable to understand that both his agenda and his leadership were considered to be the major problems South Africa was facing. The harmony that emerged among those that attended the conference, the agreement they expressed about the need to end apartheid, and the understanding that was demonstrated between Africans and whites all combined to create a situation the kind of which South Africa had never experienced in the past. This was too much for Botha to understand.

Frank Chikane, General Secretary of the South African Council of Churches and one of Africans invited to the two-day conference, remarked, "In the past we had written whites off in our struggle against apartheid. All whites were problems because they were seen as synonymous with the brutality and suffering experienced by blacks. Now we see that because we have a common destiny in South Africa we must come together to shape that destiny. That is why we have been invited to this conference."[35] Nico Smith, an Afrikaner from the Dutch Reformed Church who resigned his position in the church to minister to a black community in Pretoria, predicted that the church would not be able to break down the wall of apartheid short of supporting an all out war. Smith added, "Apartheid would have to be broken to climb over violent forces. The churches will have to break the walls of apartheid knowing that our black brothers will be there with us."[36]

Two ideas came out of the conference. The first was that opposition to Botha's leadership was now coming from a group of people he had always depended on for support. These included the business community, who had previously benefited from the application of apartheid, and from members of the Dutch Reformed Church, whose theology of the inferiority of Africans was the basis of their support of apartheid. The second was that the position taken by the Dutch Reformed Church and by the conference was a great encouragement to the ANC. From this point on, the battle lines were being drawn as the combatants braced for an all out struggle. The ANC saw that the forces of apartheid were steadily receding, weakened by a combination of forces Botha could not control. The final chapter of his term of office was being written in a dramatic fashion.

## SHOWDOWN WITH DE KLERK: THE FALL OF BOTHA

When the U.S. Congress voted 244–132 on August 11, 1988, to impose new economic sanctions against South Africa, it signaled the beginning of the end of Botha's term of office. A week earlier, on August 5, some 143 persons conscripted into the South African army refused to serve. The loss that the Nationalist Party suffered in the special election held in May 1983 came as proof that Botha was no longer providing effective leadership. When he suffered a mild stroke on June 18, 1989, many members of the Nationalist Party felt that he must be replaced as leader. Among those who felt this way was F. W. De Klerk, chairman of the Nationalist Party in the Transvaal and minister of education in the Botha government.

From August 1988 to September 1989, the struggle between Botha and de Klerk entered a new phase—de Klerk showed determination to bring Botha's term of office to an end, and Botha struggled to stop what he thought was a usurpation of his power. De Klerk, twenty years younger than Botha, was at first considered a hard-liner, the Richard M. Nixon of South Africa.[37] But as de Klerk played a role in creating the political tragedy unfolding for Botha, he was forced to change positions and adopt a more liberal stance, very much like Mikhail Gorbachev of the Soviet Union. Archbishop Desmond Tutu expressed the fear that if de Klerk succeeded Botha, he would become president of South Africa and would be worse than Botha, Vorster, and Verwoerd. Indeed, de Klerk was forced to make a hard choice: to maintain his traditional attitude toward sustaining apartheid and subject South Africa to more isolation and economic sanctions, or to accept the fact that apartheid was condemned unreservedly by the international community and so had to end.

If de Klerk succeeded Botha, he would have an opportunity to initiate fundamental change in national policy at the very beginning of his term of office, and he did not have to carry the excess baggage of apartheid as his three predecessors did. In March 1989 the Nationalist Party decided to cast a ballot for party leader. There were four candidates for the position—de Klerk; Berend du Pleussis, the moderate Minister of Finance; Christiaan Heunis, leader of the party in the Cape Province and one of Botha's close associates; and Foreign Minister Roelf Botha. When the votes were counted, de Klerk had received 59 votes of the 130 ballots cast. Du Pleussis received 30 votes, Heunis received 25 votes and Roelf Botha received 16 votes. De Klerk then became president of the Nationalist Party. Botha was forced to give up the position of party leader in favor of de Klerk, but the confrontation between the two men intensified from March to September with Botha losing ground to de Klerk.

On August 14, 1989, de Klerk led fifteen of South Africa's senior politicians within the Nationalist Party to Tuynhuys, the official residency of the president, to demand Botha's resignation. This was the first time in the history of South Africa that cabinet members had decided to ask their leader to resign. In the confrontation that ensued between Botha and the conspirators, Botha characterized de Klerk as someone "with a smile on your face and a dagger in your hand."[38] Among the fifteen cabinet members who asked Botha to resign was Magnus Malan, until this moment a close friend and confidante of Botha. Recognizing that Botha was a marked man, Malan played the role of Brutus, saying, when he turned against Botha, "I wish I could bypass this day,"[39] but regretted that circumstances compelled him to support the other fourteen cabinet members in demanding his resignation. The time for Botha to defend the laager was over.

In one last political gasp, Botha lashed out his anger at the fifteen conspirators. When de Klerk tried to tell him that they were motivated to take this action because of his poor health, Botha thundered back, "Look, you are going too far. I am fit. Is any one of you in possession of a medical certificate that proclaims you to be healthy? Let me hear, how many of you are sitting here with pills in your pockets while you drag my health into this mud? Oh, so that is going to be your new tack, your new propaganda, playing with the ANC."[40] Calling them hypocrites and telling them they were weak and useless, Botha indicated that he had the right to fire them all. He flatly refused their suggestion that he appoint an acting president. In responding to the conspirators, Botha was living up to his reputation as the Old Crocodile.

This crisis continued until de Klerk was elected acting president of South Africa at the end of August 1989 to replace the ailing Botha, who was expected to resign due to poor health. In this action Botha's term of office had come to an end, even though he refused to accept the fact that he was no longer president of South Africa. On September 20, 1989, de Klerk was elected president of South Africa by the Nationalist Party. For both the Nationalist Party and South Africa, de Klerk's assumption of the office of president represented a new and decisive phase in the country's history. On May 6, 1990, Botha, then 74 years old, resigned from the Nationalist Party saying that he did not want to be a member of a party that was about to negotiate with the ANC against the interests of Afrikaners.

In his turn, de Klerk responded by saying that Botha's resignation was unfortunate and was based on a wrong interpretation of what de Klerk's administration was trying to accomplish. He also said that he did not want to repudiate Botha because he had rendered the country valuable service in defending the laager.[41] However, the two men entered a new phase of bitterness with de Klerk accusing Botha of refusing to see the writing on the wall and failing to acknowledge the hard fact that the laager could no longer be defended as it had been defended in the past. Botha, in turn, accused de Klerk of wanting to turn over the country to an ANC government much sooner than Afrikaners would wish. It is clear that Botha did not want to go quietly into oblivion. But for all practical purposes the era of the supremacy of apartheid had come to an end and the period of negotiated transfer of power to the African majority was about to begin. For de Klerk, this was the period of seeking accommodation and of seeking a meeting of the minds with Africans on the best strategy of storming the laager.

The extent of the tragedy of Botha's reign of terror in his efforts to defend the laager came to light in 1996. In 1995 President Nelson Mandela named the Truth and Reconciliation Commission, chaired by Archbishop Desmond M. Tutu, to investigate the various forms of the brutality that millions of black South Africans suffered during the iron fist policy initiated by Botha.[42] Mandela and his administration concluded that before they could set the country on the road to reconstruction and self rediscovery, it was necessary to bring into the open all forms of abuse of power and the suffering to which the application of apartheid had subjected Africans. The terms of the Tutu Commission included inviting members of the Botha administration to come forward and give testimony so that the truth of abuse of power by its members would be known. Caught between their fear of possible indictment and the need to conceal the abuse of power, members of Botha's administration faced an agonizing dilemma of choice. Finally, some decided to come forward to confess the wrongs they had committed.

Among those who came to testify was General Johan van der Merwe who confessed to giving orders in 1988 to blow up the headquarters of the World Council of Churches in Johannesburg because of its opposition to apartheid. The blast injured twenty-three people. Van der Merwe also admitted that he ordered the military units under his control to infiltrate a group of antiapartheid activists and provided them with booby-trapped hand grenades which would explode as soon as the pins were pulled.[43] Van der Merwe then offered a startling confession about his orders, saying that the plan had been initiated by Adriaan Vlok, Botha's notorious Minister of Law and Order. Van der Merwe said that Vlok's instructions had come directly from Botha himself. It was revealed that since September 1977, when Steve Biko and forty other African political activists opposed to apartheid were killed, the number of those killed by the orders of the apartheid government rapidly increased until the end of apartheid in 1994. Indeed, defense of the laager was built on the blood of many black South Africans. Mandela and his government were at a loss to know exactly what to do with the report of the Tutu Commission. Such was the tragedy of defending the laager.

As the Tutu Commission began to subpoena officials of the Botha administration implicated in the atrocities, many came forward to confess their role in order to receive amnesty. They had until December 15, 1996, to come forward or face indictments. More than 2,000 submitted applications for amnesty in exchange for testimony.[44] However, the man who carried paramount responsibility for these atrocities, Pieter W. Botha, then 80 years old, sat in virtual seclusion in a retirement home on the south coast of the Cape Province and may never be brought to trial. *Time* concluded, "Embattled and isolated, he refuses to give interviews or even to pick up the telephone. An aide who answered a call described the unrepentant hard-liner as unapproachable. Yet if auguries are to be credited, the swelling inquiry may spill over and reach even the Groot Krokodil (Great Crocodile), as he is known in Afrikaans. Last week, after rains caused the Touws River to burst its banks, Botha's living room was knee-deep in water, symbolic perhaps of what Tutu hopes will one day come a flood of justice."[45] Such as the extent of the tragedy that Pieter W. Botha inflicted on South Africa in his effort to defend the laager. The task of undoing that tragedy, of bringing the laager down, was not easy.

## SUMMARY AND CONCLUSION

From the time he assumed the office of prime minister as successor to John Vorster in 1978, through the time he assumed the office of president in 1983, to the time he was replaced by F. W. De Klerk in 1989, Botha regarded apartheid as absolute in every way. He was unwilling or unable to see that the more he resisted change in the application of apartheid, the more he came under intense pressure to recognize it as a major national problem. Right up to the end of his term of office, Botha remained solidly convinced that apartheid remain the cornerstone of the South African economic, social, and political system and that any other course of action would spell disaster for Afrikaners. He did not think that it was possible to ensure the position of political power for Afrikaners without sustaining apartheid. But in seeking to sustain this position, Botha, like his predecessors, was sealing his own political fate.

Whatever Botha thought, whatever he did, whatever policy he formulated, he knew that he had to submit to the supremacy of apartheid. His dedication to apartheid made it impossible for him to perceive the issues and problems that apartheid caused the country from any other perspective. The holy alliance that he believed existed between himself and apartheid would lead to the ultimate salvation of Afrikaners. This was his mission, his entire purpose for being. For anyone to suggest an alternative course of action or a different frame of mind was to become unfaithful to that mission and purpose. He did not want to be the first Afrikaner to break with the traditions of the past, or to envisage a different course of national endeavor from the one he was pursuing. Only his removal from office would bring this kind of thinking to an end.

To Botha, no cause was more important than his belief that he had a mission to accomplish, a national purpose designed for him by destiny and providence. The election of 1981, the constitutional proposals of 1983 that made him state president, and the Nkomati Accord of 1984 represented the political action of a man whose vision of the country he led was inseparable from the mental framework of a national leader whose mission was to enshrine the supremacy of the system he found in place when he assumed office.

Unable to comprehend the rapid pace of change forced upon his country by events inside and outside South Africa, Botha tried to maintain a system that he did not realize would lead to national disaster. He did not know that apartheid had become the Pied Piper of South Africa leading him, as well as the Afrikaners whose political interests he represented, to the cave of political oblivion. He was caught totally by surprise when the Nationalist Party replaced him with F. W. de Klerk as party leader and president of South Africa. Such was the tragedy of apartheid; Botha had become a victim of it as were the rest of the people of South Africa. His efforts to defend the laager had backfired. What prospects did de Klerk face? The next chapter offers some answers.

## NOTES

1. From 1960 to 1983, South Africa maintained both the office of president and prime minister. The office of president was only titular, but the office of prime minister carried the normal functions of government. In 1983, the office of prime minister was eliminated and those functions were assumed by the president.

2. Founded in 1912, the ANC was the oldest nationalist organization in Africa. Since it was outlawed in 1964, the ANC continued to exert considerable influence of the politics of South Africa until de Klerk rescinded the ban in Feb-

ruary 1990, paving the way for it to play a major political role in the transformation of South Africa.

3. The World Council of Churches, statement on raids in southern Africa, April 25, 1975.

4. Zimbabwe Chapter of the British Council of Missionary Society, "Violence in Southern Africa: A Christian Assessment," October 28, 1970. Old Mutare Methodist Archives.

5. Some members of Vorster's administration were diverting funds, supposedly to be used to combat economic sanctions, into personal back accounts.

6. Under apartheid laws, the people of South Africa were classified into four major racial groups: whites, Coloreds, Indians, and Africans (officially known as Natives until 1986). These classifications determined who a person was, what he did, where he lived, his income, as well as the kind of employment opportunities he had. All employment opportunities were classified according to these groups.

7. Under the state of emergency, the government took any action it thought necessary. There was nothing those arrested under its provisions could do to defend themselves except appeal to the government itself.

8. Front-line states were defined in 1969 as black independent countries that shared common borders with white-ruled countries. In 1969, Tanzania and Zambia were front-line nations because they shared common borders with Mozambique, still under the Portuguese colonial administration. Zambia was a front-line state because it shared a common border with Zimbabwe, which was a under the grip of Ian D. Smith. In 1975, Mozambique became a front-line state because it had a common border with South Africa.

9. Colin Legum, "The Nkomati Accord and its Implications for the Front-line States and South Africa," in *Confrontation and Liberation in Southern Africa: Regional Directions after the Nkomati Accord*, ed. Ibrahim S. Msabaha and Timothy M. Shaw (Boulder, CO: Westview Press, 1987), p. 89.

10. Ibid., p. 93.

11. The dam was built in 1972 by the Portuguese colonial government using cheap African labor and the financial assistance given by South Africa. The major purpose of the dam was to provide South Africa with electricity so that it could enhance its industrial productivity, believed to benefit Mozambique.

12. South Africa, *Panorama* 29, no. 5 (Pretoria, July 1984): 2.

13. Ibid., p. 3.

14. The Nkomati Accord, an agreement signed by P. W. Botha of South Africa and Samora Machel of Mozambique, March 16, 1984. Los Angeles: The South African Embassy.

15. For detailed discussion of this development, see Dickson A. Mungazi, *The Cross Between Rhodesia and Zimbabwe: Racial Conflict in Rhodesia, 1962–1979* (New York: Vantage Press, 1981), p. 207.

16. Robert Davis and Dan O'Meara, "Total Strategy in Southern Africa: An Analysis of South Africa's Regional Policy since 1978," in Msahaba and Shaw, eds., *Confrontation and Liberation in Southern Africa*, p. 239.

17. Ibid., p. 240.

18. Ibid., p. 242.

19. In 1648 European states signed the famous Treaty of Westphalia bringing to an end the Thirty Years War that had ravaged Europe from 1618 to 1648.

20. South Africa, *Panorama* 27, no. 5 (May 1984): 2

21. Ibid., p. 3.

22. Botha claimed that South Africa had a Western-oriented system of free enterprise while Mozambique had adopted a socialist system.

23. Botha, comments made after the signing of the Nkomati Accord, March 16, 1984. Los Angeles: South African Embassy.

24. Ibid.

25. Machel, comments made after the signing of the Nkomati Accord, March 16, 1984. Los Angeles: South African Embassy.

26. In October 1964, Nikita Khrushchev (1894–1971), who assumed the office of General Secretary of the Communist party in the Soviet Union in 1958, was removed from office and was succeeded by Leonid Brezhnev because of his behavior both at home and abroad, especially at the United Nations in 1959.

27. Gwendolen M. Carter and Patrick O'Meara, eds., *Southern Africa: The Continuing Crisis* (Bloomington: Indiana University Press), 1987, p. 132.

28. Ibid., p. 133.

29. This was in reference to Botha's constitutional plan to allow Coloureds and Indians representation in the legislature.

30. Gwendolen M. Carter, "South Africa: Growing Black-White Confrontation," in Carter and O'Meara, eds., *Southern Africa: The Continuing Crisis*, p. 133.

31. Ibid., p. 34.

32. Ibid., p. 135.

33. Ibid., p. 136.

34. *Newsweek*, January 27, 1986.

35. Ibid., September 27, 1987.

36. Ibid.

37. *New York Times*, May 11, 1989, p. 51.

38. Allister Sparks, *Tomorrow is Another Country: The Inside Story of South Africa's Road to Change* (Chicago: University of Chicago Press, 1995), p. 89.

39. Ibid., p. 90.

40. Ibid., p. 91.

41. *Washington Post*, May 7, 1990, p. 5.

42. *Time*, November 4, 1996, p. 59.

43. Ibid.

44. Ibid.

45. Ibid.

1. F. W. de Klerk with President George Bush at
the White House, September 1990. "White
domination must come to an end." Photo: South
African Information Service.

2. Cecil John Rhodes (1853–1902), the moving force behind British colonial adventure in Africa. "Our concession is so gigantic it is like giving a man the whole of Australia." Photo: Zimbabwe National Archives.

3. Nelson Mandela in prison at Robben Island. "Apartheid is a crime against humanity." Photo: South African Information Service.

4. Ian D. Smith, prime minister of colonial Zimbabwe from 1964 to 1979. "The mantle of the pioneers has fallen on our shoulders to sustain civilization in a primitive country." Photo: Zimbabwe National Archives.

5. The statue of J. C. Smuts in Cape Town. Smuts served twice as prime minister of South Africa, from 1919 to 1924, and from 1929 to 1948. "Smuts had serious difficulties in carrying out his programs." Photo: The author, 1994.

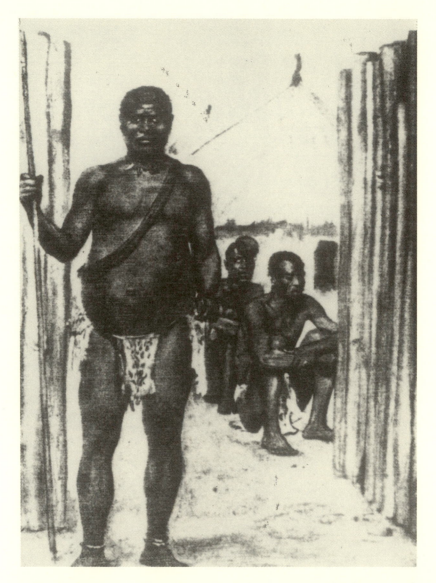

6. King Khumalo Lobengula of Zimbabwe. "Hour after hour, week after week, month after month the king argued with remarkable success with the Cambridge men. He tore to shreds their thesis on the advantage of granting Rhodes the concession." Photo: Zimbabwe National Archives.

7. R. F. Botha, South African foreign minister, F. W. de Klerk, and James Baker, U.S. secretary of state at a press conference at the State Department in Washington, D.C. "Time has come for South Africa to restore its pride and lift itself out of international isolation." Photo: South African Information Service.

8. Godfrey Huggins, prime minister of colonial Zimbabwe from 1933 to 1953. "The Europeans in this country can be likened to an island in a sea of black. The Natives must not be allowed to invade that island." Photo: Zimbabwe National Archives.

9. Soweto, South Africa. "The journey to the transformation of South Africa must begin with a single step from Soweto." Photo: The author, 1994.

10. African children in Smith's rural Zimbabwe. "During the height of the Rhodesia Front the plight of most African children deteriorated rapidly." Photo: The author, 1974.

11. The youth of Soweto looking to the future. "Soweto represented the ultimate decay of the South African system under apartheid. It also represented the rising hope for the future." Photo: The author, 1994.

12. Robert G. Mugabe, president of Zimbabwe. "Mental emancipation is both the instrument and modality of political and economic emancipation and cannot be taken for granted." Photo: Zimbabwe National Archives.

# 4

# Chasms in the Laager: The Fall of Edgar Whitehead and the Rise of Ian D. Smith

> The mantle of the pioneers has fallen on our shoulders to sustain civilization in a primitive country.
>
> Ian D. Smith, November 11, 1965

## THE CHARACTER OF THE RF GOVERNMENT

From December 16, 1962, to March 3, 1979, Zimbabwe, the former British colony of Rhodesia, was governed by the Rhodesia Front Party (RF) which espoused a racial philosophy that Africans and Christian organizations[1] considered so oppressive that a devastating civil war broke out in April 1966. The leading members of the RF included Ian D. Smith, Winston Field, Clifford Dupont, Peter van der Byl, Andrew Skeen, John Mussett, William Harper, Lord Graham, Lance Smith, Arthur Smith, and David Smith,[2] who all lived and operated under the philosophy and political creed that Africans must never hope to attain a social equality with whites.

This was the first time since the inception of the colonial government in September 1890 that Zimbabwe had been subjected to this kind of political philosophy and behavior of a few white men, who were so obsessed with sustaining white political power and defending the laager that nothing else seemed to matter. In their own way, these men became the Don Quixote of the new era of white supremacy, tilting the giant windmills of the rising tide of African nationalism. In effect, they too, had become the Pied Piper of the old colonial objectives, believing that they were leading their white fellow colonists from their fear of the advent of an African government to their envisaged utopia of absolute white political power. Defending the laager became their sole motivation. Instead, they eventually led their followers into the cave of political oblivion because they lost the struggle against Africans.

In the context of the political environment which had produced the RF, Ian D. Smith's political philosophy—*No black majority government in Rhodesia in my life time, not in a thousand years*—became an obsession, a mission that he believed he was called upon to accomplish as the sole legitimate disciple, and, indeed, the vicar, as well as the rightful successor to Cecil John Rhodes, Leander Starr Jameson, Earl Grey, and Godfrey Huggins. He believed that he was the ultimate defender of the laager in Zimbabwe. It is a strange coincidence that the concept of a thousand years was first expressed by Cecil John Rhodes in 1896 and then by Adolf Hitler in 1934. For Smith and his RF government, there was no other course of action to follow, no other policy to define and pursue, and no other perspective from which to view the perilous nature of the problems they were creating as a government.

It is important to understand that it was this philosophy the RF used to declare Zimbabwe unilaterally independent on November 11, 1965. The RF believed that this action was the final coup to those who threatened their defense of the laager. The RF took this fateful action in an attempt to foil the efforts Africans were making toward self-actualization. Ian D. Smith believed that he was, in effect, staging a *kamikaze* assault on the rising tide of African nationalism. Defense of the laager could not co-exist with African political aspiration. He regarded his own objectives as a mission that no other colonial official had accomplished in the past and that only he could do. Therefore, in refusing to initiate dialogical interaction with Africans, Smith failed to realize that this action would turn out to be an ill-conceived strategy resulting in his own ultimate self-deception, which would render him unable to defend the laager. His own demise also became the demise of the RF itself. This chapter provides answers to the following questions: Who was Ian D. Smith? How did he come to power? What kind of policy did he define and pursue? What was the effect of implementing that policy? What exactly did he and his government do to defend the laager? Before we furnish answers to these questions, it is necessary to discuss the chasms that developed in the laager because of the political behavior of his predecessor, Edgar Whitehead (1905–1971).

## WHITEHEAD'S POLITICAL GAMBLE AND FALL

There were two critical events that began to unfold in Zimbabwe in 1959 that help to explain the rise and fall of Edgar Whitehead. The first event is that, as Prime Minister from 1958 to 1962, Whitehead felt so threatened by the growing influence of the African National Congress (ANC) and its threat to the laager that he outlawed it on February 28. The ANC had criticized the inadequacy of the political policy of his administration because it was designed to promote and protect the political, social and economic interests of whites and keep the black majority in a subservient position. Whitehead was unable to tolerate this kind of criticism from a group of people he and his predecessors considered unqualified to pass such a judgment. Africans refused to subordinate themselves to inadequate colonial political policy. In turn, Whitehead said he was determined to nip this threat to the laager in the bud. But in doing so, he set the two racial groups on a confrontational course.

The second event that took place in 1959 was the enactment of the African Education Act, which, for the first time in the history of African education,[3] created a unified teaching service for African teachers. Under its provisions, African teachers with a college education would serve under the same conditions as white teachers with a college education.[4] Whitehead had reason to consider this legislation a milestone, a major improvement in the education of Africans. He believed that it would resuscitate his own failing political heartbeat and restore the fast-disappearing confidence of Africans in his government. But to his surprise and dismay this legislation was opposed on two fronts. The first front was that Africans opposed the fundamental principle that played a major role in producing it—namely, Whitehead's view that he knew best the kind of education Africans must have. The fundamental Victorian attitude that the white man knew what Africans wanted is why Africans rejected it, not because it was inadequate.

The African Education Act was also opposed by the Dominion Party (DP), forerunner of the RF, for an entirely different reason. The DP was outraged by what it considered a threat to the principle of white political power, the preservation of the laager, and the idea that Africans should receive an education that would help them claim social equality with whites. The DP believed that for Whitehead to allow the African teachers with a college education to serve under the same conditions as white teachers with a college education was to erode the philosophy that the white man must remain superior to Africans. This would pose a serious threat to the defense of the laager. The DP considered it inconceivable that anyone in the country would think that racial equality in the educational process could become a reality simply because Whitehead appeared to suggest that it should.

The DP concluded that the enactment of the African Education Act of 1959 would signify the reduction and eventual loss of white political power, putting Africans at a political advantage. It concluded that, under these conditions, they would be rendered unable to defend the laager. This is why the DP did everything in its power to stop the act before it became law. The DP made no secret of its plan to have the colonial government retain absolute power to control African education in order to give whites a decisive advantage. This is also why the DP argued that for Africans to receive equal educational opportunity would mean that the white man would have no basis to claim that the government must remain at all times in what its members called "in civilized hands," meaning white government. Because the DP did not wish to see a transfer of power to Africans, it tried to mobilize all its resources as members of the opposition in Parliament to kill the bill before it became law. While it failed in this fundamental objective, the political bitterness and hatred of the educational advancement of Africans became the hallmark of its political behavior in the future.

With only thirteen seats in a parliament of thirty seats, as opposed to seventeen seats for the United Federal Party (UFP) which Whitehead led, the DP had no chance of stopping this bill. However, the anger and the fear of what was likely to happen in the future were so intense that the DP took it upon itself to send Whitehead into political oblivion and wipe out the educational aspirations of Africans before they became a reality. But the DP had to wait for an election in 1962 before it could put its own philosophy into action as an RF government. The fact that the African Education Act was opposed by both Africans and the DP suggests that Whitehead faced a problem which no previous colonial government leader had ever faced. He did not know that in African opposition lay the elements of threatening the laager, and that in its own way the DP was causing chasms in that laager.

## CHASMS IN THE LAAGER: THE CONSTITUTION OF 1961 AND THE DP'S OPPOSITION TO IT

The political crisis arising from the African Education Act of 1959 was minor when compared to the one that the constitution of 1961 caused. What the DP did not know at the time was that the British government had told Whitehead in 1959 in no uncertain terms that it was impatient with the negative attitudes of the colonial government toward the development of Africans and the suffering which they had endured under the infamous Land Apportionment Act[5] of 1929. It was only natural that Africans should have mixed reactions to this gesture on the part of the British government. This is why some members of the DP argued that the constitution of 1961 was designed to bring about a black government.

But Africans themselves felt that, having been denied legislative representation since 1890, fifteen African seats to represent an African population of 3.8 million against fifty white seats to represent 0.25 million whites, was a slap in the face.

To make sure that white voters fully understood both the terms of the new constitution and the implications of their vote, Britain required that the constitutional proposals be submitted to a national referendum before they were adopted. What sent shock waves through the political spine of the DP members was the key provision of the new constitution that the government demonstrate its unquestionable commitment to the political advancement of Africans. Political reality forced Whitehead, so he thought, to accept this requirement as a condition of his continuing to receive support from the British government.

But in trying to play the colonial political game according to the rules set by the British government, Whitehead created a dilemma for white voters: to reject the new constitutional proposals and deny themselves an opportunity for their future political security, or to approve them and so indirectly help accelerate the political advancement of Africans. A former member of the DP commented in 1983,

We knew that whatever we did, we could not win. Britain had made it clear that the exploitation that it believed we subjected Africans to through a self-serving political policy had to stop. The granting of independence to Ghana in 1957 was a clear signal of what Britain intended to do in all its colonies in Africa. We thought that we were fighting only the African aspiration for advancement, we did not know that we were, in effect, caught between a rock and a hard place, a dilemma which we could not resolve. The laager that we thought we were defending was being attacked from all directions.[6]

For the DP, the referendum posed a formidable political problem of how to react. The DP did not have an effective leadership that would help put forth its views in a way that voters would understand. The DP was also still struggling to recover from the shock of the passage of the African Education Act of 1959. As a result it could not demonstrate a thorough grasp of the importance of this issue. Indeed, the DP was in a state of decay, unable to overcome its anger at the passage of the African Education Act. This helps to explain the agonizing situation that it now faced in what it believed was an even greater threat from Britain in demanding that the colonial government demonstrate its commitment to the political development of Africans.

Early in 1962 the DP reached the conclusion that the African Education Act of 1959, the constitutional proposals of 1961, and the British requirement for a rapid political advancement of Africans combined to constitute a set of conditions that its members could not accept. The DP never understood that this was, indeed, the beginning of a decisive struggle between the colonial establishment and Africans. Its preoccupation with the desire to retain political power in white hands closed the minds of its leaders to a constructive analysis of the situation. It could not, therefore, come up with a possible solution to a complex problem which it had, in fact, created through its political philosophy.

Aware that the DP espoused a political philosophy which the voters would not support, Whitehead tried to exploit the situation to maximize his own political advantage as his way of defending the laager. He therefore vigorously campaigned for the approval of the constitutional proposals, presenting a point-by-point argument to persuade the voters to approve them. For this reason, he received wild applause on February 8, 1961, when he argued, "Southern Rhodesia[7] will of course not have achieved complete independence in the international sense, but the United Kingdom participation in our internal affairs will have ceased."[8] Whitehead thought this candor would gain him the support of the voters.

But William Harper, the unpopular DP spokesman, was booed as he attempted to rebut, "I do not believe it is possible to achieve independence under these proposals."[9] Harper was, in fact, right. That white voters did not believe Harper cast a longer shadow on the DP's credibility than the one which trailed it during the debate on the African Education Bill in 1959. Rapidly moving events quickly established the knowledge that, indeed, the DP had earned its reputation as members of the colonial establishment who opposed any form of advancement of Africans. That is how the colonial establishment had succeeded in defending the laager in the past. But conditions and times had changed. The DP appeared unable to bounce back from the verge of political extinction following the announcement of the referendum results on July 27, 1961. The referendum showed 41,949 "yes" votes and 21,846 "no" votes. Therefore, Whitehead scored a resounding victory and sank the DP's hopes to a low point. The euphoria which characterized Whitehead's reaction to the results of the referendum can be understood in terms of his argument that the extreme elements of both the DP and the African politicians had been dealt a death blow. He raised his head high as he boasted that only he had the ability to defend the laager.

The excitement of the victory carried Whitehead a little too far when he promised that racial discrimination would be ended by repealing the infamous Land Apportionment Act. In making this promise, he created a bigger problem for himself than the DP had faced in opposing the African Education Bill of 1959. However, in the wake of the demise of the DP, Whitehead was riding the crest of the wave of popularity among white voters. All that the DP could do, for the time being, was to pick up the pieces of its shattered political philosophy, not the mantle which its members thought Rhodes had left behind, swallow its pride, and nurse the painful wounds of a humiliating defeat. The anger of both the thought of equality with Africans and the lost referendum became even more intense with the passage of time and had reached a new level by the time the elections were held in December 1962.

Three key issues must be raised at this point with respect to the DP's attitude toward all forms of the development of Africans. The first issue is that its members included men of extreme racial views which forced them to lay claim to being the only true disciples of Cecil John Rhodes, Leander Starr Jameson, Earl Grey and Godfrey Huggins. The leading members of the DP included Desmond Lardner-Burke, William Harper, Winston Field,[10] Ian D. Maclean, William Cory, Ian D. Smith, Desmond Frost, Clifford Dupont, John Mussett, John Gaunt, and Lord Graham. They all believed that keeping political power in the hands of whites was a necessary condition of limiting the political advancement of Africans, which could not be ensured if they were given equal educational opportunity. Therefore, the DP saw educational opportunity for Africans as a definite form of African political advancement, just as the British were demanding. For this reason, the educational opportunity for Africans became a major issue in the election campaign of 1962.

The problem which the DP faced as a political party is that its racial views and political philosophy were too extreme to offer a realistic alternative solution to the conflict which was rising faster than most people realized. For Africans, the choice between the UFP and the DP was really a choice between two evils, a painfully slow pace to an African government under the UFP and a steady progress to racial domination under the DP. Given the attitude of the British government and the rapid rise of African nationalism, Africans felt that they were better off to risk their future with the UFP. This is why the few of them who could vote cast a "yes" ballot in the national referendum of 1961. But by the time the general elections were held in 1962, new realities had come into play. For both Whitehead and the DP it was a time of reckoning.[11]

In 1962 the DP succeeded in having white voters wonder if Whitehead was leading them along the road to their future political security or to the dreaded African government. This led to the second key issue—namely, that the DP showed an intense dislike of British principles regarding the place of Africans in the colonial society, especially the requirement that they be given an equal educational opportunity in order to ensure their political advancement. Britain reserved the responsibility of protecting Africans by the constitutional provision of 1923. This added a sinister twist and increased the intensity of the dislike the DP had for anything the British government did or tried to do. This is why Britain's decision to retain this responsibility in the constitution of 1961 infuriated the DP. In addition to the increasing tension caused by rising African nationalism, this aspect of the colonial situation set the British government and the DP on a confrontational course beginning in 1962 when the RF became the government.

The breakdown in communication between the DP and the British government would later prove crucial in the Africans' struggle for political independence. In 1962 the British government saw things from an entirely different perspective from that of the DP. This created elements in the relationships between the two sides that were critical to the emerging conflict. Although Africans were opposed to Whitehead's policy, they had no respect for the DP either. This is how a triangle of badly strained relationships emerged among Africans, the UFP, and the DP, with the British government playing the role of an umpire, calling the plays from the Whitehall dug-out. The laager was being encircled in ominous ways. The DP thought that the referendum was the bottom of the 9th inning with bases loaded with the UFP players. The Africans watched this game between two white teams with intense interest, hoping to catch the home run ball before they became players themselves.

The third key issue that must be raised at this point is the difference in perception of the educational opportunity for Africans as viewed by the UFP and the DP. This difference furnishes yet another example to illustrate that the white man could no longer regard Africans as mere spectators of a political game in which only whites could play. Remembering that this kind of conflict existed in 1958 between Garfield Todd and Whitehead, the situation between Whitehead and the DP in 1962 acquired more powerful dimensions. As the election campaign of 1962 got underway, the views of white voters began to change from enthusiastic support of Whitehead to doubts and misgivings about his policy, his ability to defend the laager under increasingly complex conditions represented by the British position, and African opposition. Once these chasms began to develop in the laager, there was nothing Whitehead could do to patch them.

## EDUCATIONAL OPPORTUNITY FOR AFRICANS AND THE RF POSITION IN THE ELECTION CAMPAIGN OF 1962

Wishing to consolidate the victory he had scored in the referendum of 1961 and to regain the confidence of Africans that he had lost by declaring the state of emergency on February 28, 1959, Whitehead called a snap election. He approached the election campaign with a sense of self-confidence, and, thus, a sense of self-deception. He suddenly announced in April 1962, that new general elections would be held in October. He believed that because the stricken DP was in a state of total disarray, it would never be able to launch an effective campaign against his policy. Whitehead also concluded that the DP had failed to attract any sizable support of white voters in the referendum of 1961 because of its argument that the constitutional proposals were a sell-out to white interests. Therefore, the DP was unlikely to succeed in raising any new issues that would attract the interest and support of voters in the general election of 1962. Events would prove that Whitehead was wrong in that assumption. However, he believed that he had never had it so good; everything seemed to go his way. He did not know that he was about to play his last card and that his political career was about to come to an untimely end.

To conclude that the announcement of the impending elections added insult to the DP's injured feelings and shattered political objectives is to recognize the sorry state in which it found itself. In the words of a political observer, "the DP had become a political rubble, a bunch of subdued white racists whose obsession with the myth of white supremacy was leading them to a political dead-end street."[12] William Harper, recognizing the shattered image of the DP, resigned from the party following the announcement of the impending general election. This resignation precipitated a major crisis within the DP. No person was willing to risk his reputation and political career by associating himself with it in any way since its reputation had been tarnished beyond repair.

Indeed, to belong to or support the DP in any way was to secure a one-way passport to political extinction. Since its demise from the referendum of 1961, the DP had been associated with everything that was wrong and negative in the white man's political behavior. The political fortunes of the DP were turning into ashes in the incinerator of the conditions it had created. Its members relentlessly flogged the dead horse of an issue which more moderate whites had accepted as a necessary condition for their continued political survival, the political advancement of Africans.

These were the circumstances under which Whitehead, in a state of euphoria, announced a series of changes that he believed would satisfy the demands of the British government, pacify Africans, and silence his critics and political opponents. If this happened, he believed his political career would be secured for many years to come. But before he knew it, public opinion began to change in favor of the DP. When he announced that the Land Apportionment Act of 1929 would be repealed in order to integrate the colonial society, the DP went into a state of panic. When he promised to end racial discrimination in employment and in public facilities, and to open public service to Africans for the first time since they were excluded in 1931 by the provision of the Land Apportionment Act, the DP was outraged. When Whitehead promised to include African junior ministers in his next administration, the DP felt insulted. When he predicted that an African government was possible within fifteen years because the government would guarantee an effective system of education to produce well-trained Africans to run it, the DP thought he had gone too far. When he announced that he was naming a high-level commission of inquiry into African education,[13] the DP thought he must be removed from office because he had become a romantic adventurer.

There is no doubt that Whitehead sincerely believed the white man's future in Zimbabwe would only be secured by giving Africans a reasonable opportunity for advancement. The rise of African nationalism, combined with British demands, must have convinced him that the philosophy of white government for a thousand years was not really something to work toward. One white man later recalled that the idealogy of colonial officials "regarding Africans as uncivilized, fit only to train to function as laborers must belong to the past, along with its founder Cecil John Rhodes, and his disciples, Leander Starr Jameson, Earl Grey and Godfrey Huggins. We were living in a new era where the white man had to choose, to recognize that his own security was invariably linked with the advancement of Africans within the framework of a genuine spirit of equal partners, or to try to perpetuate colonial rule and face the possibility of strained race relationships leading to a major conflict in the near future."[14]

Whitehead's apparent advocacy of the kind of social reform he wished to implement suggests that he was indeed at least sensitive to the demands of the times, especially the aspirations of Africans. But how can his change of views from advocating the maintenance of white political power during the Todd years to advocating change during the election campaign of 1962 be explained? His refusal to operate "under colonial principles of privileges"[15] made his conflicting positions on racial equality questionable to both whites and Africans.

## THE RF STRATEGY FOR WINNING THE ELECTION

Early in 1962, the DP felt it necessary to disband because of the state in which it found itself: baseless and without proper structure and leadership. Its members recognized their inevitable fate. They knew they had to shake off the negative image that was associated with their extreme racial philosophy. Fearing the political malaise that had sent Garfield Todd into political oblivion in 1958, DP members adopted a totally different strategy to remain alive as a political party. In May 1962, the DP decided to dissolve and appealed to the number of small fragmented parties that included the United Group, the Southern Rhodesia Association, and the conservative members of Whitehead's own UFP to unite and form a new political party known as the Rhodesia Front (RF). The formation of the RF was an event that was destined to alter forever the course of politics and the character of race relationships in Zimbabwe. In the pursuit of its own policy, the RF led the country to one of the bitterest conflicts in Africa.

The change of name from the Dominion Party to the Rhodesia Front had a psychologically boosting effect. The members of the new party struggled to create a new policy that whites could support. But the RF needed time to reorganize itself and to structure an election platform which would demonstrate not only familiarity with the critical issues of the day, but also a degree of moderation that would appeal to the voters. That the RF drew its membership from various splinter political parties whose members had divergent political views made it much harder for it to have a unified platform. The only thing that its members shared in common was their uncompromising opposition to the political advancement of Africans. This is why they made Whitehead's educational policy a major election issue and the focus of their ire.

As the campaign got underway, the RF began to grow from weakness to strength. It became confident that it could be the party to defend the laager. Its rallying point was its unqualified opposition to Whitehead's policy of inclusiveness. Fearing to expose its own ignorance of the issues, the RF simply elected to focus its major attention on attacking the education of Africans as the greatest threat to white political power since 1890. It therefore presented a slate of candidates who had the emotional appeal and the ability to express themselves in a way which gave the appearance of moderation. Slowly, as the RF struggled to present itself as a party capable of understanding the critical issues the country was facing, the negative image that had tarnished the DP began to fade. In doing so, the RF was laying a new claim to be the custodian of the laager.

When it felt strong enough, when its members knew that public opinion was slowly shifting from supporting Whitehead to itself, and when it drew larger crowds to its political rallies than the DP had done, the RF launched a vicious campaign against Whitehead's educational policy. John Gaunt, Ian D. Smith, Winston Field, Desmond Lardner-Burke, Lord Graham—all wealthy and powerful—provided the leadership that the RF needed to earn the respect of white voters. However, none of these men seemed to comprehend the serious implications of their extreme racial philosophy on the future of the country. Their only concern was to do everything in their power to halt and reverse the course that Whitehead had charted for the expected political advancement of Africans.

The difference between the UFP and the RF relative to their respective election platform was as clear as the difference between day and night. In a move that was intended to convince both Africans and the British government of his sincerity in seeking to promote the political advancement of Africans, Whitehead vigorously courted the African vote, even though he knew that in accordance with the constitutional provisions of

1961, it counted no more than 5 percent of the total vote. He warned white voters that their understanding of the issues was critically important to their long-term security and interests. For the first time in the history of Zimbabwe, a white politician was warning his fellow colonists that their future lay in regarding Africans as equal partners in building a country. But Whitehead did not present a clear program of involving Africans in that partnership. His appeal to white voters became nothing more than just empty words. He was clearly losing his defense of the laager.

Whitehead argued that to extend equality of educational opportunity to Africans would demonstrate the goodwill of whites and would bring about the racial harmony and cooperation essential in building a politically stable society. He also argued that race was no longer a criterion to determine a person's place in society. He warned that the alternative to this course of action would be the extreme racist government of the RF, which would drag the country toward a major racial conflict from which the whites would emerge the losers and Africans the winners.[16] But the postponement of the election from October to December did two things that worked against Whitehead. The first thing is that it gave the RF more time to present itself to the voters as a party that understood the issues.

The second thing is that it showed Whitehead and his UFP to be in a state of disarray, unsure of themselves and of the issues facing the country. In urging white voters to reject the racist policies of the RF, Whitehead invited both races to work together for a secure country in which everyone was free to pursue their own goals. He even promised that he would use the two-thirds majority he had received in the referendum to build a strong administration that would ensure the interests of all people.[17] He promised to include Africans in his next administration to demonstrate the importance of racial cooperation in accordance with the British requirements. He promised to improve the social and economic position of Africans so that they would have confidence in the future. With this confidence as a response to a constructive government policy, Africans were more likely to seek cooperation with whites for the benefit of all.

As expected, the RF took the exact opposite position on all issues. It argued that the critical problem that whites faced was a rapid political advancement of Africans as a result of the misguided policy of the Whitehead administration. It argued that for Whitehead to consider the possibility of an African government within fifteen years was a betrayal of the principles that had elevated the white man to a position of power over Africans. It concluded that for him to promise Africans a repeal of the Land Apportionment Act was to surrender the Magna Carta of the white political security in the country. It argued that for Whitehead to operate by the British requirements was to lack a vision of a national leader cast in an environment of the colonial conditions in Africa. It blamed Whitehead for giving Africans a false sense of hope for the future based on racial equality.

While Ian D. Smith, Winston Field, William Harper, Lord Graham, and John Gaunt were not dynamic speakers, they augmented their political limitations with the intensity of their belief, the poignancy of their feeling, and the depth of their conviction. Suddenly it was a new ball game, the struggle for the right to defend the laager had shifted in favor of the RF. The fortunes of the UFP and those of the RF were being reversed in a way that no one could have conceived only a few months earlier. However, the irony of the RF's political behavior is that it was contesting an election under a constitution that it had vigorously opposed as members of the DP. To add a touch of pathos to this tragic turn of events, Africans also opposed the UFP but for an entirely different reason. As a defender of the laager, Whitehead was under siege from both directions.

The conflict between Whitehead and Africans regarding the UFP's policy succeeded in persuading white voters to believe the message promoted by the RF that it had a sacred mission to rescue the country from the vicious jaws of African nationalism and from Whitehead's appeasement of the British government's demands. Africans believed that they had a duty to take their country back from their colonial usurpers, who had ruled it with impunity since 1890. Thus, Whitehead became the target of both Africans and the RF, each firing political rounds in rapid succession from two different strategic points. Whitehead was unable to make any sense out of this situation. He failed to grasp why Africans were unhappy with his policy. The RF simply exploited the African opposition to Whitehead's policy to warn white voters of the consequences of including Africans in the government. In the conflict that emerged in this kind of environment he was steadily losing defense of the laager.

As the RF grew from weakness to strength, white voters listened to its political message more closely than they had to that of the DP. That the RF focused on a single election issue—the education of Africans—and ignored the rest, forced Whitehead to play the political game according to rules he simply did not understand. In this manner the RF was taking control of the campaign itself. Whitehead's argument that his educational policy would lead to an African government within fifteen years was a strategy which the RF used effectively to persuade the voters that if he was returned to power they would have no future in the country. Indeed, the RF shared and was guided by the views expressed by Ethel Tawse Jollie, who said in the legislature in 1927, "We do not intend to hand over this country to the Native population or to admit them to the same social and political position that we ourselves enjoy. Let us make no pretense of educating them in exactly the same way as we do the whites."[18]

In speech after speech and at rally after rally, the RF invoked the memory and the claimed political wisdom of earlier leaders whose views and ideas were considered infallible in defending the laager. That infallibility was equated with the educational process and the view that social integration must never be considered. Indeed, this is why Ian D. Smith said during an interview in 1983, "We were advised that the standards would fall if we integrated the two systems of education."[19] The RF believed that defending the laager would not be ensured in a social climate of racial integration. The standards that Smith was talking about were really not educational at all, but political. In the view of the RF members, the more Africans were educated, the more they would demand equal treatment in society, and the more they received equal treatment, the less whites could lay a claim to exclusive political, social, and economic superiority on the basis of education alone. This was Smith's definition of the fall of standards, which he and his RF, government wanted to prevent at all costs. According to the RF the only way to maintain standards was to maintain strict racial segregation in all aspects of national life. Defending the laager required this approach.

To make it possible for whites to continue to make and justify the claim of social superiority, the RF concluded that they must continue to enjoy a disproportionate share of the educational pie and to make no pretense of educating Africans in exactly the same way as whites. This is how, in its political campaign of 1962, the RF succeeded in turning public opinion against Whitehead. However, the task of attuning Africans to this philosophy was much harder. In fact, the RF would never accomplish this objective.

Instead of listening to the British government's warning of the possible consequences of negating the political advancement of Africans through denial of educational development, the RF promised to strengthen the system of education as it had existed before the enactment of the African Education Act of 1959 and within the framework of the Land Apportionment Act.[20] This is why it considered the Land Apportionment Act the foundation on which it would build the fortress of white political power. It would also regard it as the Magna Carta of the white control of national institutions. Its members believed that this control must never be eased in the slightest[21] for generations to come, just as Rhodes had urged seventy years earlier.

With the strong financial support given by the wealthy and more radical members, the RF went on the offensive and presented a slate of candidates for all fifty white seats. It exercised extreme care and caution in selecting each candidate from men whose loyalty to party principles was absolute. It carefully trained them to refrain from discussing any

issue, other than the political advancement of Africans through education. It trained them to avoid mistakes that might cost them the election.
The RF candidates were also trained to arouse the passion and the hatred
of the possibility of educating Africans beyond a capability for manual
labor.

The RF candidates were also trained carefully to arouse fear of the
consequences of reforms that they believed Whitehead was trying to introduce in order to appease Africans and the British government. Indeed,
in basing its entire election campaign on the single issue of the education
of Africans, the RF set out to prove that this was the most important
issue of the election. This is why it adopted the uncompromising position
that since Africans "must at all times be subservient to the white man,
they must never be educated in the same way as the whites,"[22] In this
manner, Africans would assist the RF in defending the laager.

The RF argued that for Whitehead to reach a constitutional agreement
with Britain on terms that the British government dictated was a betrayal
of the operating principles that retained political power of the white man
since the founding of colonies in 1890. Voters began to listen to the RF's
message more closely than they had done at the beginning of the election
campaign. This shows how fast opinion was shifting against Whitehead
in favor of the RF. In the words of a liberal white man, "the RF members
truly believed that Africans would use their education to dismantle the
colonial government and not to promote their own advancement. They
feared that Rhodes' mantle, which they believed they had inherited,
would fall from their shoulders. This is why they argued that the process
of decolonization, or storming of the laager, in Africa must be halted
above the Zambezi,[23] and that its members felt that they had the dis-
tinctive honor of being the ones to do it."[24]

There is no doubt that the RF had a perfect plan of using the educational process to retain absolute white political power. The laager must
be defended at all cost. Since 1958, when Africans began to claim their
right to vote under the provision of the federal constitution of 1953,[25] the
government designed an effective method of restricting the number of
African voters to no more than 5 percent of the total vote. Therefore, the
federal constitution put into place two voters rolls. The "A" roll was for
those voters who earned an annual income of $2,300 and had four years
of secondary education. The "B" role was for those Africans who earned
an annual income of $900 and had ten years of schooling.[26] On the one
hand, due to limited educational opportunity for Africans, very few even
qualified for the "B" roll. On the other hand, whites had no difficulty
meeting the voting qualifications for the "A" roll because they had
a monopoly on both educational opportunity and income. The RF
knew that this was the basis of its political power, which must never be
given up.

By 1961 a new racially discriminatory practice had come into being. When the number of voters on the "B" roll reached 20 percent of the number of voters on the "A" roll, no one else would be allowed to register till the next election.[27] But there was no limit to the number of voters who could register on the "A" role. Because all of the voters on the "A" roll were white, and all voters on the "B" roll were African, the government instituted racism in the electoral process in a very powerful way. This form of colonial racism remained in practice until the elections of 1980, the year the RF collapsed and an African government was installed.

During the election campaign of 1962, the RF promised that it would make it harder for Africans to meet the educational qualifications that they needed to claim the right to vote, even on the "B" roll, where each ballot cast counted only 25 percent of the ballot cast on the "A" roll. This shows just how determined the RF was to uphold its educational policy as an essential tenet and instrument of its political philosophy. There is no doubt that the RF saw this as an effective strategy of increasing the number of white voters and decreasing that of African voters. Educational opportunity was the key to it all.

While this plan was totally repugnant to both the British government and to Africans themselves, the RF managed to convince white voters to believe that it was in their best interests to support it by returning it to power. By the time the elections were held on December 14, 1962, white voters had been converted to the RF's line of thinking. In this manner they reinforced the defense of the laager. Thus, Whitehead and the British government were stunned when the RF won thirty-five seats, and the UFP won only fifteen seats. The remaining fifteen were won by Africans in accordance with the provisions of the constitution of 1962. These numbers rendered Africans ineffective in storming the laager.

Whitehead's fall from political power resulted from his inability to reconcile himself to the conflicting positions which he took. This explains why only a few Africans believed him when he said on December 10, 1961, "Our constitution demands the spirit of tolerance. We are determined to have a society in which everybody can express his own views without fear."[28] In this broadcast to the country, Whitehead was explaining why he was outlawing the National Democratic Party (NDP), which Africans had formed after he outlawed the ANC in 1959. Therefore, when he launched his "Build a Nation" and "Claim Your Vote" campaigns, only 8,000 of the 50,000 qualified Africans responded. It is evident that Whitehead became a victim of his own gross miscalculations.

The inconsistency in his political behavior and his failure to recognize the African's political consciousness resulting from their lack of adequate educational opportunity created a situation of confrontation in Parliament itself on November 15, 1961. On that date, Ahrn Palley, a white member who represented African interests, expressed regret over the delay in naming a commission of inquiry (the Judges Commission). Palley wanted to ensure that the commission fully understood its terms of reference, which must "include, among other things, finding ways of ending the shortage of finance for Native education, the relationship between Native education and white education, the problems arising from the shortage of accommodation."[29]

Whitehead demonstrated his intolerance and arrogance by instructing his minister of education, Milton Cleveland, to respond, "By setting up a commission of inquiry, we are quite deliberately inviting criticism of the system of Native education."[30] This situation shows how Whitehead had become confused by the conditions of the times. Cleveland went on to add that neither Palley nor any other member of Parliament had any right to interfere in an area of responsibility reserved for the government. By all counts, this reaction came from an administration that had lost its sense of purpose and direction. Cleveland joined his leader in the cave of political oblivion as the RF captured the spotlight.

## WINSTON FIELD AND THE RF'S POLICY

A question must now be asked: Now that the RF won the general election of 1962, what kind of policy did it initiate? The answer to this question is important because it shows how, as a government, the RF intended to formulate its own program of action that it considered consistent with its basic political philosophy and principles. A very strange aspect of the political behavior of the RF is that not only did it contest an election in 1962 under a constitution that it vigorously opposed as members of the DP, but as the RF from 1962 to 1965 it also used that same constitution and the African Education Act of 1959 to try to reverse Whitehead's programs.

Another phenomenon occurred in the behavior of the RF as it took office in December 1962. Although it had won the election by opposing Whitehead's policy toward Africans, it was constantly haunted by the specter of a violent reaction from them. The RF feared that Africans might give the British government an excuse to intervene militarily to stop it from leading the country along the path of self-destruction. The RF drew its membership from extreme and divergent elements of the fragmented dissident political parties making it very difficult to improve its image as a political party able to exercise responsibility in handling the affairs of the country. The major problem that the RF faced as it took office was that it did not have an effective recognized leadership.

Out of desperation, the RF named Winston J. Field, a wealthy farmer from Marondera, to lead it into the general election of 1962 and to serve as the next Prime Minister. Field was a man of considerable personal charm and character and a leader who believed that the RF should behave in a manner that must be consistent with British requirements. It was his opinion that the RF government should not adopt a policy so radical that it would arouse the suspicions of Africans and doubts of the British government. Field, in the opinion of the RF members, immediately seemed to take the stand that Garfield Todd and Edgar Whitehead had taken. Would he therefore face the same political fate which they faced?

While Field believed that the RF must formulate a moderate policy, its members immediately became apprehensive because of his apparent compromising position on issues which they considered vital to the sustenance of white political power. Therefore, the conflicting positions that the influential members of Field's administration took demonstrated that the RF still lacked an essential understanding of the serious implications of its policy and political behavior. The best that Field could do, therefore, was simply to give way to the pressure of the extreme elements of his administration. These elements included Ian D. Smith, a wealthy farmer from Shurugwe; Clifford Dupont and Desmond Lardner-Burke, both wealthy lawyers; and Lord Graham and William Harper, both wealthy business executives. In this political environment, irked by the wealthy, the powerful, and the ambitious, was the beginning of a major conflict within the RF itself.

From the beginning of his administration, Field alienated himself from the RF by declining to embrace its policy fully based upon its philosophy. Like Todd and Whitehead, Field was doomed from the start; Field was facing the kind of fate that Botha later encountered. The anger that had brought the RF together to fight against Whitehead's policy now transferred into a larger arena in which it fought the dual of ideological conflict among its own members. The RF was caught between its desire to portray itself as a moderate and responsible political party and its obsession with maintaining the basic elements of white political power. The irrationality that was central to its behavior and action could not be eliminated until its downfall in December 1979. Field's unwillingness to reverse the policy that Whitehead had put in place created a major problem of political leadership for the RF. However, instead of reversing the progress that Whitehead had made, the RF interpreted it by making regulations that were consistent with its racial philosophy and political views.

Therefore, from the moment that he took office on December 17, 1962, to the time that he was ambushed in a political coup led by Ian D. Smith on April 12, 1964, Field hopelessly tried to assert his leadership, influence, and authority in an extremely hostile environment. Enforcing regulations from the African Education Act in a way that hurt the educational and political advancement of Africans was his own way of dealing with his own political limitations and of giving way to the pressure from his radical cabinet and party members. Thus, at the very beginning of his administration, Field became a beleaguered leader who simply lost control of the situation. He stood castigated by Africans, suspected by his own party, and distrusted by the British government. He did not have the ability to overcome this triangle of opposition.

The background that gave rise to the confused and emotional condition that manifested Field's leadership and the RF political behavior must be understood. Since the release of the Waddilove Manifesto[31] on February 9, 1946, white politicians felt threatened, not only by what was happening in African education, but also by the increasing trend of thinking among some missionaries that Africans were not getting their fair share of the educational pie needed to enhance their political advancement. From Godfrey Huggins to Ian D. Smith, the government detested the missionary view that "We believe that a satisfactory educational policy awaits a clear enunciation of principles regarding the African's place in society, economic and political life of the country, and that the formation of definite lines of development by Africans must be made so that they reach the full and unrestricted citizenship which we believe is unquestionably their right."[32]

This was also the basis that the Kerr Commission of 1951 used to argue in favor of a real partnership between the government and the mission schools in developing a dynamic educational system for Africans.[33] But the thought of partnership in the educational development of Africans is really what all colonial governments detested without any reservation. This is the situation that the RF was now facing, a situation that was increasingly becoming more difficult to control than during the time of Whitehead. How could Field resolve this difficult problem?

## THE RF'S RESPONSE TO THE EDUCATION FOR AFRICANS

While he was opposed to the intent of the African Education Act of 1959, Field used the regulations his administration formulated from it to re-assert the RF philosophy. The RF won the election in 1962 by opposing the educational development of Africans because it carried serious implications for their political advancement. It was therefore natural for the RF to define its own policy by responding to the educational program Whitehead had put in place. We must now examine how the RF reacted to this policy to give us a clear idea of what it was likely to do in the future. Section I of the African Education Act of 1959 empowered the minister of African education to establish a board known as the Unified African Teaching Service (UATS), whose function was to consider any matter pertaining to African education with special reference to the employment conditions of the African teacher. The board, of course, reported to Whitehead's minister of education, Milton Cleveland, who had initiated a practice of naming people from various areas of education, both missionary and government, so that different viewpoints were taken into consideration in making decisions.[34]

But Arthur Smith, the RF minister of education, changed this practice and appointed RF zealots who offered no viable alternatives and who saw their main function as one of implementing the RF philosophy and policy. This meant that the UATS became merely a rubber stamp board ready and willing to endorse and completely support any RF policy. To strengthen his approach to African education, Field named the secretary for African education as chairman of the UATS, and instructed him to conduct business in accordance with the RF's political objectives. This ensured that the deliberations of the UATS strengthened the fundamental principles of the RF.

Section II of the African Education Act specified that anyone over the age of eighteen could become a teacher and a member of the UATS provided that he was employed full-time in either a government school or missionary school of accredited standing, and that his appointment had been approved by the secretary for African education himself. But during the RF administration, an additional requirement was made requiring a teacher to serve a probationary period of one year and fulfill other duties indirectly or directly related to his teaching duties as a matter of duty without additional pay.

In terms of Section IV of the African Education Act, teachers who had rendered a faithful service for six years could apply for a leave of not longer than one school term. Once on leave, the teacher was at liberty to use his time as he pleased. Under the original legislation, there were three types of leave: a general leave of absence, study leave, and sick leave. As soon as the RF took office, it introduced a new requirement that the grant of any leave was a privilege, and that no teacher would claim it as a right. The RF let it be known that a teacher to whom leave was granted could be required to return to his duties before the leave period expired. What is significant about the changes the RF made in its own regulations arising from the Education Act of 1959 was not only its impact on the conditions under which African teachers served, but also the demonstration of both its lack of concern for the welfare of African teachers and its desire to reverse the progress that had been made.

A key provision of the African Education Act of 1959 was the creation of a disciplinary committee that had the power to enforce discipline among African teachers. The original committee consisted of three members appointed by the secretary for African education and two members recommended by representatives of the missionary schools. While the committee had the power to recommend action relative to the discipline of teachers, it was required to state the reasons for its action. In this regard, the function of the original disciplinary committee was similar to that of the American Grand Jury. But the RF made two major changes in both the committee's composition and function. The first change was that it increased its membership from five to six and appointed all the members of the committee from among the RF enthusiastic supporters. The second change was that the RF gave the new committee power that made it more of a trial court than a committee functioning on educational issues.

To understand how intensely the RF disliked the Judges Report of 1962, which stated that the colonial government must seek a dramatic improvement in the education of Africans as a means of enhancing their political advancement, two examples of its reaction are helpful. The first reaction was evident on January 31, 1969, when Arthur Smith told Geoffrey Atkins during an interview for the Rhodesian Television that, "The Judges Commission came forward with the recommendation that the annual increase on the expenditure for African education should be 12% per annum. We do not believe that such a large figure is in fact needed."[35] There is no doubt that the RF was fully committed to the curtailment of the educational development of Africans and that discrediting the Judges Report was the best way of doing so. As far as the RF was concerned, the Judges Report was a dead issue. After Africans were persistently denied an equal opportunity for educational development, the RF demonstrated its total lack of interest in this important matter by arguing that 12 percent per year was too large.

The second example occurred on September 2, 1969, when Andrew Skeen, a military man who had entered politics during the elections of 1962 and was a spokesman for the RF, expressed views that were more extreme than many of his colleagues. He wanted both the British government and Africans to know what the RF's policy really was regarding the educational development of the African population. Skeen was quite blunt when he said, "We in the Rhodesia Front Government are determined to control the rate of African political advancement until time and education make it a safe possibility. We also wish to have the power to retard it. We cannot say time. Ten, fifty, or a thousand years must elapse before Africans can ever hope to achieve political equality with whites."[36] In less than fifteen years, Africans successful stormed the laager.

In this manner Skeen was actually demonstrating the RF's contempt of one of the key recommendations of the Judges Report. Ian D. Smith himself said in relation to the Judges Report, "I believe that if in my lifetime we have an African Nationalist government in power, then we will have failed in the policy I believe in. If we can stave the advent of the Nationalist government off now, then I believe we can stave it off forever. If, as a government, we fail to do this, then I do not believe we deserve to be charged with the responsibility of handling the affairs of Southern Rhodesia."[37] Smith was basing his prediction on hope rather than on his ability to defend the laager. This was the ultimate illusion of a leader who had lost proper perspective. At that time, successful defense of the laager demanded something more substantial than the RF and Smith were able to give.

There is no doubt that the RF's obsession with preventing the advent of an African government was a preoccupation that dictated both its entire political behavior and its educational policy. The question now is: Did the RF believe that there was a clear causal relationship between its curtailing the educational development of Africans and perpetuating its political power? That its members actually believed this is exactly what A. J. Peck, legal adviser to the RF, meant when he argued in 1966 that for whites to allow Africans to advance educationally would end white political power.[38] Peck concluded, "I make no apology for this policy."[39] One effective means of curtailing the educational development of Africans, which the RF used, was to increase disparity in government spending. Table 4.1 show the disparity between expenditure for white students and black students for the periods indicated as the RF's method of defending the laager.

**Table 4.1**
**RF Expenditure for Education**

| Academic Year | Per White Student | Per Black Student |
| --- | --- | --- |
| 1964–1965 | $197.30 | $18.40 |
| 1965–1966 | 206.00 | 18.90 |
| 1967–1968 | 300.00 | 28.00 |
| 1969–1970 | 746.00 | 68.00 |

Source: Zimbabwe Monthly Digest of Statistics, November 1981.

## AFRICAN RESPONSE TO THE RF POLICY AND THE RISE OF IAN D. SMITH

The victory that the RF scored in the general elections of 1962 coincided with the inauguration of the Zimbabwe African Peoples Union (ZAPU), which replaced the banned NDP. Up to now Africans had helplessly watched the political situation in their country from the sidelines. Before Whitehead outlawed it on September 20, 1962, ZAPU had been designing a strategy that was in direct conflict with the goals of his government. What frightened Whitehead was a statement of policy and principles that ZAPU issued on December 9, 1961, in which it stated, "We are concerned only with our determination to fight for an immediate liquidation of the social, economic, political, and educational exploitation of the African population by the colonial forces."[40] This was a clear statement that what Africans intended to do was to storm the laager.

In this statement ZAPU was, in effect, serving notice that it would take an aggressive stance in opposing the government policy in the future. This is demonstrated by what Africans did from the moment the RF took office in December 1962. Leopold Takawira, a leading member of ZAPU, put the African strategy into proper perspective when he said, "We are no longer asking the whites to rule us well, we now want to rule ourselves."[41] This position shows that, in their own way, Africans were stating clearly that defense of the laager and their struggle for self could not co-exist. Going further in 1962 to state the principles that would guide them in their determination to define and give a new meaning to their political endeavors, Africans, under the leadership of both ZAPU and ZANU, issued a declaration, "Today we say one man, one vote. Tomorrow we will say one African, one vote."[42] In other words, Africans were saying it was a matter of time before they stormed the laager.

It is evident that the crisis, which was rapidly developing between the RF government and Africans, took a turn for the worse with the RF's own action. As part of its policy to strengthen the political gains that it had made in the elections of 1962 and to make Africans feel the full weight of its power, the RF suddenly and without any prior warning, began to raise fees by $1.25 per student per term in African primary schools. It ignored the fact that this was a departure from a previous practice of providing subsidized education because parents paid taxes to support the schools. This reality was of no concern to the RF government.

The RF also ignored the fact that white students had been enjoying free education since 1935. Therefore, its action in raising tuition convinced Africans of the need to adopt a strategy of confrontation. They believed that the policy of raising fees was designed for the sole purpose of curtailing the educational opportunity for their children. They knew that the $40 per month they earned as an average income would not enable them to pay the fees. They also knew that this situation systematically eliminated thousands of African students from attending school. The significant point is that the RF thought it had found a strategy to control their educational development so as to restrict their political advancement just as Andrew Skeen said.

Beginning in 1963, Africans decided to do something to register their dismay with the RF policy. Throughout the country, they joined hands in protest marches. In Bulawayo, Africans also protested against what the Director of Public Relations called a colonial scandal—that there was only one secondary school with a total enrollment of 300 students out of a total school population of 160,000.[43] In Harare, alone, Africans effectively organized a boycott of the school, setting in motion what proved to be the ultimate action of a people who now realized that they must end the conditions that controlled their lives before there could be adequate educational development to pave the way for their political advancement. By 1964 they organized into groups that set the school buildings on fire, forcing enrollment to drop from 20,000 to 200 by the end of that year.[44]

When Field sent the police and the army to restore order and keep the schools open, Africans responded by attacking them with stones and sticks. Thus began the final phase of the struggle that lasted until the end of the RF itself in December 1979. Africans' quest for education as a prerequisite of their political development had taken a back seat to the struggle for political independence as a prerequisite of their educational development. In his study *The Colonizer and the Colonized*, Albert Memmi of Tunisia argues that this strategy arises from the consciousness of the colonized and that as long as the colonizer exploits their education, he will sustain his position of political power. Memmi concludes that the only way to end the political power of the colonizer is to eliminate the colonizer himself.[45] In other words Memmi seems to suggest that storming the laager must include eliminating its defenders.

This explains why, from 1963 to 1964, hundreds of African students boycotted classes forcing 80 percent of the schools to close and demanded fundamental changes in the political structure itself. Attacking the educational institution that the RF government used to strengthen its own political power was synonymous with attacking the symbol of an exploiting institution itself. As Africans forced the educational process to a halt, Charles S. Davies, the RF secretary for African education, was forced to admit, "African education in 1964 might well be called the year of troubles. School boycotts, burning, and intimidation were used to bring the educational process to a halt. In Salisbury[46] alone the enrollment at one point fell from 20,000 to 200. Some teachers were involved in all this. Some teachers were forced to join the political parties."[47] Winston Field was engulfed by events he did not understand and so could not control. As the situation rapidly deteriorated, he simply did not know how to solve it. In 1988 Pieter Botha would encounter a similar problem.

This is the situation that forced Ian D. Smith to lead a political coup that removed Winston Field from the position of prime minister on April 12, 1964. Field had been caught in a triangular power struggle: the British demands for a rapid educational advancement of Africans, the negative reaction of Africans themselves, and the desire of the extreme elements of the RF to perpetuate white political power as a demonstration of their loyalty to Rhodes's racial philosophy. Field was forced into retirement and died in 1969, a lonely man deserted by members of the RF and despised by both the British government and Africans. But within eighteen months after Smith assumed the office of prime minister, he found the combination of British demands for African political advancement and African opposition to the policy of his administration too difficult to handle. Indeed, Smith was at the end of the road as he made a fateful decision on November 11, 1965, in declaring the country independent unilaterally. Stating the reason for this action, Smith went on to add, "The mantle of the pioneers has fallen on our shoulders to sustain civilization in a primitive country."[48]

## SUMMARY AND CONCLUSION: BONDING AFRICANS TO THE RF LAAGER

The discussion in this chapter leads to four conclusions regarding the RF policy. The first conclusion is that the RF saw disparity in the educational process as a means of achieving two objectives: to sustain its position of privilege and to convince Africans that no matter how hard they tried, they would never hope to achieve total equality with whites. To achieve both objectives, the RF demonstrated its intolerance for the efforts Africans were making to secure a meaningful educational opportunity as a condition of their political development.

The second conclusion is that, in making a concerted effort to sustain the myth of African inferiority, the RF was also attempting to strengthen the myth of white superiority. In this setting, the RF blamed Africans for the inadequacy of its own policy. This is exactly why Smith told the author during an interview on July 20, 1983, that, "Before the Second World War, Africans did not believe in education, they thought it was something that always belonged to the white man."[49] Smith's administration practiced this myth to design a policy for Africans while the RF used this myth to justify its denial of equal opportunity to Africans.

The third conclusion is that the more the RF tried to maintain educational disparity to control the political development of Africans, the more Africans themselves made an effort to find ways of liberating themselves from it. Therefore, in their respective action to strengthen their own positions, both the RF and Africans charted a new course to a major conflict between them.[50] Rev. Ndabaningi Sithole, a veteran politician and a founding member of both the ANC and ZAPU, put the reality of this situation into proper perspective when he told the author in 1983, "In its own way, the Rhodesia Front government sought to perpetuate itself by imposing its political philosophy on us. In our own way we became determined to eliminate our oppression. This is the environment that was leading to a major conflict."[51]

The fourth and final conclusion is that it is quite clear that the policy of the RF government was intended to strengthen its political hold on the country by attuning Africans to its own purposes. This was stated clearly in its statement of goals in 1967 when it said, "Exactly the same conditions will apply to the African students as the white students. In regard to the cost of attending a university, grants will be given only to those who bond themselves to the state."[52] In this policy position, the RF was trying to bond Africans to the laager. One must therefore conclude that the single most important purpose of the RF's educational policy was to retain disparity in the educational process so that it would be possible to retain the principle of white political power as yet another form of defending the laager. Where would this lead the country?

## NOTES

1. Christian organizations refer to religious organizations, both Catholic and Protestant.

2. There were four Smiths in the RF government. These were Ian D. Smith, prime minister from 1964 to 1979; Lance Smith, minister of international affairs; David Smith, minister of agriculture; and Arthur Smith, minister of education. They were not related by blood, but by a political and racial philosophy.

3. Throughout the colonial period there were two departments of education, one for Africans and the other for whites.

4. Southern Rhodesia, *The African Education Act*, 1959.

5. David Martin and Phyllis Johnson, *The Struggle for Zimbabwe* (Harare: Zimbabwe Publishing House, 1981), p. 68.

6. A former member of the RF during an interview with me in Harare, July 15, 1983. The white man declined to be identified because, he said, "I do not wish to appear to excuse myself from the policies the RF pursued and try to give the impression that we were a bunch of racists."

7. There were two Rhodesias, both of them under British control. Southern Rhodesia was named Rhodesia in 1964 when Northern Rhodesia became the independent nation of Zambia, led by Kenneth Kaunda until 1994.

8. James Barber, *Rhodesia: The Road to Rebellion* (London: Oxford University Press, 1967), p. 95.

9. Ibid., p. 96.

10. Field (1904–1969) served as the first RF prime minister from 1962 to 1964. He was removed from office in a political coup led by Ian D. Smith, just as F. W. De Klerk removed Pieter Botha from the office of president in 1988.

11. A white man, during an interview with me, in Harare, July 17, 1983.

12. A white political observer, during an interview with the author, in Harare, July 14, 1983.

13. The Judges Commission, which Whitehead named in 1961, submitted its report shortly after the RF assumed the government in 1962. The RF made no secret of the fact that it did not like the report because it was fundamentally opposed to it in principle.

14. A white man during an interview with the author in Mutare, Zimbabwe, July 21, 1983.

15. Albert Memmi, *The Colonizer and the Colonized* (Boston: Beacon Press, 1965), p. 21.

16. This is exactly what happened from April 1966 to December 1979. The African government that the RF dedicated itself to preventing was actually installed on April 18, 1980.

17. Martin and Johnson, *The Struggle for Zimbabwe*, p. 68.

18. Southern Rhodesia, *Legislative Debates*, 1927.

19. Ian D. Smith, the last colonial prime minister of colonial Zimbabwe who served from 1964 to 1979, during an interview with the author in Harare, July 20, 1983.

20. The RF amended the infamous Land Apportionment Act of 1929 by enacting the more infamous Land Tenure Act in 1969, which divided the country into two halves, one for whites, the other for Africans. The Land Tenure Act is one of the major causes of the war of independence beginning in April, 1966 because its provisions imposed severe limitations on the educational development of Africans.

21. Barber, *Rhodesia: The Road to Rebellion*, p. 158.

22. A white man during an interview with me in Harare, Zimbabwe, July 29, 1983.

23. Reference to Zambia, which gained political independence in October 1964 under an African government.

24. A white man during an interview with me in Harare, Zimbabwe, July 29, 1983.

25. The federation consisting of Southern Rhodesia, Northern Rhodesia, and Nyasaland, lasted from 1953 to 1963 and was dissolved because of African opposition.

26. Franklin Parker, *African Development and Education in Southern Rhodesia* (Columbus, OH: Kappa Delta Pi, 1960), p. 60.

27. Ibid., p. 61.

28. Southern Rhodesia, *Parliamentary Debates*, 1959–1961.

29. Southern Rhodesia, *Parliamentary Debates*, November 15, 1961.

30. Ibid.

31. The Waddilove Manifesto seems to represent the starting point in the serious conflict that existed between the colonial government and the church. Differences between political ideology and theological perception could no longer be subdued.

32. *The Waddilove Manifesto: The Education Policy of the Methodist Church*, a statement of policy, February 9, 1946. Courtesy of the Old Mutare Methodist Archives.

33. Southern Rhodesia, The Commission of Inquiry into Native Education (Alexander Kerr, Chairman), 1951, p. 17.

34. Southern Rhodesia, *African Education Act*, Section 1, 1959.

35. Arthur Smith, RF minister of education, during an interview with Geoffrey Atkins of the Rhodesia Television, January 31, 1969.

36. Andrew Skeen, RF spokesman, in *Rhodesia: Parliamentary Debates*, September 25, 1969.

37. Larry Bowman, *Rhodesia: White Power in an African State* (Cambridge, MA: Harvard University Press, 1972), p. 70.

38. A. J. Peck, *Rhodesia Accuses* (Boston: Western Islands Press, 1966), p. 70.

39. Ibid., p. 71.

40. ZAPU: Statement of Principles, December 9, 1961. Courtesy of Zimbabwe National Archives.

41. Frank Clements, *Rhodesia: A Study of the Deterioration of a White Society* (New York: Frederick Praeger, 1969), p. 150.

42. Ibid., p. 151.

43. Southern Rhodesia, The Annual Report of the Director of Public Relations, 1963.

44. Southern Rhodesia, The Annual Report of the Secretary for African Education, 1964.

45. Memmi, *The Colonizer and the Colonized*, p. 97.

46. During the colonial period in Zimbabwe, Salisbury was the capital city, named after Lord Salisbury in 1890 in honor of the British prime minister at the time. Salisbury was renamed Harare by the black government that assumed office on April 18, 1980.

47. Southern Rhodesia, The Annual Report of the Secretary for African Education, 1964.

48. Ian D. Smith, *Rhodesia's Finest Hour: Unilateral Declaration of Independence*, November 11, 1965. Salisbury: Zimbabwe National Archives.

49. Ian D. Smith, during an interview with the author, July 20, 1983.

50. Ndabaningi Sithole, during an interview with the author, in Harare, July 20, 1983.

51. Ibid.

52. Rhodesia Front, Statement of Policy and Principles, January 16, 1982. Zimbabwe National Archives.

# 5

# F. W. de Klerk: The Man and His Mission

The time has come for South Africa to restore its pride and to lift itself out of the doldrums of growing international isolation, economic decline, and increasing polarization.
F.W. de Klerk, Inaugural address, September 20, 1989

## CONFLICT BETWEEN BOTHA AND DE KLERK

On August 14, 1989, Pieter W. Botha, recently removed from the office of president of South Africa, complained that, while he was being subjected to pressure to resign from office, his cabinet members failed to come to his aid in defense of an administration of which they were a part. He argued that, in failing to do so, these cabinet members were in violation of a universal principle that members of an administration must always come to aid of another member who was under attack. Botha went on to blame F. W. de Klerk for leading the rebellion that he initiated in 1988. On the same day, Botha went on television to explain the nature of the new conflict that was rapidly developing between himself and de Klerk. He said that one of the issues causing this conflict between the two men was de Klerk's decision to travel to Zambia to hold discussions with President Kenneth D. Kaunda about ways of reducing tension in all of southern Africa. De Klerk had watched what was happening between South Africa and members of SADCC in their respective action to maintain their own economy. He felt, as a result, that he had to do something to solve the problem before it became more complex.

There was a widespread belief in all of southern Africa that Botha was against de Klerk's trip to Zambia, not because he felt it was not necessary, but because he was looking for an early opportunity to undercut de Klerk in every way possible as revenge for leading the rebellion that removed him from office and as leader of the Nationalist Party. Botha argued that he could not support de Klerk's trip because Kaunda had given active support and refuge to the members of the outlawed ANC nationalists who were waging a guerrilla warfare against the apartheid government from bases in Zambia. Indeed, the president of the ANC, Oliver Tambo (1917–1995), a close associate and friend of Nelson Mandela, had been directing ANC operations from bases in Zambia for purposes of storming the laager and bringing the government of South Africa to an end. In this context, Botha was quite accurate in his reasons for opposing de Klerk's visit to Zambia. That was exactly the reason de Klerk used in deciding to make the trip.

Botha also argued that de Klerk was making the visit to Zambia without obtaining assurances from Kaunda that he would stop supporting the ANC nationalists in launching raids into South Africa. He said that it was necessary to obtain these assurances before making the trip in order to enhance the prospects of a successful trip. Botha recognized that, due to lack of experience, de Klerk was vulnerable to exploitation by the veteran Kaunda who had been mellowed by experience in international relationships. These were the reasons that Botha used to conclude that he could not support the trip de Klerk was about to make. Botha concluded, "I am of the opinion that it is inopportune to meet with President Kaunda at this stage."[1] But de Klerk himself was not persuaded to give up the trip or to try to obtain assurances from Kaunda along the lines that Botha suggested. He had reason to believe that the trip would serve a useful purpose in the cause of all the people of southern Africa.

De Klerk also argued that if Botha had been controlled by the opposition that was expressed against holding a summit conference with Samora Machel, then the Nkomati Accord could not have been reached. He expressed his belief that just as Botha had used dialogue to reach an accord with Machel, it was necessary for him to use the same dialogue to establish a basis of understanding of the regional issues with Kaunda so that solutions could be found on problems of relationships in southern Africa. He also argued that dialogue with any national leader in southern Africa would provide an opportunity for the parties to come to an understanding of the issues from their proper perspective. De Klerk was aware that if he gave in to Botha's opposition to the trip given that Botha was a national leader under fire, his own credibility as the acting chairman of the Nationalist Party and acting president of South Africa would have been seriously compromised.

De Klerk, therefore, decided to make the trip on the basis of these considerations. Indeed, the meetings with Kaunda were very productive, establishing a basis of understanding between them as to what must be done to solve the problems. Kaunda was quick to point out to de Klerk that, as long as apartheid remained the policy of South Africa, it would be very difficult to address all other problems of southern Africa. De Klerk seemed to agree but made no promises to end this sinister policy. He returned to South Africa with somber thoughts about what he heard from an African leader who felt obligated to support his fellow Africans, members of the ANC, who were waging a struggle to end apartheid. For the first time, de Klerk came face to face with the hard reality that apartheid was condemned all over the world. Contrary to the advice that de Klerk had received from Botha to obtain assurance from Kaunda to stop supporting the ANC nationalists, Kaunda instead reiterated his commitment to that support. Once Africans made the decision to storm the laager it would be reversed.

Botha also disclosed information he said was at his disposal about de Klerk's conduct within the Nationalist Party. He stated his belief that even before he suffered a mild stroke, de Klerk was busy working against him, as he and his rebellious associates were motivated by the excuse that, at the age of 73, Botha was no longer providing an effective leadership for both the Nationalist Party and the country. Defending the laager demanded energy and efforts that would be more strong in the hands a younger leader. In the presidential election campaign in the United States in 1996, Republican candidate Bob Dole was 73 years old. His Democratic opponent and incumbent, Bill Clinton, was 50 years old. Clinton did not make Dole's age an issue, although some Americans thought that at the age of 73 Dole was too old to run for president. Dole's fall from a poorly constructed platform in Chico, California, on September 13 while he was campaigning reinforced this view. The presidential debate held between the two men on October 6 did not help Dole.[2] De Klerk and his rebellious associates were saying that effective leadership was needed to defend the laager and address the enormous problems that South Africa faced in its relationships with other countries of southern Africa. They believed that Botha was no longer able to play that role effectively, and, therefore, had to be replaced.

Botha's response was that he was operating under the Nationalist Party policy and principles. Obviously, Botha took offense to what he considered a conspiracy led by de Klerk and his associates. Botha was infuriated by what he characterized as a callous attitude on the part of the conspirators and lashed out angrily at them saying, "It is evident to me that after all these years of my best efforts for the Nationalist Party and for the government of this country, as well as its security, I am being ignored by members of my cabinet. I consequently have no choice other than to announce my resignation."[3] Events would later prove that Botha had no other choice of action or reaction.

After Botha's television appearance, de Klerk and Roelf Botha (no relation to the embattled president), foreign minister, took exception to the former president's remarks and issued a response saying, "We are sad that a man who has done so much for his country has to retire under these unhappy circumstances. We felt that his state of health justified this action on our party."[4] De Klerk and Roelf Botha went on to add that the question of leadership of both the Nationalist Party and the country was so crucial that it could no longer be avoided. That is exactly the line of thinking that Ian D. Smith and his associates utilized in removing Winston Field from the office of prime minister in colonial Zimbabwe in September 1964. Roelf Botha and de Klerk also argued that the conflict between them and Botha was also caused by his failure to see the need to initiate fundamental change in policy to suit new conditions and meet the needs of the present. They said that Botha was so much a part of the past that he was unable to project the future required by rapidly changing conditions in southern Africa.

In a gesture that was intended to rally support for their opposition to Botha, de Klerk and Roelf Botha acknowledged the fact that, "It was an ignominious finish to the career of a politician who began as a Nationalist Party organizer fifty-four years ago"[5] Indeed, Pieter W. Botha was first elected to Parliament in the elections of 1948 when Daniel F. Malan, the founder of the modern Nationalist Party, was elected and served as prime minister until 1954. Botha was named Defense Minister by John Vorster in 1966. He served with dedication, operating under the principles that the Nationalist Party had outlined to sustain apartheid. When de Klerk and Roelf Botha said that Botha was unable to project a future different from the past, they never questioned his dedication to the sustenance of apartheid as a loyal defender of the laager. Until Vorster resigned, disgraced by scandal in 1978, he could count on Botha to demonstrate loyalty to both him and the Nationalist Party because defending the laager demanded it. Botha was then the natural choice as successor to Vorster, serving as prime minister from 1978 to 1983 when a constitutional amendment abolished the office of prime minister in favor of that of president. Botha served as president from 1983 to 1988, when he was replaced by de Klerk.

Until that year, Botha combined the offices of party chairman and president of South Africa. From this perspective Botha exercised enormous power over the Nationalist Party and the country. On September 20, 1989, when de Klerk was installed as president of South Africa, Botha's term of office unceremoniously came to an end. The bitterness he expressed over the manner in which he was removed from office is understandable. His resignation was a surprise to even his close and trusted associates and cabinet members. He said that he wanted to become a unifying force for the Nationalist Party and for South Africa without the burden of party and government leadership. But with the kind of conflict that emerged between himself and de Klerk, Botha was denied the opportunity to play that role. His fall from power effectively ended his lifelong ambition of ending his political career as a statesman.

## DE KLERK'S POLITICAL PERSONALITY

Now that de Klerk had succeeded in replacing Botha as president of both the Nationalist Party and of South Africa, what kind of leadership would he provide? Would he function as a member of the ruling party, and provide an agenda for action different from Botha's? Would he be able to come to terms with Africans and recognize the need to bring apartheid to an end? To furnish answers to these questions is to provide a profile of a man and leader whose political skills had not been tested. Questions about de Klerk's political skills and knowledge is the reason Archbishop Desmond M. Tutu expressed his fear that his election as leader would result in more repression of Africans because, without experience, de Klerk was likely to give in to pressure from the extreme elements of the Nationalist Party, and not give in to the demands Africans and the international community were making to dismantle apartheid.[6]

A study of the conditions that produced de Klerk would show that Tutu's fear and doubt were not entirely without basis. When de Klerk was born in Johannesburg on March 18, 1936, South Africa was going through a difficult time. In that year J. B. Hertzog, who served as prime minister from 1924 to 1939, was leading a campaign to remove Africans from the voters role[7] because he did not think that they were qualified to exercise such a big responsibility associated with citizenship. Apartheid had its origins in this kind of thinking. Successive leaders of South Africa entertained this idea in one form or another. But it was Daniel Malan who actually gave effect to it. Hertzog feared the political power that Africans were rapidly gaining through the influence of the ANC, which had been formed in 1912. Hertzog believed that the only way to eliminate the threat that Africans were posing to the monopoly of the political power Afrikaners enjoyed was to eliminate them from the political process.

In 1924 the Labour Party, a predominantly English-speaking party, and the Nationalist Party, a predominantly Afrikaans-speaking party, formed an election coalition to oppose the South African party led by J. C. Smuts, an Afrikaner and the revered hero of both world wars who supported the policies of the British Empire. When the clouds of conflict were rolling across the skies in Europe in 1936, beginning with the civil war in Spain, Hertzog and Smuts found themselves on opposite sides of the issues. Smuts supported the British position, but Hertzog supported Germany. As soon as Hertzog assumed office, he joined forces with Daniel Malan. Soon the two men were building the Nationalist Party on a platform opposing the objectives of the British Empire. Although Hertzog and Malan were both from the Cape Province, they had wider support that extended to all four provinces of South Africa. In the Transvaal, the home province of Paul Kruger, anti-British and anti-African sentiments became the twin towers of the Nationalist policy.

There, in the Transvaal, de Klerk's father, Jan de Klerk, was an active member of the Nationalist Party. He also served in several cabinet positions for fifteen years including that of Minister of Education, a post he held until 1969 when he became president of the senate. De Klerk's uncle, G. J. Strijdom, succeeded Malan in 1954 and served as prime minister of South Africa until his death in 1958. De Klerk's older brother, Willem de Klerk, served for some time as editor of a daily Afrikaans newspaper, *Die Transvaler*, which was based in Johannesburg. As he was growing up, de Klerk was introduced early into the anti-African environment that became part of his education. This background meant that de Klerk came to public life having been well groomed.

The young de Klerk took his formal education very seriously and graduated in 1958 from Potchefstroom University with the degrees of Bachelor of Arts and Bachelor of Law (cum laude)[8] at the age of 22. He then worked as an attorney's clerk in Pretoria before he joined a law firm in Vereeniging in the Transvaal. As a student, de Klerk participated in many university activities and served as a member of the student representative council. He was offered the position of professor of law at his Alma Mater in 1973, but declined because he was already a member of Parliament representing the Vereeniging district, an extremely conservative constituency known for its hardened attitudes toward Africans. That is the reason de Klerk was elected. De Klerk rose rapidly in the Nationalist Party's inner circle. In 1978, shortly before his forty-second birthday, Pieter W. Botha appointed him to his first cabinet post. As minister of education, the post that his father had held under Vorster's administration, de Klerk tried to stop the admission of African students into universities traditionally designated for whites.

It would seem that de Klerk was basing his policy on what Paul Kruger, president of the ill-fated Transvaal Republic, said during the height of his political power in 1889: that Africans must understand that they belonged to an inferior class whose major role in society was to obey instructions from white men in order to learn to be productive laborers.[9] As de Klerk grew up, his relationships with Africans were based on this Afrikaner fundamental philosophical tenet. By the time he entered politics, there was nothing in his background and upbringing that would suggest an alternative approach to the question of race other than the application of apartheid. On July 1, 1985, de Klerk became chairman of the Ministers' Council of the House of Assembly. He and his wife, Marike Willemse, whom he met at Potchefstroom University where she was studying for the degree of Bachelor of Commerce, had three children, two sons and one daughter. Like all Afrikaners, the de Klerk family was considered religious. For years that had been a prerequisite for defending the laager.

Although de Klerk felt secure in his position of president of South Africa and chairman of the Nationalist Party, he was worried by the possibility that the method he used to remove Botha from office could easily translate into a belief among voters that the party was in total disarray and therefore could not be trusted with the responsibility of defending the laager. This could lead to a loss of credibility among Afrikaner voters. Zach de Beer, co-leader of the relatively liberal Democratic party, said on this aspect of the Nationalist Party, "It is obvious to all that the Nationalist Party is sharply divided on the vital issues of consultation and negotiations. This constitutes a very real credibility problem for the Nationalist Party leadership."[10] This suggests the conclusion that the cracks in the laager could not be patched. David Welsh, professor of political science at the University of Cape Town, added, "I do not think that we can expect a dramatic break through with de Klerk. But at least he is rational and, although his track is not record on apartheid, he appears to be on the learning course."[11]

Observers acknowledged the fact that de Klerk, who had a record of vigorously defending apartheid and the laws enacted under it, wanted to use Botha's resignation to have the Nationalist Party close ranks behind him in order to resolve the deep divisions that were developing within itself. Pieter W. Botha was the one person he could not count on. However, given the nature of the problems the Nationalist Party was facing, it was not possible for de Klerk to govern without the state of emergency that Botha's predecessor, John Vorster, imposed at the time of the Soweto uprising in June 1976. But de Klerk also knew that to continue the state of emergency would create greater problems in his relationships with Africans than it did with Botha.

It was a well-known fact that de Klerk was leaving a tarnished record in the national Ministry of Education to assume the office of president at a critical period in the history of South Africa. It was not clear as to whether his designation as Botha's successor changed his political spots or whether it had given him a new vision for the future of the country. Indeed, de Klerk was "a conformed right winger with a long record as a defender of white privileges."[12] Africans and members of the international community wanted to know where a right wing Afrikaner with unacceptable apartheid credentials would lead the country. This was not a rhetorical question, it was real and demanded a response. Whether de Klerk was able to furnish a response would be determined by what he and his administration were planning to do in this critical area of national life.

As minister of education in Botha's administration, de Klerk was an outspoken advocate of segregated universities. In 1987 he issued a series of controversial regulations to make government subsidies to the nation's best universities depend upon their commitment to effectively control campus unrest. In chapter 4 a discussion was directed at the same practice that the Rhodesia Front government initiated in colonial Zimbabwe. The courts, recognizing the danger that such regulations posed to higher education, rejected them and placed de Klerk in an uncomfortable situation. De Klerk, like Ian D. Smith in colonial Zimbabwe, also pressured university governing councils to agree to additional conditions that he intended to use to limit any campus activity he considered incompatible with his own definition of activities normally associated with universities. Would he succeed as president of a country under siege when his accomplishments as Minster of Education were mediocre?

There is another important factor that may indicate de Klerk's political personality. In normal political situations, like those that exist in true democracy, the conflict that emerged between Botha and de Klerk occurs quite often. For example, Margaret Thatcher, British prime minister for a decade, lost her position in a dispute between herself and members of her cabinet over her increasing autocratic style of leadership. Chapter 4 has also concluded that, in 1964, Ian D. Smith led a cabinet coup that removed Winston Field from the position of prime minister in colonial Zimbabwe. What made de Klerk's challenge of Botha's leadership unusual and successful is that, since 1948, the Nationalist Party ruled the country, uninterrupted, without any opposition from other parties or rebellion from within itself.

But when opposition finally came from within its own ranks, it signaled something new that had to be addressed. De Klerk knew that he would succeed in his effort to unseat Botha. He and his fellow conspirators saw Botha as the successor to the corruption of his predecessor, John Vorster, and made no effort to get rid of it. In closing ranks behind de Klerk, the Nationalist Party members believed that they were getting rid of the tarnished image of a party that had provided a utopia for Afrikaners since 1948. In removing Botha from the position of leadership, members of the Nationalist Party believed that they were erasing the dark shadows and legacy of Vorster's term of office. If Botha thought that he was the Caesar of the new South Africa, de Klerk certainly regarded himself as its Brutus, plotting and masterminding the conspiracy that undercut him.

In spite of the ultraconservative stance of his background, indications

are de Klerk had a political personality that was likely to help him initiate change in the structure of apartheid. These indications came in early
June, 1989 during an interview he had with Ned Temko of *World Monitor*.
Asked what message and issues he would send and seek to bring before
the voters in South Africa on the elections to be held in September, de
Klerk responded, "We are reaching out towards a new future. We will
have to bring drastic change about. In the final analysis the good must
be fairness to all the people of South Africa, or a square deal for each
and every section of our population. White domination, we have clearly
stated, must come to an end. But that cannot be exchanged for another
form of domination."[13] In saying that the end of white domination must
not be replaced by another form of domination, de Klerk was actually
admitting that the Nationalist government, as architects of apartheid,
had been exercising the kind of domination recognized across the world
as a major cause of conflict in South Africa. He was actually saying that
he did not want the ANC to exercise that domination in the future.

Temko then asked de Klerk how seriously he saw the political threat
from the extreme right wing groups in South Africa. De Klerk responded,

All things new are on the ground, that threat is not very serious. They represent
in the vicinity of 20 percent of the white electorate. We think that the parties to
the right have a fatal flow in their policy. That is, they do not make provision
for the reasonable aspirations of the people of color. We think that the parties to
the left of us have a fatal flaw in their policy as well in that they do not make
sufficient provision for the need for the protection of minority rights in this country. It is only my party which brings those two together into a package, and that
is why I have no doubt that we are looking forward to a very good election
result on September 6.[14]

For de Klerk to indicate that white domination must come to an end was
to recognize that fundamental change had to take place in the political
system as imperative to any thrust for political reform. The question was
whether he was he equal to the task of bringing about that reform. His
political personality enables one to see him as a persuasive leader with
an unusual ability to see both sides of an issue. This was his greatest
asset.

During the struggle to remove Botha from office, de Klerk presented
himself as a conservative who regarded apartheid as the salvation of
Afrikaners. But as soon as he was elected leader of the Nationalist Party,
he surprised everyone, including his co-conspirators, by appearing to
espouse liberal views. The rank and file of the Nationalist Party were
quite upset to see this kind of change in the views of a man who had
been in tune with popular views on the issues facing South Africa. Such

a personality conflict is often difficult to measure, and in the case of de Klerk it was an even more difficult task. De Klerk was on his way to bringing about change in South Africa the like of which had never been seen in the history of the country. Still, there was doubt and skepticism within South Africa that de Klerk was the right man to assume the leadership of a deeply troubled country at a critical point in its history. Such was the political personality that de Klerk brought to this dramatic scene.

The doubt that Desmond M. Tutu expressed when de Klerk was elected leader of the Nationalist Party in August, 1989 appears to have been confirmed when Frank Chikane, Allan Boesak, and Tutu held a meeting with de Klerk in October. From the manner in which the meeting was conducted and de Klerk's attitude, Tutu quoted Chikane as saying to de Klerk,

You are asking the world to give you a chance. You are telling black people of South Africa that the door to a new South Africa is already open but it is not necessary to batter it down. You say that you must talk to representative leaders. Today, as I left to come and take advantage of your open door policy, a leader of the democratic movement wanted to consult me about this meeting. To claim to be representative I needed to hear his views. I asked him to travel with me. But he told me that he could not because a government restriction order imposed during your presidency prohibits him from leaving the Johannesburg magisterial district. People are saying your actions do not match your words.[15]

Tutu went on to state that Chikane did not mention the 3,000 political prisoners who were still held in South African jails after the release of Walter Sesulu on October 15, 1989, and other ANC leaders a little later. Tutu concluded that de Klerk's claim of initiating fundamental change in the politics of South Africa was inconsistent with both the policy of the Nationalist Party and his own words. Tutu repeated his earlier view that de Klerk was being held hostage by the extreme elements of the Nationalist Party and that he did not have the freedom to pursue a policy that would mean, in effect, the end of apartheid. It was one thing for de Klerk to lead a political coup against Pieter W. Botha, but quite another to initiate the kind of policy that would place South Africa on the road to harmony, peace, and development. De Klerk needed to know that, with the passage of time, Africans would become more determined to end apartheid in their own way. If they did not receive cooperation from whites, they would be doubtful if Afrikaners would have a future in South Africa. It was up to de Klerk to make a bold move toward dismantling apartheid entirely. Nothing less would satisfy Africans.

In reality Tutu argued that de Klerk should not hide behind the extreme elements of the Nationalist Party to forestall progress toward ending apartheid; he must face the problems that his own party had been creating since 1948. Tutu concluded by challenging de Klerk to assert the appropriate leadership role to solve the national problems because, he argued, "Enormous obstacles still stand in the way of the free political activity that is needed to get negotiations about a new political arrangement in South Africa."[16] In saying what they did, both Chikane and Tutu were bringing de Klerk's political personality to the test. His ability to pass that test would determine his legacy in the political annals of South Africa.

Another critical dimension of de Klerk's political personality began to emerge in June 1989 when he made an unofficial tour of Europe. Among the European leaders he would hold discussions with were Margaret Thatcher of Britain and Helmet Kohl of Germany. De Klerk was making this pilgrimage, not to persuade his hosts to accept the fact that apartheid must remain the central tenet of the South African political system, but to set the stage for his victory in the elections scheduled for September 6. If he won the election, there would be no doubt that his claim to the presidency of South Africa would be substantiated. In making this pilgrimage to Europe, de Klerk hoped that he would be asked to explain his intentions on the future of South Africa away from the controversy that would surround such an explanation if it was made in the country. In this way anticipated favorable reaction to his agenda expressed in Europe would minimize any negative reaction at home.

De Klerk's political personality was primarily shaped by his background in the Transvaal, "the province where the Nationalists are more vulnerable to the conservatives with their dream of pure apartheid."[17] De Klerk, therefore, knew that he needed to balance his understanding of the need to ease the dominance of apartheid and the need to retain its essential components. Where could such a balancing act lead him, the Nationalist Party, and South Africa? De Klerk seems to have had an answer when he said, "Each racial group must have the right to administer its own affairs."[18] This was vintage apartheid language that its framers had been talking for half a century. Was de Klerk ignoring the attitude of the international community? Was he suggesting that Africans were responsible for administering their own affairs like they had been doing in the Bantustan homelands? Were they expected to maintain their own streets, their own schools, their own hospitals, their own telephone services, build their own facilities such as water supply and electricity? In this system, where would de Klerk place the common balancing wheel that was needed to sustain the new social order he said he would seek to promote? De Klerk did not seem to have immediate answers to these questions.

However, common sense would suggest that if de Klerk chose to cling to his notion of group rights, any effort that he might make in bringing about political change would be influenced by apartheid. He needed to

know that apartheid could not be reformed. Any programs initiated under its gaze could not amount to anything substantial. On the one hand,
members of the Nationalist Party would be uncomfortable with his attempt to invade the shores of apartheid even though the change he, like
Botha before him, was trying to initiate was only marginal. On the other
hand, the international community and Africans would not accept only
cosmetic change; they would want to see significant and irreversible
change. In this context de Klerk did not have to come to sit on the fence
of apartheid and hope that things would be all right, he had to jump on
one side of it and claim his territorial boundary.

It would appear that de Klerk would need an election to help him
decide his options. He recognized that he faced two choices: to do nothing about apartheid and allow things to deteriorate, or to take the bull
of apartheid by the horns and wrestle it to the ground before it could
gore him. This is why he made a pilgrimage to Europe and to Zambia.
For him to come back from those trips and do nothing would be to
become disloyal to a great national cause that he was placed in a position
to change. The elections scheduled for September 9, 1989, would be crucial in helping him exercise those options. The results would define his
political personality far more profoundly than anything he had done in
the past.

One other reason why de Klerk undertook the pilgrimage to Europe
was to persuade the European nations to ease the economic burden
placed on his shoulders by the application of sanctions. He was made to
understand in no uncertain terms that, as long as apartheid remained
the policy of South Africa, there was no prospect of ending the sanctions.
He returned to South Africa fully convinced that whatever he did at
home must take into account the reality of the response of European
nations to his action on apartheid. Maintaining sanctions was their response if he decided to retain it. This is the reality that de Klerk's political
personality was brought to bear upon.

Although de Klerk held the view that his domestic agenda must not
be influenced by the reaction of nations in Europe, he was realistic
enough to acknowledge the fact that the application of apartheid had
ramifications that extended far beyond the borders of South Africa. This
acknowledgment compelled him to recognize the pressure that was coming from the international community as a more important factor than
reaction from the home front itself. But de Klerk was also realistic
enough to recognize the truth that the call to dismantle apartheid was
more strongly made at home by the various organizations and people
who were more affected by it than the international community was. The
time for de Klerk to decide whether he would continue to defend the
laager or help Africans to storm it was rapidly approaching.

## DE KLERK'S POLITICAL PERSONALITY AND
## FAMILY MATTERS

Another indication of what de Klerk was likely to do about apartheid came on January 10, 1991, in a matter that was very personal. On that day it was reported that his son, Willem, 24 years old, had fallen in love with Erica Adams, also 24, the daughter of Deon Adams who was classified under apartheid as Coloured[19] and was the leader of the mixed-race Labour Party in the Cape Province. *Die Burger,* a daily Afrikaans newspaper in Cape Town, disclosed the information that Willem had been engaged to Erica for some time. *Die Burger* stated that South Africa's population registration laws, which formed the centerpiece of apartheid, officially classified Willem as white and Erica as Coloured. This means that she had both white and black ancestry.

It is important to remember in this South African version of Romeo and Juliet that the Nationalist Party had made interracial romance and marriage a criminal offense. The party did this by promulgating the Prohibition of Mixed Marriages Act of 1949 and by the Immorality Act of 1957. Although both laws were repealed in 1985, attitudes among Afrikaners have to this day remained hostile to such marriages. Willem and Erica met while they were studying public relations at Cape Technikou, a college-level institute specializing in engineering. They had been dating for nearly two years before they decided to get married. What was de Klerk going to do, defend the laager or help storm it?

As soon as Willem completed his course of study, he left to take additional studies in public relations in Britain, where he was expected to remain for six months. Erica wore the decorated ring on her left hand and posed for photographs taken by reporters of local newspapers. However, she declined to confirm whether she and Willem were engaged. When pressured to respond, Erica simply said, "We cannot give details of our relationship because personal circumstances in our situation make it impossible. We might say something at a later stage."[20] Erica's reluctance to respond to questions from the press is fully understood in the context of the attitudes of Nationalists and Afrikaners toward romance and marriage across the color line. This reluctance was even more imperative because the father of the young man she was about to marry was an Afrikaner to the core, a Nationalist, and president of the country.

There was no indication as to whether Willem had taken Erica to meet his family, or whether Erica had taken Willem to meet hers. Perhaps this is the reason why de Klerk himself decided to issue a statement in which he neither confirmed nor denied the report of the engagement except to say that his son's relationships were a private family matter. However, de Klerk went on to say, "He did not inform me that he was planning to get engaged. In fact I have only recently become aware of the relationship between him and a student friend. My son is 24 years old and has been out of the house for quite a while already. As an adult man he is in a position to make decisions of his own. I regard the relationship as a private family matter, and I believe it should be handled as such."[21]

The Press Association of South Africa received a similar response when it reached Erica's father. His answer to the question of whether his daughter was engaged to Willem was, "My policy is not to talk about my family matters in public."[22] In these responses both de Klerk and Adams were placing their families in a situation that demanded an articulation of national issues. Both men came to recognize the fact that family matters, though very private, could not be separated from national matters because they were parents of very public figures. Therefore, the press had a legitimate interest and right to expect answers to the question of whether their children were engaged to be married.

The point that must be made here about the relationship between Willem and Erica is one that de Klerk would rather forget. History says that Afrikaners' Dutch ancestors who first arrived at the Cape in 1652 had been fathers to children by the Khoi and San women who lived in the area at the time. The Coloured population, numbering 3 million in 1991, came originally from this practice. Although there was no immediate reaction from Afrikaner politicians to the relationship between Erica and Willem, de Klerk feared that the right-wing Conservative Party would try to exploit the issue to embarrass him and ruin his national agenda. Therefore, de Klerk needed to be very cautious about how he responded to this situation within his own family because it could very well affect his handling of the apartheid crisis. This was be a real test of his political personality.

## DE KLERK DEFINES HIS MISSION

It is ironic that de Klerk began to question the effect of apartheid when he was leading a rebellion against Botha. Pressure from the international community, opposition from the ANC, criticism from church leaders, and threats from the front-line states all combined to convince him that the long-term interests of Afrikaners would be served, not by strict enforcement of apartheid, but an alternative approach or apartheid would have to be maintained at a high cost. The conditions that he was facing in trying to sustain the infamous policy were very different from those that earlier administrations faced. De Klerk began to imagine a South Africa without apartheid. He also began to perceive a nation that must overcome the oppression of its envisaged future different from the past. The more he thought about these possibilities the more he became convinced that there was only one option left, and that was to begin bringing apartheid to an end.

By 1991 de Klerk had become convinced that it was in the best interest of all the people of South Africa to dismantle apartheid, to storm the laager. He decided to start on this mission by repealing the Group Areas Act of 1950 that segregated neighborhoods by race. He also considered repealing the Land Act of 1913, which allocated 87 percent of the land to whites and the remaining 13 percent to Africans. He felt that a new constitution must be written to eliminate the population registration laws that were so discriminatory against Africans. De Klerk concluded that whatever he suggested would not meet the demands of the international community and Africans as long as vestiges of apartheid remained in place. This meant that in the very near future he would have to face the possibility of an African government. The victory that he scored in the election of September 6, 1989, provided him the mandate he needed to carry out the task of dismantling apartheid. He could no longer delay the storming of the laager. Since 1948 every national leader in South Africa demonstrated his commitment to defend the laager. De Klerk was the first to lead a crusade to storm it. It had served an unholy purpose and had to go. Instead of watching Africans storm by themselves, he decided that it was better to help them. The task was accomplished by a new constitution that gave Africans the political power they had struggled for. In turn, Mandela named de Klerk vice-president.

## FACTORS INFLUENCING DE KLERK'S MISSION

But in order to carry out his mission, de Klerk needed to understand four critical factors about South Africa. The first is that South Africa was at the most serious crossroads in its history. There were signs that the situation could easily grow into a major civil war that Afrikaners could not win. South Africa began to experience this crossroads when Botha succeeded Vorster in 1978. Corruption in Vorster's administration did not end there; it extended into Botha's administration. Suddenly the Nationalist Party, once considered infallible, now found itself unable to do anything right. The callous manner in which it implemented the dimensions of apartheid left little room for doubt that it had gone too far.

The second factor is that no matter what de Klerk did, it was totally insufficient to reform the policy of apartheid. His only option was to persuade the Nationalist Party to agree to his program of bringing apartheid to an end. It had become the monster whose appetite for oppression had become insatiable.This is one hard reality that the *Christian Science Monitor* of March 1989 took into account in concluding that, although de Klerk's record was "one of staunch conservative stance, even by Nationalist Party criteria, he was making statements that suggested the need to initiate change."[23] The *Christian Science Monitor* suggested that an open-minded approach would enable de Klerk to examine all options before he launched his mission to rescue his country from a major disaster. In the final analysis de Klerk must be guided by the same argument that Desmond M. Tutu had been making for many years: that the security of the whites in South Africa rested squarely on the political advancement of Africans. In order to make this possible, de Klerk had to recognize that apartheid had to go.

The third factor that de Klerk had to take into account in carrying out his mission of helping Africans storm the laager was to convince the rank and file members of the Nationalist Party of the wisdom of his approach to the problems of South Africa. This aspect of his mission constituted a critical phase of fulfilling his agenda. Without the support of the Nationalist Party, de Klerk would carry the same label as Botha did—that he was dictatorial in his approach to national problems. If this happened, Botha would be vindicated in his criticism of de Klerk. In order to succeed in this approach, de Klerk needed to avoid the arrogance and tyrannical methods that Botha used. Given the climate that existed in both the country and the international community, de Klerk had an advantage that Botha did not have: public perception that after forty-seven years in office the Nationalist Party must give way to a new order. That de Klerk was at first recognized as a conservative gave him the credibility that he needed when he finally took the initiative in the process of bringing about fundamental political change.

The fourth and final factor that de Klerk needed to take into account in launching his mission for fundamental political change was to obtain the support of the front-line states and the international community. He was aware that the only way to get that support was to end the state of emergency unconditionally and agree to dismantle apartheid. During a trip to Europe, de Klerk came face-to-face with the harsh realities that apartheid had to go if South Africa hoped to carry on normal business relationships with the rest of the world. The imposition of economic sanctions completely isolated South Africa, costing it millions of dollars. Athletes from South Africa, were not allowed to participate in the Olympic Games until the summer games held in Atlanta in 1996.

De Klerk knew that the support of the front-line states and OAU was crucial to the success of his mission. He was also aware that the Nkomati Accord of 1984 was heavily criticized for its lop-sided clauses favoring South Africa and that Machel had entered into negotiations with Botha from a position of weakness. De Klerk's support of the accord was tempered by the reality that African states did not like it because it enshrined the basic elements of apartheid. To convince both the international community and the front-line states, de Klerk needed to promise to dismantle apartheid in order to create a nonracial society. If de Klerk was sincere in taking these four factors into account, he would be able to carry out his mission of transforming South Africa much more efficiently than he would without them and bring about the happiness of everyone in the country.

De Klerk knew as soon as he assumed the office of president on September 20, 1989, that he had to do something dramatic to alter the course that apartheid had charted for South Africa since 1948. He also knew that cosmetic changes would continue to plague the country and push it into a state of degeneration. This is why, in his inaugural address, de Klerk stated that he was pledging himself to the creation of a new climate that he said would "make it possible lift the nationwide state of emergency, or at least to gradually move away from it."[24] He also indicated other components of his mission as he promised to "work relentlessly to rescind discriminatory legislation, to continue releasing political prisoners and give urgent attention to a bill of human rights for all races."[25] If de Klerk was able to operate by this pledge, there would be no reason why he would not receive the support he needed to complete his mission. It appeared that the worst opposition was likely to come from within the Nationalist Party itself. But given the circumstances of the situation that they faced, the members of the Nationalist Party knew that their future lay in the security of Africans.

Wishing to stress the importance of his mission to transform South Africa, de Klerk went on record to assure Africans and the international community of his irreversible commitment to fundamental political change in South Africa in accordance with their expectations. He was compelled to add, "The time has come for South Africa to restore its pride and to lift itself out of the doldrums of growing international isolation, economic decline, and increasing polarization. We are aware that we have raised expectations during the past months. We intend to live up to them because we believe in what we believe, in what we advocate. We are quite prepared to be tested against our understanding. We cannot accept responsibility for over enthusiastic or even revisited versions of our policy."[26] De Klerk also added that he was aware of other unreasonable expectations which he said had been created. In many cases some expectations were so unrealistic that change would not come immediately. He pleaded for patience.

De Klerk appeared genuinely moved by both the impact of the inauguration itself and the implications involved for him and South Africa. He was quite deliberate in what he had to say in the inaugural speech. His eyes welled up with tears several times during the address, especially when Rev. P. W. Bingle, a close family friend and confidant, spoke of de Klerk in human terms and suggested that the new president had a divine mission to promote fundamental political change to save his country from self-destruction. Bingle concluded his remarks by pleading for everyone to come to de Klerk's assistance for the good of the country. Bingle warned his fellow South Africans that the alternative to de Klerk's initiative would be a major national disaster. This course of national development was to be avoided at all costs.

Although de Klerk's inaugural address was received well by the international community and moderate whites, die-hard Afrikaners considered it a betrayal of the principles that they believed had been applied to sustain their political power. However, de Klerk did not show how Africans responded to his address. The South African Press Association quoted Archbishop Desmond M. Tutu, the famous foe of apartheid, as saying that he hoped that de Klerk "will demonstrate that he is serious about his vision for a new South Africa because that is the vision we want."[27] It was a mission to rescue South Africa from the banks of a major national disaster. Allan Boesak, another implacable foe of apartheid, said that de Klerk had six months to produce tangible results as a manifestation of the accomplishments of his mission. Boesak cautioned de Klerk that if he failed he should expect strong reaction from Africans. That reaction might very well lead to a civil war. De Klerk knew that he had only one chance to bring about change in South Africa by peaceful means. Boesak also reminded de Klerk of the statement that he (de Klerk) made when he became leader of the Nationalist Party in February 1989 when he spoke of a "totally changed South Africa which would rid itself of past racial antagonisms and would be free of domination or oppression in whatever form in which all reasonable people and groups in South Africa would cooperate in building a new society."[28]

De Klerk was also fully aware that Africans and the international community expected him to dismantle apartheid much faster than he believed conditions would allow. They were not quite sure that the dismantling of apartheid formed the core of his mission. They wanted to remind him that any delay in that course of action would result in a combination of intensified international sanctions and opposition from Africans to create a set of new conditions which he would be unable to control. De Klerk was also influenced by the expression of his view that while white minority domination must come to an end, it must not be replaced by domination by Africans. To off-set this possibility, de Klerk tried a new constitution that would protect the rights of minority groups.

Considering the fact that, while the Nationalist Party had been ruling the country since 1948, it never thought of constitutional provisions to protect the rights of Africans, Africans reacted negatively to de Klerk's proposal. If accepted, this constitutional proposal would be tantamount to giving the white minority veto power. This had never been done in all of Africa, and Africans would not allow it to happen for the first time in South Africa. De Klerk should have known that at the beginning of his mission. De Klerk should also have known that the white minority government led by Ian D. Smith in Zimbabwe tried this tactic, but it fell flat on its face. How could it work in South Africa? In making this proposal de Klerk must have known that it would raise serious questions about his sincerity in seeking a fundamental change in the politics of South Africa. De Klerk was also aware that in making the proposal he would lose credibility among Africans. But he felt he had to make it in order to place it as item on the agenda.

In assessing the strategy to fulfill his mission, de Klerk added that, in order to accomplish it, his administration would make initiatives to resolve what he called those matters which so frequently are raised as obstacles by the apparatus of government. Those matters included the continuing imprisonment of Nelson Mandela and hundreds of other African political prisoners, and the continuing state of emergency which was first imposed in 1964 when the ANC was outlawed and its leaders were arrested and sent to prison. De Klerk did not suggest a timetable or target date by which to release them as part of his initiative. As long as these Africans remained in prison, there was little chance that he would convince Africans that he meant well in setting an agenda to accomplish his mission. Without setting such a date, it was doubtful whether he could prove that he was committed to that mission.

As part of his mission, de Klerk also addressed the importance of South Africa's cooperation in developmental programs of the entire region of southern Africa. He challenged the front-line states to rise to the occasion and respond to his call for the benefit of all the countries. De Klerk concluded his challenge to the other countries of southern Africa saying, "use your influence constructively to help us attain the goal of peaceful resolution of our problems."[29] He was quite persuasive in saying that, in trying to help South Africa solve its problems, the countries of southern Africa would demonstrate their good intentions to their neighbor. This is how they would also help themselves. He suggested that there was no reason for the hostility that was so prevalent in earlier times toward South Africa because his administration was committed to ending apartheid.

With reference to the continuing wave of antiapartheid protest in South Africa, de Klerk assured South Africans that his administration would continue to deal with unrest, violence, and terrorism with a firm hand in order to create the climate of dialogue so critical to the quest for solutions to the country's problems. In discussing this dimension of his mission, de Klerk seemed a victim of amnesia that characterized the reaction of his predecessors to retain apartheid. He seemed to forget that what he called terrorism was, in effect, a demonstration of an uncompromising opposition to a system that was in itself violent and so meted out terrorism to Africans who were its victims. He mentioned the fact that Nationalist government terrorism did not come from those who protested against apartheid, but from the government's imposition of oppressive conditions created by the application of apartheid.

De Klerk asked everyone in South Africa to cooperate in seeking to accomplish his mission and warned of the consequences of failure in that endeavor saying, "If we fail in our mission the ensuing chaos, the demise of stability and progress will forever be held against us. Where necessary a completely new approach to remove obstacles would be used."[30] He went on to indicate that discussions and negotiations between everyone who was interested in finding solutions would be held. Any radical organization that wished to stop the use of violence would be welcome to sit down with other parties to negotiate the future of South Africa. This represented a rare opportunity for all South Africans to come together and pool their minds to create the best constitutional arrangement that could be designed.

De Klerk concluded his inaugural address by warning his country that the eyes of the world were on South Africa. He suggested that there was determination among all South Africans of goodwill—all the 27 million Africans and the 4 million whites—to find solutions to the problems of ending apartheid so that the future would be better for all the people. He said that, in order to give credence to his mission, he must abolish the infamous Ministry of Information which, for years, operated as if it was under the direction of Joseph Goebbels.

De Klerk stated that this move was necessary to bring about the South African version of glasnost. Instead of trying to boost South Africa's image, the new strengthened department was expected to have a more constructive role of seeking to improve communication between the government and the public. Under conditions of earlier times, the Ministry of Information would be quick to issue statements following violent confrontation between the military or the police and the opponents of apartheid, always blaming other parties and exonerating the action of the government. De Klerk was forced to take this action following an incident on September 6, 1989, when the police killed fifteen of the hundreds of Africans who were protesting elections held for whites only.

All this was happening on the heels of an election in which the Nationalist Party lost three parliamentary seats, but still won the majority. That was all de Klerk needed to carry out his reform. In spite of the parliamentary losses, de Klerk interpreted the results of the election as a mandate to continue his mission. While his move to restructure the police and change the structure of the Ministry of Information were plausible, de Klerk made no effort to change the structure of the government itself to save the duplication that was required by apartheid in the name of efficiency. De Klerk might have thought that a radical change of the government might have weakened his approach to reform. But in failing to reform, the message was that he intended to maintain the status quo despite his claim to the contrary.

In August 1989, while he was chairman of the Nationalist Party, de Klerk failed to distance himself and his party from apartheid when it was under severe worldwide criticism. While he did not defend it, he did not admit that it was a thing of the past and that a new approach needed to be made. He told an election meeting held in the affluent district of Hougton near Johannesburg that, "Apartheid is the policy of the Conservative Party. Don't try to hang it around the neck of the Nationalist Party."[31] Since when was apartheid the policy of the Conservative Party? It must have come a total surprise to hear de Klerk make such a claim instead of admitting that apartheid was the policy of his own party, but it needed change to suit new conditions.

However, what de Klerk was referring to in his denial is not clear because everyone knew that the Nationalist Party formulated the policy of apartheid as part of its election platform in 1948. If de Klerk denied his party's responsibility for introducing apartheid, how could he realistically introduce reform as part of his mission to bring apartheid to an end? De Klerk and his government were beginning to portray apartheid as an albatross that, indeed, was hanging around their political necks. In launching his mission, de Klerk was heavily influenced by the fortress of opposition forces.

De Klerk concluded that it was better to initiate reform immediately than to wait and try later when Africans would have lost confidence in him. In the past, backed by a formidable army and the police, the Nationalist government suppressed Africans under the state of emergency laws. At that time the antiapartheid forces were weakened by harsh conditions that had been created. However, different organizations, both political and civic, began to gain strength in cooperation while the Nationalist government was losing it. In 1988 de Klerk felt that it was time to initiate change that he believed would leave his name in the history of South Africa as one who had a vision of the future. But the truth of the matter is that he and the Nationalist government were at the mercy of conditions they could no longer control. What they were doing was trying to put their best foot forward so they did not appear to operate from the position of weakness. However, everyone in the country knew that the laager had been stormed and that Africans were about to erect a new edifice that would accommodate the aspirations of all South Africans. The laager that Afrikaners built and so fiercely defended was too small.

## SUMMARY AND CONCLUSION

This chapter began with a discussion of the conflict that emerged between Pieter W. Botha and F. W. De Klerk as the final act of creating cracks in the laager. The purpose of that discussion was to show how differences in the political philosophy between the two men compelled de Klerk to recognize the need to initiate action in setting a domestic agenda and action in southern Africa as a region in an effort to minimize the effects of the storming of the laager. The conflict began with de Klerk's decision, as soon as he was elected chairman of the Nationalist Party in 1988, to travel to Zambia to hold discussions with Kenneth Kaunda on ways of reducing tension in southern Africa. When Botha expressed opposition to the intended trip, conflict between the two men took on dimensions that neither man anticipated.

As the conflict between the two men intensified, it soon became clear that Botha would lose not only the competition with de Klerk, but also the leadership of the both the Nationalist Party and of the country. This conflict placed both South Africa and the Nationalist Party at a cross-roads. De Klerk had to rise to the occasion to rescue both his party and the country from the brink of disaster. From this conflict de Klerk gained the strength to accept the challenge of initiating fundamental change in the political system. He then launched a mission to bring about that change. The challenge and the task were by no means easy.

When the Nationalist Party came to know all the pertinent issues in dispute between Botha and de Klerk, its members rallied behind de Klerk to make it possible for him to carry out his mission. It must be understood that in initiating the kind of reform he had in mind de Klerk was not motivated by human considerations toward Africans, but by a desire to stop a possible bloody civil war that would take away everything Afrikaners had. The discussion in this chapter shows that he was successful in putting in place the elements of the mission he intended to launch. The next challenge that de Klerk faced was to negotiate with Africans about the nature of the political change he had in mind. It remained to be seen if Africans would agree to the kind of the new South Africa that he wanted to create. However, the fall of the laager presented an opportunity that Africans would not allow to pass. This was their time to rethink the future of the country without the laager.

## NOTES

1. *News York Times*, August 15, 1989, p. 9.

2. On November 5, Dole lost the election to Clinton, exactly as polls had indicated. Clinton's margin of victory was 379 electoral votes against 159 for Dole. Some observers attributed Dole's loss to his age.

3. *New York Times*, August 15, 1989, p. 9.

4. Ibid.

5. Ibid.

6. *Washington Post*, February 3, 1989.

7. Nelson Mandela, *Long Walk to Freedom: The Autobiography of Nelson Mandela* (Boston: Little, Brown and Company, 1994), p. 42.

8. South Africa, *President F. W. De Klerk: First Year in Office* (Washington, D.C.: South African Embassy, 1990), p. 10.

9. Alex La Guma, ed., *Apartheid: A Collection of Writings on South African Racism by South Africans* (New York: International Publishers, 1971), p. 32.

10. *Christian Science Monitor*, August 16, 1989.

11. Ibid.

12. Ibid.

13. F. W. de Klerk during an interview with Ned Temko in the *Christian Science Monitor*, June 5, 1989.

14. Ibid.

15. Desmond Tutu, "Judge de Klerk by His Actions," in *New York Times*, October 20, 1989.

16. Ibid.

17. *The Economist*, June 24, 1989.

18. Ibid.

19. It has been stated in chapter 3 that under apartheid laws the people of South Africa were placed into three racial groups. These were whites, Coloureds, and Africans. The Immorality Act of 1957 prohibited people of different racial groups from marrying. They could only marry within their own racial group.

20. *New York Times*, January 11, 1991

21. Ibid.

22. Ibid.

23. *Christian Science Monitor*, March 10, 1989.

24. F. W. de Klerk, "Inaugural Address," September 20, 1989. Los Angeles: South African Embassy.

25. Ibid.

26. Ibid.

27. Ibid.

28. Ibid.

29. Ibid.

30. Ibid.

31. *Christian Science Monitor*, August 27, 1989.

# 6

# Ian D. Smith, the RF Policy, and Conflict from Efforts to Defend the Laager

> Mr. Speaker, I move that this House take note that there is widespread alarm and despondency amongst the African population of this country.
>
> M. M. Bhebe, M.P., August 19, 1970

## RF'S ATTITUDES TOWARD AFRICANS IN PARLIAMENT

From its formation in December 1962 to the end of its administration in December 1979, the RF did not hesitate to show disrespect for any display of intellect by Africans. In this regard, its members remained loyal to the philosophy of the two men they regarded as their mentors, Cecil John Rhodes and Godfrey Huggins, who argued that Africans had the minds of children.[1] Soon after winning the general elections of 1962, the RF was tormented by the realization that this was the first Parliament to have black faces sit opposite white faces in a chamber, which, up to that point, had been an exclusive club and a sacred shrine for the white man. For the new constitution to allow Africans to storm this laager was unacceptable. Aware that its opposition to the constitution that made this possible had been futile, the RF now felt compelled to launch a crusade directly against the African members of Parliament themselves. Ian D. Smith himself directed this crusade in order to preserve the shrine the RF regarded as sacred.

The presence of fifteen Africans in Parliament also constantly reminded the RF members about the real possibility of a black government in the future. They never attempted to hide the fact that they were outraged by the British insistence that Africans take their place in Parliament and never forgave Whitehead for agreeing to a constitutional provision which made it possible for Africans to question the absoluteness of the political power of the white man.[2] This is exactly why the RF detested the thought of engaging in parliamentary debates with Africans. This was an act they believed forced the RF to endure the attack of the laager. Therefore, from the very beginning of its administration, the RF introduced a new element of racial prejudice in Parliament itself. This dimension of human interaction had a profound impact on the ability of the African members of Parliament to function effectively and fulfill their responsibility to their constituencies.

One of these fifteen African members explained in 1983 the effect of the RF's attitude toward them saying,

The fifteen of us began to feel belittled, ridiculed, and out of place. No white members ever came to chat with us during intercessions, they all avoided us. They hated our presence in parliament, and even made fun of us. They laughed at us for what they claimed was a lack of experience on our part in parliamentary procedures. The Rhodesia Front used our presence to practice political target shooting and make cheap shots at what its members considered a notion that 15 black persons could engage in a debate with 50 white men on issues of national importance. This is how the RF made us feel small and out of place. Its negative attitude toward us impaired our ability to discharge our proper parliamentary and constituent responsibilities.[3]

This was the RF's ultimate defense of the laager.

In one way or another, the RF repeatedly humiliated the fifteen African members of Parliament under the various provisions of the Land Apportionment Act. For example, they slept and stayed in separate hotels. White members and African members had nothing in common outside the Parliament building. Even in Parliament itself when the African members tried to speak during a debate, some RF members left the chamber in disgust, others shouted them down. Some continued their own private conversations, others simply laughed. African members began to ask themselves what they were doing in a colonial parliament. Who could expect fifteen Africans to change things when there were fifty white men? They began to realize that their presence was nothing more than a token show of democracy that the RF successfully exploited for its own political gains and to reduce Africans to the level of being political misfits.[4]

Although the number of African seats was increased to sixteen by the RF constitution of 1969, it was still so small that the attitude of the RF toward African members even worsened. For example, in June 1979, when he learned that some African members suggested wearing formal wigs as a symbol of the respect that they believed must be shown their office, Peter van der Byl, RF Minister of Information, Immigration and Tourism, did not hesitate to show his disrespect of both the suggestion and Africans themselves saying in reaction, "What do they want wigs for? They can just sprinkle a little powder on their heads."[5] Wearing of wigs was for years a practice that the colonial legislatures in Africa adopted from the British tradition. The RF discontinued it in 1965 as a demonstration of its displeasure with British principles of promoting the political development of Africans.

If the RF had the audacity to belittle Africans in Parliament only six months before its collapse, then common sense would suggest that it was even more abusive of Africans in general during the height of its power from 1966 to 1978. To belittle Africans in Parliament was part of the RF's strategy of making light of the issues that they tried to address. In this manner those Africans were either completely silenced or intimidated. Table 6.1 indicates the sixteen African members of Parliament and the constituencies they represented as of 1970.

**Table 6.1**
**African Members of Parliament in 1970**

| Name | Constituency | Name | Constituency |
| --- | --- | --- | --- |
| Bhebe, M. M.[6] | Ntshonalanga | Masenda, L. P. | Mabvazuwa |
| Chikonyera, T. M. | Highveld | Moraka, W. S. | Motojeni |
| Gandanzara, N. A. | Manica | Mungate, A. T. | Zambezi |
| Gondo, J. M. | Kunyasi | Namate, D. M. | Tuli |
| Hove, J. B. | Pioneer | Ndhlovu, L. A. | Insukamini |
| Khabo, J. M. | Pagati | Sadomba, R. T. | Nemakonde |
| Mahlangu, L. J. | Mpopoma | Sifuya, E. G. | Kariba |
| Makaya, R. C. | Lowveld | Watungwa, E. G. | Harare |

Source: Rhodesia: *Parliamentary Debates*, August 19, 1970.

To conclude that the African members of Parliament during the RF administration suffered from the effects of an identity complex is to recognize the political dilemma that they faced. On the one hand, the RF resented their presence without reservation. On the other hand, Africans whose interests they represented did not appear to have placed any trust and confidence in them. One of them suggested, "The Africans considered us to be in full cooperation with the RF in the pursuit of its policies. They wanted to know how we could easily allow ourselves to be used by the RF against their interests. They did not know that parliamentary decisions are determined by vote. How could sixteen Africans influence the outcome of the vote against fifty white men? It actually turned out that their concerns were based on solid ground. We offered nothing more than a token opposition to the RF, which used our presence to strengthen its own political power. Where would we go from here?"[7] These sixteen Africans were viewed by Africans in the districts they represented as attuned to support the defense of the laager.

## RF'S POLICY AND CRISIS IN PARLIAMENT: THE EFFECT OF BHEBE'S MOTION

Soon after it took office in December 1962, the RF converted its opposition to the constitution of 1961 into an instrument of demeaning Africans to serve its own political ends. Now it turned its attention to make major capital political gains out of its opposition to the presence of the sixteen African members of Parliament. Every time the RF presented legislation to Parliament, even though it was against the interests of Africans, its members claimed that they had the support of the African members. What they meant was that the African members could do nothing to stop it. But these African members repeatedly argued that they opposed the entire RF legislative agenda.

For example, in 1969 the RF introduced new legislation for a new constitution, the infamous Land Tenure Bill, which entrenched racial segregation in every aspect of national life. The sixteen African members voted against it while all fifty white members voted in favor. The RF used the outcome of the vote to claim that it had the support of the African members as a whole. The RF had never had it so good. Indeed, the RF was having the best of both worlds. From 1969 to 1979, all the 50 white seats in Parliament were held by the RF members, it had become absolute in every way. There was no white opposition since the UFP suffered a humiliating defeat in the special election held in 1964. Any semblance of opposition came from the sixteen African members. Indeed, during the RF tenure, Zimbabwe was an absolute one party state, fully controlled by the RF.

With the perception of its invincibility, the RF launched a $3 million campaign in 1968 to attract a million new white immigrants from Europe by promising them the best education in the world. This caused the *Rhodesia Herald* of November 12, 1968, to mourn the deterioration of African education and urged the RF government to do something to reverse the trend. In its editorial the paper argued, "Of all the new things Europeans have brought into the lives of Rhodesian Africans, none is more appreciated, none more welcomed, none more sought after than schooling. Since the Second World War, the African desire for schooling has been insatiable."⁸

These were the factors that produced an environment in which African members of Parliament tried to arouse a new nationalistic feeling against what they saw as harmful effects of the RF's educational policy. But, distrusted by their own people and belittled by the RF, the Africans knew that the odds were heavily against them. For them the choice was to sink or swim in the troubled political water that threatened to wreck their fragile political boat. They were caught between the futility of their cause and an avalanche of African criticism of their failure to influence the direction they believed their education must take. They felt they had to do something to regain the trust and confidence of the people they believed they represented and to register their protest against the RF's educational policy.

After spending several weeks in designing their strategy and carefully checking the accuracy of their facts, the sixteen African members of Parliament felt they were ready for a showdown with the RF, to launch an assault of the laager, by making an assault on its educational policy. The day was Wednesday, August 19, 1970. After a thorough preparation and rehearsal, all sixteen members took their seats some thirty minutes before the beginning of the session. The visitors' gallery was packed with whites and a few Africans seated in a remote corner. His voice quivering and almost choking with emotion, M. M. Bhebe, the member for Ntshona-langa, having been recognized by the Speaker in accordance with parliamentary procedure, stood up at 2:24 P.M., and, as if unsure of himself, straightened out his tie and buttoned his jacket. With a tense and serious look on his face, Bhebe said, "Mr. Speaker,⁹ I move that this House take note that there is widespread alarm and despondency among the African population of this country about the administration of African education."¹⁰

As usual, the RF members belittled the motion and saw Bhebe as a Sancho Panza of the African political Don Quixote urging his master to tilt the giant wind mills of the RF presumed invincibility. The RF had neither any appreciation of the intensity of his feeling nor any understanding of the seriousness of his motion. However, as soon as Bhebe made the motion and before he even took his seat, J. M. Khabo, the member for Pagati, seconded it. Therefore, the Speaker had no choice but to have the motion debated. There was a mixed reaction from the RF members. "Some inwardly expressed an outrage: how dare Africans question the absoluteness of its power and the right to design an educational policy for Africans in accordance with its philosophy? Others responded with laughter and wondered why the African members decided to waste their time on such a futile endeavor. Some looked puzzled, others appeared angered by the whole thing. Some were making inaudible sounds as if they were in a pub."[11]

But futile as their efforts might have been, African members of Parliament believed that this was their only chance to demonstrate what they believed was the gross unfairness of the educational system and to expose the RF itself. The forcefulness with which each member expressed his views showed that the structure of the colonial system must be dismantled if a major racial conflict was to be avoided, and time was running out. Bhebe must have had these and other considerations in mind when he went on to elaborate his motion. He argued that the RF had shown no interest whatsoever in implementing the major recommendations of the Judges Report. To Bhebe this proved its intention to retard the development of African education as Andrew Skeen had said the previous year. He also said that the reason the RF was trying to force the church organizations out of the education of Africans was because part of its strategy was to perpetuate white political rule by creating a gulf between the church and Africans. He stated that the conflicting positions which the RF were taking regarding African education was leading to fragmentation of some very important elements of the educational process. For example, the RF policy had left Grade III without a teacher, and this caused a disruption in the normal progression of elementary schooling.[12]

Bhebe spared no efforts to register what he believed was the root cause of alarm and despondency among Africans about the RF's educational policy. He took special exception to the fact that it had used the excuse of limited financial resources to curtail their educational development. Bhebe argued that this was the reason the RF was withdrawing a number of grants which had been traditionally paid to African schools. In addition to this the RF arbitrarily imposed a policy of 5 percent cut in salary grants for African teachers of primary schools, adding, "I do not think that the $1.25 which the Minister of Education now requires of each primary student will meet the requirements of African education. It will result, instead, in reducing the number of students from primary schools because their parents will not be able to pay."[13]

Bhebe expressed one of the most disturbing features of the RF educational policy when he discussed the relationship which existed between the Ministry of Education and that of Internal Affairs since the announcement, by Lance Smith on September 2, 1969, of the 5 percent cut in salary grants for African primary teachers. As a result of the relationship between what was happening at the primary level and at the secondary level, the education of the African child suffered a severe setback. In arguing that the policy of a 5 percent cut would negatively affect the development of secondary education, Bhebe was in fact recognizing the ultimate purpose of the RF educational philosophy for Africans. This is why he argued that poor education at the primary level means poor education at the secondary level. He concluded that this was the reason the RF was pursuing the policy it had announced on April 20, 1966. The educational policy of the RF was the cornerstone of the laager. It could not be changed without putting the laager itself into peril.

Bhebe cautiously touched upon an issue that was central to the RF's educational policy, that of expansion in African education in general. Making sure that Africans understood this, he carefully and slowly let his intense anger and frustration take control of his emotion when he said, "Expansion of primary schooling is necessary for the expansion of secondary education. It is disturbing to find that the government deliberately withholds funds needed to make this expansion possible."[14] Bhebe must not have been fully aware that since it took office, the RF did not see the importance of expanding African education in the way he was discussing. While everyone else thought that education in 1970 had changed enough to require a corresponding change of thinking about African advancement, the RF never lost sight of its vision of building a white utopia in an African setting by controlling the educational development of Africans.

Quoting the recommendation of the Judges Report that "Marriage should not bar a woman teacher from the privilege of permanent appointment. Special regulations should apply in the event of childbirth,"[15] Bhebe had raised a point that was close to the cause of Africans' unhappiness with the RF policy. Since Victorian times, female teachers all over the world suffered a disability through educational inequality that in turn made them second-class citizens. But in Africa, including colonial Zimbabwe, an additional hardship was imposed and perpetuated because it added a dimension that deprived them of both an opportunity for education and for employment. Africans always believed that female teachers were better than male teachers, especially for the elementary grades, and that married female teachers were even better than single teachers because they were more permanent. Whether this belief was right was beside the point. The point was that Bhebe wanted Africans to know that, in raising it as an important educational issue relative to the RF's educational policy, he had represented their interests well, and that the RF must now be held responsible for the serious flaws that were evident in its policy.

While he still had the floor, Bhebe wished to maximize the opportunity he had to cover as much ground as possible. Therefore, he relentlessly criticized the RF for not allowing African children to start school until they reached the age of seven and he decried the practice of keeping enrollment at forty-five students for each class in the primary school. Because it was hard for the teacher to pay full attention to all the students, Bhebe argued, they were inadequately prepared to undertake secondary education. This in turn provided the RF with a good excuse to conclude that Africans could not benefit from academic secondary education thereby pushing 37.5 percent of the graduates of primary schools to vocational education and industrial training as Earl Grey and William Milton had done during the formative years of the colonial government. In essence, Bhebe was saying that the RF's educational policy was compatible with traditional colonial educational policy toward Africans.

In concluding that "These are the facts that have caused alarm and despondency among the African people,"[16] Bhebe was saying, in effect, that because the RF was doing nothing right, either its whole policy must be overhauled, or the RF itself must be replaced by, not another white colonial government, but by an African government. That the RF did not appreciate his indictments indicates that there was no solution to the problem. For Bhebe to suggest the possibility of replacing the RF government with an African government is indicative of the reality of the conclusion that the colonized would continue to endure the agony of colonization and suffer a lack of educational development as long as the RF policy continued. Although this was not the kind of thinking that the RF members would tolerate, Bhebe had the strength of character to put on record his profound unhappiness with the RF's educational policy. He wanted his fellow Africans to understand how deeply he felt about the problems.

But for all his outrage and unreserved condemnation of the RF's educational policy, Bhebe demonstrated serious limitations and contradiction in his political action over the next two years. For example, on February 10, 1972, he wrote a letter to me urging me to support the laager by expressing support for the lop-sided agreement that had been reached on November 24, 1971, between Ian D. Smith and the British government on terms of ending the constitutional crisis caused by the Unilateral Declaration of Independence (UDI) on November 11, 1965. Many observers concluded that approval of the agreement would have legalized UDI and would have taken fifty years for Africans to have control of the government. The key requirement for Africans to claim their right to vote was the provision that, "You have been at a secondary school for two years or more and you have been earning $25.00 a month for the last two years, or own a house, building, farm, or land worth $600.00."[17] The RF was fortifying the laager in many ways.

In this letter Bhebe listed eight reasons why he thought I should support the proposals. Three of these reasons relate to the education of Africans:

1. There will be improved schooling facilities for Africans.

2. There will be improved teacher training facilities for Africans.

3. There will be equal pay for African teachers who have the same qualifications as white teachers.[18]

Bhebe must not have been aware of the actual facts. The development of education for Africans was the last thing the RF wanted to see. He also did not take into account the fact that Britain acquiesced to the provision that one must own a house, building, farm or land worth $600 when, in fact, under the terms of the Land Tenure Act of 1969, which strengthened the racial character of the Land Apportionment Act of 1929, Africans were not allowed to buy land at all.

Responding on March 1, 1972, I reminded Bhebe of the major flaws of the proposals and stated why I would not support them, stating, "All the eight reasons you gave asking me to support the proposals are merely secondary, and not important at all. The most important element of the proposals, which has been left out, is the question of a black majority government. When is it coming? I find myself unable to help legalize UDI by giving the proposals my support."[19] However, no one would wish to deny Bhebe the opportunity to put on record his total opposition to the RF educational policy. He would not be denied the publicity he needed to prove to his constituency that he was representing their interests well by attacking the laager. The charges that he made against the RF educational policy were sufficient to arouse the indignation of Africans all over the country. Therefore, Bhebe, indeed, succeeded in his efforts.

Bhebe's ability to articulate the concern of Africans about their opposition to the RF educational policy set the stage for the other black members of Parliament to support the motion. This is why J. M. Khabo, the member for Pagati, who seconded the motion, was also the first to speak after Bhebe in support of it. Wishing to highlight the charges that Bhebe had made and at the same time level new ones, Khabo listed a number of reasons why he seconded the motion. Pointing out the inconsistency in the RF educational policy, he reminded the House that the successive colonial governments had argued that Africans were uncivilized and irresponsible. He wanted to know if, in forcing the local communities to assume the responsibility of finding the 5 percent balance in the primary teachers salaries, the RF now thought that they were in fact civilized and responsible enough to be entrusted with the responsibility of financing part of their own education.[20] This is the kind of thinking and talking that the RF feared would come from the African members of Parliament.

There is no doubt that Khabo intended this rhetoric to register his displeasure with the RF's attempt to perpetuate the Victorian myth that Africans were uncivilized. Ian D. Smith himself had acquired a unique notoriety for repeatedly insulting the African culture by characterizing it as uncivilized and primitive.[21] Angered by A. L. Lazell's remarks that

African members were irresponsible for supporting the motion, Khabo was even more blunt in expressing his outrage against what he considered an RF conspiratorial action. He, of course, was referring to the partnership between the notorious Ministry of Internal Affairs and the Ministry of Education in formulating an educational policy that he believed was against the educational development of Africans.

That Khabo expressed his belief that the educational policy introducing the 5 percent cut in salary grants for African primary teachers was intended to mislead Africans into believing that there was a positive cooperation between the two ministries in developing their education shows how well Africans understood the seriousness of the issue they were debating. When he concluded that the real intent of this unholy alliance was to coordinate the RF's efforts in curtailing the educational development of Africans,[22] the debate had aroused deep emotions that neither side could control.

Indeed, Khabo's concern over the partnership between the two ministries was really not without foundation. He knew that since the enactment of the Orders-in-Council of 1894, which created a system of colonial administration from which the Department of Native Affairs came into existence, the colonial government instituted what Africans, over the years, regarded as an extremely oppressive machine. The Department of Native Affairs recruited local Africans to serve in a police force, which, in fact, terrorized its own people in the name of maintaining law and order. It also issued the notorious pass books with severe penalties for violation.

In enforcing provisions of the Land Apportionment Act of 1929, the Native Land Husbandry Act of 1951, and the Native Councils Act of 1957 in a way which reduced Africans to the level of bare existence, the colonial government used the Department of Native Affairs to effectively control the life of Africans and force them to endure the educational agony that made it possible for whites to profit from the cheap labor which they supplied.[23] Khabo was even more vehement in expressing his belief that Africans were now fully aware that the Department of Native Affairs under the RF had become a new symbol, even an agent of their oppression. Wishing to reduce the effect of this negative reaction from Africans, Khabo argued, the RF changed the name from the Department of Native Affairs to the Department of Internal Affairs in 1965. But this new department instituted an oppression of its own. Like Bhebe, Khabo wanted to remind his fellow Africans that in the partnership between the two departments in designing their educational policy, Africans had jumped from the frying pan into the fire.[24]

To substantiate his argument, Khabo pointed out that the African parents were already responsible for erecting and maintaining school buildings, teachers' houses, buying school furniture, paying fees, and meeting other expenses. He concluded by arguing that for the RF to impose the 5 percent cut in salary grants for African primary teachers was to add insult to injury, adding, "We feel that this is unfair to Africans."[25] Questioning the policy of a government which did everything for white students and nothing for African students, Khabo particularly wanted his fellow Africans to remember that white students had enjoyed free and compulsory education since 1935.

Like Bhebe, Khabo warned the RF that pursuing its educational policy as it did was, in effect, creating an environment for a major conflict. Of course, some RF members laughed at this suggestion, while others were irritated by what they regarded as an incitement of hostility against the whites. But what really angered them was "the thought that Africans could challenge the RF's authority and power and resented the constitutional provision which made it possible for Africans to do that."[26]

Khabo reserved his severest attack of the RF's educational policy for his discussion of the effect of the salary scale for the African teachers who were paid 60 percent of what the white teachers were paid. Of course, the RF would argue that African teachers had a different educational background and training than white teachers. That is what Khabo argued was basically wrong with the entire system of education under the RF. A commencing salary of $77 per month for primary teachers carried a message that for any African to decide to become a teacher was to indicate his wish to live in poverty.

Concluding that the ultimate effect of this policy was to discourage Africans from becoming teachers so that the RF would have a good excuse that it was not expanding African education because there were not sufficient funds and too few teachers, Khabo put the RF on the defensive. This had a profound effect on the Africans' decision to confront the RF itself. Appealing to the RF to reconsider its policy, Khabo concluded, "We must consider the educational interests of the child. If we do not, we will not achieve a satisfactory objective."[27]

In accordance with the strategy that the African members had designed, Khabo left it to his colleagues to oppose other aspects of the RF educational policy which were causing alarm and despondency. E. G. Sifuya, a member for Kariba, argued that in forcing Africans to pay taxes, the RF was in fact having the lion's share of the educational pie. In arguing that this was a strategy to perpetuate the RF power of Africans, Sifuya actually recognized the real intent of the total RF educational policy, namely to condition Africans to accept the view that after UDI, they must stop hoping that Britain would one day come to their rescue. Sifuya also argued that it was clear that the RF wanted Africans to know that their future lay in their cooperation with the RF policies. In concluding, "I would like the Minister of Education to know that this is what has caused alarm and despondency among Africans,"[28] Sifuya urged the RF to rescind its policy before it was too late.

One after another the African members of Parliament added indictments against the RF educational policy. In stating that the policy was designed to serve its own interests, Africans mounted a united effort, not just to influence the change of policy, but also to alert Africans of the danger to come if they failed to do something soon. Disregarding an interjection from Jack Christie, an RF member, R. T. Sadomba, the member for Nemakonde, argued that the overall effect of the RF educational policy would be to create second-class citizens out of Africans.[29]

Completely aware that the RF did not take what they were saying seriously, the African members did everything in their power to let it be known that they were not playing games. This is why N. A. Gandanzara, the member for Manica, began by cautioning the RF members as he began to speak in support of the motion when he said, "When we speak of these concerns, we are not wasting time, but we are stating the reasons why there is alarm and despondency among Africans about the government policy toward their education. It is true that Africans are unhappy about the disparity in the educational process. The government policy is either intentionally designed to retard African education or it is designed to trigger the reaction from Africans so that it uses tear gas tactics against its opponents."[30]

Gandanzara raised two critical points that no previous speakers had discussed. The first was his argument that because the RF was the first colonial government to have Africans in Parliament, it insulted their intelligence in order to intimidate and silence them. He warned the RF that it was in its own best interests to respect Africans and their ability to contribute to a crucial national debate about an important national policy. Its persistent disregard of Africans would cost it dearly.[31] The second point that Gandanzara raised was that, in trying to force Africans to accept its policy of community development, the RF was forcing its educational policy on them, and it would backfire.

If the RF was still hoping that it would succeed in this direction, it would be well advised to direct its efforts toward a reevaluation of its entire policy instead. The Africans had made it clear that they had rejected its definition of their development. Gandanzara, as well as his fifteen African colleagues, had neither the patience nor the tolerance of the RF's excuses for not providing Africans an equal educational opportunity. All sixteen African members of Parliament felt that they had a mission to accomplish: to advise the RF in no uncertain terms and that if confrontation came between it and Africans, it could not say that it had not been warned.

In appealing to the RF to start all over in designing a more realistic educational policy for Africans, Gandanzara concluded, "I appeal to the

Minister of Education to make a serious reconsideration of his policy and take our views into account because if a 5 percent cut is implemented, it will mean a cut not only in teachers' salaries, but also in educational facilities in general."[32] What Gandanzara really meant is that the policy of a 5 percent cut meant in effect a cut in the little that had remained in the education of Africans. In implementing its policy, Gandanzara said that the RF demonstrated its lack of sensitivity to the concerns of Africans. If this insensitivity continued, why should Africans be asked to exercise reason and moderation? He urged the RF to demonstrate moderation by taking the views that they had expressed into consideration in the interest of good racial relationships.

L. A. Ndhlove, the member for Insukamini, attempted to convince both Africans and the RF that the most serious problem which they encountered was the RF's negative attitude toward the educational development of Africans and that the RF had gone further than any other previous administration in not only promoting this attitude among whites, but also in basing its educational policy on it. Expressing his view that Africans would expect meaningful educational change only through a change of government from the RF to Africans, Ndhlove was in effect urging Africans to coordinate their efforts in seeking an unconditional end of the RF government itself. The only other viable alternative was for the RF to end all forms of racial discrimination in the educational process.[33] Of course, Ndhlove had no illusions that the RF would even consider doing this.

In terms of colonial parliamentary procedures, it was not possible for every African member to put on record his opposition to the RF educational policy. However, for those who spoke this was an opportunity of a lifetime; no one would want to be left out of this great cause. But the Speaker of the House of Assembly felt that the African members had had their place in the sun and, on August 25, 1970, allowed Arthur Smith, the minister of education, to respond to the charges. To conclude that his performance was less than satisfactory is to recognize that he failed to convince Africans of the wisdom of the policy of his government.

It is quite clear that Smith wanted Africans to know that the policy of a 5 percent cut could not be reconsidered, adding, "If the Church authorities feel that they must hand over their schools on account of their inability to met the 5 percent cut and there is no council to whom they can hand over, then, the government will take over the responsibility until such a time that a properly formed and efficient council can assume the responsibility. I have, therefore, difficulty in appreciating the mover's motion."[34] In arguing that the reason for the 5 percent cut was that the RF wanted to save money toward establishing secondary schools, Smith must have forgotten that he told Geoffrey Atkins of Rhodesia Television on January 31, 1968, that the real reason for the policy was to force the African to accept the idea of community development.

The conviction with which Smith defended the policy of his government demonstrated a negative attitude of the RF that Ndhlove recognized as the main problem in the relationship between Africans and the government itself. Smith preferred to make his remarks in terms of generalities showing no feeling for the concerns Africans had expressed. This attitude did irreparable damage to immediate relationships between the two sides. From this attitude Africans, both in Parliament and in general, concluded that the only way for them to have a meaningful educational opportunity was to end the RF itself. This is not the position that Africans chose to take, it was one that the RF forced upon them in an effort to sustain racism.

## RF'S POLICY AND THE CHRONOLOGY
## OF EVENTS LEADING TO THE CIVIL WAR

The high road to the war of independence began on June 17, 1963, when Africans, representing forty districts and organizations throughout Zimbabwe, met in Gweru and unanimously adopted a resolution that they immediately transmitted to the governor, Sir Humphrey Gibbs, rejecting the RF policy of community development that had clear implications for apartheid. The reasons for this rejection included the knowledge that the policy was intended to force Africans to accept less opportunity for their development than whites. It was also being arbitrarily imposed on them in order to serve the ultimate interests of the RF. The delegates concluded their resolution with a warning, "We totally reject and resent this policy and petition the intervention of Her Majesty's government because we visualize a tragedy ahead."[35] As an official appointed by the British government to represent it, Gibbs was in total agreement with Africans and was visibly hostile to the RF policy and racial philosophy. This development was the beginning of a serious constitutional crisis resulting in a unilateral declaration of independence by the RF on November 11, 1965. This action did not ensure the RF's defense of the laager.

At the beginning of the new academic year in January 1964, conditions in African schools had deteriorated so drastically that African students did not believe that they were receiving any meaningful education at all. Facilities were poor and teachers were arbitrarily dismissed because they were suspected of placing their sympathy with the nationalists. The RF had arrested many for alleged political activity against it. Expenditure for education for African students had been reduced considerably. The curriculum had been so controlled that educational activity had lost its meaning. There were fewer places in schools for African students than at the beginning of 1963.

As the last school term opened in September 1964, African students were so displeased with their education that they boycotted classes forcing 80 percent of the schools to close. The students demanded fundamental changes in the structure of the government itself as a transitional preparation to a black majority government. They formed groups that clashed with the police, set buildings on fire, and destroyed any educational facilities in sight. Hundreds were arrested. This scenario was repeated in Soweto in June 1976. The educational process had come to a complete halt forcing Charles S. Davies, the RF Secretary for African Education, to declare 1964 The Year of Troubles. The RF did not seem to care.

Following the RF Unilateral Declaration of Independence, African students all over the country joined in protest marches and warned that serious confrontation would ensue from the RF's pursuit of its educational policy. Taking part in the march were students from five leading schools, including 300 from Goromonzi, 200 from Nyatsime, 200 from Fletcher, and 300 from Mzingwani.[36] When the RF dispatched riot squads to break up the march and to arrest the leaders, an explosive situation was created. On May 1, 1966, the war of independence moved nearer when an African student, who believed that both his arrest and detention were illegal, returned to the University College in Harare. When the police came to rearrest him, the college president strongly protested and argued that in its action the RF was instituting a police state. Ian D. Smith seemed to take pride in doing just that when he claimed that in a country of primitive people such as the Africans of Zimbabwe, it would have been irresponsible of his government not to have done so. A major institutional crisis was narrowly averted when the London Council of the British Union came to the president's support in his stance that he would rather resign than let the police take the student away. But the damage had been done and could not be repaired.

The spiral of confrontation moved much closer on August 4, 1967, when Michael Holman, a white student at the college was acquitted after a controversial trial following his arrest for publishing in a college student paper, *Black and White*, a poem that severely criticized the RF's racial laws and educational policies. As president of the college student body and the chairman of the representative council, Holman totally opposed the RF government. This was the reason for his arrest in July 1967. Soon after his acquittal, however, Desmond Lardner-Burke, the RF minister of law and order, ordered his immediate arrest and detention without trial under the provision of the notorious Preventive Detention Act of 1964. This was a political power that the RF had given itself in order to suppress any political opposition without regard to the recognized legal process.

When the student body marched to the parliament building to demand Holman's release, an explosive situation was created. As the police tried to break up the march, violence erupted outside the building, and Cecil Square, the colonial shrine that the RF revered and respected as a tribute to Cecil Rhodes, was converted into a battle ground. When the police closed the university and ransacked it and subjected the professors to unprecedented harassment, the final chapter of the struggle was written. Walter Adams, Terence Ranger, and other opponents of the RF policies were deported from the country as both sides braced for a bitter struggle.

By 1972, the RF was fast losing the support of those who had sympathized with it, those who felt that even though it was an illegal government by virtue of its action in issuing a unilateral declaration of independence, it must be allowed an opportunity to restore order. One white man who was a student at the college during that time told the author in 1983, "At first some of us thought that it was the only government we had, and that we must not use the same methods of violence to oppose its policies as it was using to silence its critics. But after I was brutalized, manhandled like a common criminal, I immediately changed my mind and decided to give my total support to those who were trying to bring it to an immediate end. The RF had gone too far in its use of violence. We had come to the end of the road, a parting of ways."[37]

Back in 1969, events took a perilous turn when Ian D. Smith, having reneged on the Fearless Agreement of 1968, introduced in Parliament a new racial bill which became law after only a brief debate. Because all the fifty white seats were held by RF members, it was easy to pass RF legislation. The Land Tenure Act No. 55, promulgated on March 2, 1970, divided the country into two halves, one for the 5.1 million Africans and the other for 0.25 million whites. Section 17 of that law placed the only university in the country in the white areas and required African students who wished to attend to apply for a special government permit to do so.

There was a dimension of the RF's policy that it thought, when properly implemented, would control Africans more effectively than in the past: It decided to appoint and use African inspectors of school to implement its policy. The white inspectors were having serious problems, not only in terms of resentment from Africans, but also in terms of their security. The RF also thought that appointing some African teachers as inspectors would divide the opinion of the African population about its policy. Indeed, one African teacher, who was quite excited about his appointment, told the author in Mutare in May 1974, "I am glad to have an opportunity for promotion. I do not mind too much whether or not the Smith government is using me to curtail the educational opportunity and the advancement of the African people as long as I am paid well, that is what matters to me."[38] In the past the strategy of divide and rule had yielded tangible benefits to members of the colonial government, but not any more. Many of the African teachers whom the RF used as an instrument of implementing its policy lost their positions following the installation of a black government on April 18, 1980.

The implementation of the RF's educational policy at the university had serious consequences for both Africans and the RF itself. It meant, in effect, that African students were only allowed to attend the university through the grace and generosity of the RF itself. It was no longer a right. The Land Tenure Act made it very clear that "It is to be deemed that the Minister of Law and Order will issue permits in terms of Section 17, which means that he may cancel the permit at any time."[39] When African students refused to submit any applications for the special permit on the grounds that attending the university was their right, the RF felt that its authority was being challenged. In this regard, the enactment of the Land Tenure Act helped to create a major crisis because African students refused to be subjected to a further denial of their educational rights.

The reason for requiring African students to apply was clearly to enable the RF government to build a file of the potential opponents of its policy. By 1972, more than 2,000 students had left school for this purpose. The educational process had, once more, come to a halt, except that the implications were far more serious than in 1964. Neither RF members nor Africans were concerned because both were now preoccupied with their own survival as they engaged in a bloody civil war that was costing the country heavily in terms of human life as well as in other ways.

Beginning in 1973, the nationalist guerrillas introduced a new strategy of persuading the students at a few schools that remained open to voluntarily cross the border into Mozambique, Botswana, and Zambia to receive military training during the vacation and return to their studies at the beginning of the school term. In July of that year, St. Albert closed as the students disappeared and failed to return. This was only the beginning of a new phenomenon. Schools in the rural areas such as Mutambara, Nyamuzuwe, Musami, Nyashanu, All Souls, and Manama were all closed within a few months because students disappeared to join the rapidly growing nationalist guerrilla army that was training for the sole purpose of ending the RF government. They all believed that their educational development was impossible until the RF had been eliminated. Attack of the RF laager was now coming from all directions. How would the RF defend itself?

To complicate the problems the RF was having, the World Council of Churches boosted the morale of the nationalist guerrillas to fight the RF forces by voting, on April 16, 1975, to allocate $479,000 to organizations fighting racism in southern Africa. In essence, the RF was now paying a price for trying to eliminate the church from African education in 1970. On July 25, 1975, the RF attempted to control a situation that it knew it could not. On that day the assistant provincial commissioner for Manicaland proclaimed a curfew stating, "In terms of Section 14 of the Emergency Powers Maintenance of the Law and Order Regulations, 1975, I hereby order that with effect from 6:00 P.M. on Friday, July 25, 1975, until such time as this order is revoked, no person shall be in the area described in the schedule to this order between the hours of 6:00 P.M. and 5:00 A.M. unless he is within fifty meters of a dwelling house, tent, hut, or a motorized vehicle or has written permission from the security forces."[40] The RF warned African students at the schools near the border that it was a crime for them to cross it. However, the tactic did not work as hundreds of them continued to do so.

As the casualties of the war continued to mount, the RF government was feeling a severe economic strain in addition to the military pressure from the nationalist guerrillas. On October 30, 1979, it decided to conscript Africans into its army, including students at the college. Instead of joining the army, however, the students signed a petition stating, "Our participation in your army is immoral. We are in no position to reconcile our conscience with the idea of fighting for a minority regime against the majority."[41] In refusing to assist in the defense of the laager, Africans were fortifying their own position of attacking it. For this reason, at the cost of 200,000 lives and after a futile attempt to recruit foreign mercenaries, Ian D. Smith was forced to sue for a cease-fire in September 1979 and agreed to attend a conference in London to arrange the transfer of political power from his minority government to an African majority government.

When an African government assumed the reins of power on April 18, 1980, the RF government that Ian D. Smith had predicted would last at least a thousand years had actually survived a little more than the fifteen years that Edgar Whitehead had predicted in 1962. Robert Mugabe, the Nationalist leader whom Smith had called a black Hitler, succeeded him as the first African Prime Minister of independent Zimbabwe. This chronology of events enables us to furnish the answer to the second question we posed: What was the outcome of the war? Because Africans had set their minds to achieving what many considered impossible—eliminating their colonizer—their pursuit of education had taken a back seat. They were then able to recognize the real purpose of the colonizer and to reject any tactics designed to bring about disunity among them.

## SUMMARY AND CONCLUSION:
## THE EFFECT OF THE CRISIS

From the moment the RF assumed office in December 1962, it was quite clear to Africans that it had every intention of sustaining its political position over them by strict control of their education. The crisis that broke out in Parliament in 1970 was different from previous crises in that it had five important effects. The first effect was that it destroyed the remaining fragile bridge of communication the RF and the African members of Parliament needed in order to carry out their daily duties and responsibilities. By showing that the concerns that Africans had expressed were not important, the RF went further than any previous colonial administration in creating conditions of a major conflict which would bring its own end in less than ten years.

The second effect was that the RF grossly underestimated the determination of African members of Parliament to express their views. True, one does not normally expect that, in a colonial Parliament with the government consisting of fifty white men, sixteen African men could change things. But the sixteen African men were in a situation that forced them to do or die. That they chose to do this caught the RF off guard, as they expressed their ideas in a way in which Africans understood. The publicity that this crisis generated proved to be detrimental to the RF educational policy because it enabled Africans throughout the country to understand its real intent. This understanding became the instrument by which they waged a confrontation against it.

The third effect that this crisis had was that it showed Africans that the RF really was an extreme white political party whose devotion to white political power and loyalty to the philosophy of Cecil John Rhodes were absolute in every way. They regarded it as being totally unwilling to consider any dialogue on issues of great national importance, such as the problems that it was creating by formulating an educational policy intended to sustain its own political position. In the pursuit of a national policy that was condemned by the vast majority of the people, with the exception of a quarter of a million whites, "who harvested huge economic and political gains by exploiting the education of Africans,"[42] the RF indeed exposed its weakness and vulnerability in a way that Africans fully understood and used to eventually bring it to an unconditional end.

The fourth effect that the crisis in Parliament had was that it was genuine proof that colonization had nothing constructive to offer in assisting its victims' efforts in seeking to realize their aspirations. Colonial conditions force the colonial master to either pretend the concerns that the colonized express against his policies are minor, or to distort the reality of the situation and so minimize the problem. Colonial conditions therefore place the master and his servant on opposite sides of the issue. Because the colonial master and his servant belong to two different cultures and races, the relationships that exist between them handicap their efforts to find answers to problems.

This was exactly why the RF belittled the concerns of the African members of Parliament, and this was also why Africans themselves regarded its educational policy as oppressive. Two extreme positions such as this, at this time, could only lead to a serious confrontation. The ability of the African members of Parliament to discuss an issue of great national importance placed the RF in a difficult situation, one that it wished it did not face. This is why it had opposed the presence of Africans in Parliament in the first place.

The fifth effect that the crisis in Parliament had was that the increasing demand among Africans for equality of educational opportunity and the RF's determination to sustain its own political interests were developments that convinced both sides about the rightness of their respective causes. To hear Bhebe argue in a rebuttal, "I am making it firm that when my motion says that there is alarm and despondency among the African population of this country, that is exactly what it is,"[43] is to recognize the intensity of the African hostility toward the RF educational policy. To hear Arthur Smith conclude, "I do not believe that the African members made a very good case to support their claim that alarm and despondency exist concerning the administration of African education because most of this argument is based on misunderstanding,"[44] is also to recognize the intensity of the RF hostility toward Africans' concern. This was the situation that set the RF and Africans on a confrontation course.

The immediate result of this conflict was that when the vote was taken, all sixteen African members voted in favor of the motion, and thirty-two white RF members voted against it. No white member voted for the motion. That eighteen other RF white members did not register their vote shows how minor they felt the issue was. But the consequences of their action was devastating for the future relationships between the two. The vote also showed the racial nature of Parliament itself, and the politics of the country in general. While the African members of Parliament lost the motion, they succeeded in alerting Africans across the country of the danger to come. Throughout the country, they recognized the tragedy of the RF educational policy, and accepted the inevitability of a major conflict between the two sides.

Three facts must be understood here with respect to the RF educational policy as the major cause of the civil war. The first is that the RF itself was heavily influenced by historical precedence that Africans did not need an equal educational opportunity. To conclude that the RF was more of a victim of the historical actuality is to recognize its inability to move ahead, in the spirit of mutual racial respect, for the good of the country. When Ian D. Smith told the author in 1983 that his government maintained a segregated system of education because the education of Africans was not as high as that of whites, he was actually saying that his government must never tamper with this historical actuality. When he said, "We were trying to raise the standard of education of Africans without lowering that of the whites,"[45] he was, in effect, arguing that it really was not important to extend equal educational opportunity to Africans. This was the thinking that Africans themselves totally rejected. As a product of the historical actuality, Smith and his RF administration were unable to see the situation from its proper perspective.

The second fact is that the RF went much further than any other previous colonial administration in instituting an oppressive system. The more it attempted to strengthen its policy, the more Africans opposed it. This was the spiral of conflict that was leading to an outright confrontation. Only the RF itself placed the blame for the war elsewhere, everyone else in the country placed blame at the doorstep of the RF. In this regard the Zimbabwe Chapter of the British Council of Missionary Societies explains why Africans were justified in resorting to armed struggle to regain their freedom. The council concluded that in spite of the great moral difficulties, fighting for a just cause had been generally accepted by those with a Christian conscience as justifiable, and that those who were themselves in comfort and security could not urge armed struggle on others who would face death or suffering they did not have to bear.[46]

This was the ethical and philosophical basis on which the World Council of Churches voted on April 16, 1975, to allocate $479,000 toward assisting the nationalist guerrillas in their struggle for selfhood. Where violence, colonial or otherwise, cannot be ended in any other way, then the only option open is counterviolence. But it must be understood that both the Church and Africans fully understood the difference between colonial violence and the African violence in response to it. The former seeks to perpetuate the colonial condition while the latter seeks a reconstruction of society for the benefit of all.

The third fact is that a lack of the colonizer's respect of the culture of the colonized, as exhibited by the RF, forces him to perceive their education, within the context of his own culture, as totally insufficient to bridge the gap that exists between the two. Albert Memmi, the Tunisian philosopher, concludes that this behavior explains why each succeeding colonial government persistently argued that Africans were not adequately prepared, nor would they ever be adequately prepared to engage in the rigorous process of learning so long as they remained within the confines of their primitive culture.[47] The problem that this kind of thinking had on the relationship between the colonizer and the colonized was that neither was able to appreciate the culture of the other. For example, in introducing the policy of a 5 percent cut in salary grants for African primary teachers, the RF used the pretext that it was trying to help promote the principle of self-help among Africans. But Africans themselves saw it as part of the deliberate colonial attempt to curtail their educational development.

Once the RF formulated its policy, it could not withhold or modify it in any way without feeling that it had been defeated. On their part, once Africans decided that what the RF did was wrong, it could never accept its policy without feeling the heavy yoke of colonial oppression. In their respective ways, both Africans and the RF became highly sensitive to the historical actuality that was dictating both their response and behavior. It was therefore not possible to avoid civil war. Therefore, to appreciate Africans' intolerance of the RF educational policy one must understand the effect of this historical actuality.

Perhaps this is why the United Methodist Bishop Abel Muzorewa put this in the context of the African rejection of the RF educational policy: "Every African, young and old, man or woman, educated or uneducated, rich or poor, knew that the policy of the Rhodesia Front was an act of violence, which they fully understood they had to fight in order to have a system of education that adequately responded to their needs. As long as the RF continued, we all knew that we would never have an opportunity for good education."[48] The RF government, like previous colonial governments, hopelessly failed to comprehend the close relationship that Africans believed existed between their educational development and other forms of their advancement. This fortified their willpower to storm the laager.

Far beyond the petty excuses that the RF advanced as reasons for not making it possible for Africans to receive the education that they needed, its inability and unwillingness to recognize their legitimate educational aspirations at a time that education was universally accepted as the single most important means of social development stripped it of any remnant of credibility among all fair-minded people. Indeed, in 1962 Unesco, recognizing the importance of education to individual self-fulfillment and national development, had established a model that most countries of Africa found acceptable, except, of course, colonial Zimbabwe and South Africa, the land of apartheid.[49] The model stressed the importance of providing equal educational opportunity to all people without regard to race. But colonial conditions representing the laager did not permit this to happen, hence a civil war became inevitable.

## NOTES

1. Stanlake Samkange, *What Rhodes Really Said about Africans* (Harare: Harare Publishing House, 1982), p. 46.

2. A. J. Peck, *Rhodesia Accuses* (Boston: Western Islands Press, 1966), p. 16.

3. A former African member of Parliament who served from 1969 to 1978, during an interview with the author in Harare, July 15, 1983. The man declined to be identified because, he said, "I do not want to give the impression that we were a total failure because we accomplished some things for the good of Africans." One wonders. However, in 1980, when there were eighty African members of Parliament as opposed to twenty white members, it was now Africans' turn to ridicule the white members, calling them, among other things, monkeys. For details, see PBS, *Not in a Thousand Years: From Rhodesia to Zimbabwe*, a documentary film, 1982.

4. Ibid.

5. *Newsweek*, July 2, 1979, p. 9.

6. The reader should note that the use of initials is a common practice among Africans because the white masters often used their first names in a derogatory fashion.

7. A former African member of Parliament, during an interview with the author, July 15, 1983.

8. *Rhodesia Herald*, November 12, 1968, sect. 2., p. 15.

9. In accordance with colonial practice, the speaker of legislature was considered a non-partisan office. He often resigned either his seat in Parliament or from his political party to assume the prestigious position of speaker. At that time the speaker was Albert Stumbles, a former member of Whitehead's United Federal Party (UFP). The speaker only cast a ballot in the case of a tie. Of course, under the RF this would never happen.

10. Rhodesia, *Parliamentary Debates*, August 19, 1970.

11. A former African member of Parliament, during an interview with the author, July 15, 1983.

12. Rhodesia, *Parliamentary Debates*, August 19, 1970.

13. Ibid.

14. Ibid., p. 1870.

15. Ibid., p. 1871.

16. Southern Rhodesia, *The Report of the Commission of Inquiry into Native Education* (A.V. Judges, Chairman), 1962, p. 138.

17. Rhodesia, *Parliamentary Debates*, August 19, 1970.

18. M. M. Bhebe, letter to the author, February 10, 1972.

19. Dickson A. Mungazi, letter to M. M. Bhebe, March 1, 1972.

20. M. J. Khabo, during the debate on the no-confidence motion, *Parliamentary Debates*, August 19, 1970.

21. Indeed, after five African members had supported the motion, A. L. Lazell, the RF member for Milton Park (named after William Milton), reacted, "I think that the supporters of this motion have been very irresponsible." Rhodesia, *Parliamentary Debates*, August 19, 1970.

22. For example, see Ian D. Smith, "Rhodesia's Finest Hour: Unilateral Declaration of Independence," November 11, 1965.

23. Rhodesia, *Parliamentary Debates*, August 19, 1970.

24. Ibid., p. 1873.

25. Ibid., p. 1874.

26. Ibid., p. 1876.

27. M. J. Khabo, during debate on no-confidence motion, August 19, 1970.

28. Ibid.

29. Ibid.

30. Ibid.

31. Ibid.

32. Ibid.

33. Ibid.

34. Ibid.

35. "We reject the government policy of community development," a resolution adopted by the Gweru Convention and sent to Sir Humphrey Gibbs, Governor, June 27, 1963. Courtesy Zimbabwe National Archives.

36. "African Students March in Protest Against the Rhodesia Front Education Policy," a statement issued by the students at the University of Rhodesia, November 12, 1965. Courtesy Zimbabwe National Archives.

37. A white man, during an interview with the author, in Harare, July 15, 1983.

38. An African inspector of schools during a conversation with the author in Mutare, May 25, 1974.

39. Rhodesia, *The Land Tenure Act*, Section 17, Salisbury: Government Printer, March 2, 1970.

40. The Assistant Provincial Commissioner for Manicaland, a Government Order, July 25, 1975. Courtesy the Old Mutare Methodist Archives.

41. University Students Petition against Military Prescription, October 30, 1979. Courtesy the Old Mutare Methodist Archives.

42. Rhodesia, *Parliamentary Debates*, August 25, 1970, p. 71.

43. Ibid.

44. Ibid.

45. Ian D. Smith, during an interview with the author, in Harare, July 20, 1983.

46. Zimbabwe Chapter of the British Council of Missionary Societies, "Violence in Southern Africa: A Christian Assessment," October 28, 1970. Courtesy Old Mutare Methodist Archives.

47. Albert Memmi, *The Colonizer and the Colonized* (Boston: Beacon Press, 1965), p. 151.

48. Bishop Abel Muzorewa, during an interview with the author, in Harare, July 28, 1983.

49. UNESCO, Conference of Ministers of Education in Africa, Paris, 1962.

# 7

# F. W. de Klerk and the ANC:
# A Meeting of the Minds

Practically every leader agrees that negotiations are the key to reconciliation, peace, and a new and just dispensation.

F. W. de Klerk, March 23, 1990

As we are liberated from our own fears, our presence automatically liberates others.

Nelson Mandela, Inaugural Address, May 9, 1994

## RECOGNIZING HARD REALITIES

On March 23, 1990, de Klerk, speaking to the Pretoria Press Club, offered some insights into what he was likely to do to bring about meaningful change in the politics of South Africa saying, "In the past politics was managed mainly from a security point of view. Now, politics is being managed from a moral point of view. The determining question is what is right and what is just. To do that which is just and fair is the main purpose of politics. We cannot build a safe future on injustice. It is only when justice is done to all sectors of our population that a lasting peace will come. This is the challenge to our generation. It is a challenge which I have accepted."[1] This statement was the clearest indication that de Klerk was moving toward an accommodation with the ANC and Africans. He must have taken some serious considerations into account in reaching this position. As his fellow South Africans listened, they must have thought of what these considerations were. To take this new position de Klerk was going through a major political revival.

Indeed, it was known that at the beginning of his political career, and as a third generation Afrikaner hard-liner,[2] de Klerk became the Saul of Tarsus in his time serving the Sanhedrin of apartheid to the best of his ability. However, as soon as he assumed the office of president in 1989, he encountered the Damascus Road experience in his attitudes toward Africans and so had a new vision for South Africa. He then became the St. Paul of a new era of perception preaching the message that he believed only he could preach to bring about the transformation of the country on terms Africans defined. In this political conversion, de Klerk was now ready to assist Africans in storming the laager. Apartheid had to go. The question is: Would he be able to convince Africans that he had undergone a complete change and had become a new vessel carrying a new message of peace? Would he be able to convince his fellow Afrikaners that this revival would safeguard their political interests? He had a lot of work to do.

De Klerk acknowledged the hard reality that no country can build itself and become a happy society unless its institutional structures are based on justice and equality. This was the first time in the history of South Africa that a national leader had ever acknowledged this. De Klerk's acknowledgment came as a result of recognizing the hard realities that he encountered far more than any of his predecessors except Botha, who preferred to ignore them. As he examined the options available to him, de Klerk knew they were few. He knew that the recognition of these realities constituted a requirement on his part to move decisively to resolve the conflict that apartheid had been causing for many years. He was also aware that Africans would not accept any solution short of dismantling apartheid. The question is: What were these hard realities that forced de Klerk to recognize the imperative of seeking a meeting of the minds with the ANC?

Until 1976, the massacre at Sharpeville in 1960, when the South African police fired into the crowd of demonstrators killing 69 Africans and wounding 190 others, had set the criteria for government brutality and the supremacy of apartheid. Whenever there was an occasion to demonstrate the oppressive nature of apartheid and the brutality of the system of government in South Africa, those affected pointed to the tragedy at Sharpeville. The tragedy was indelibly written in the minds of Africans as a reminder that if they failed to do something to end apartheid it would engulf them. They understood that there would be no future for them.

In June 1976, the tragedy at Sharpeville was duplicated by that at Soweto when the wrath of the forces of apartheid descended upon defenseless students who were protesting the application of apartheid to their education. Once more the memory of the harshness of apartheid was engraved into the minds of Africans to serve as yet another reminder that theirs was a struggle against a violent system. Then, in 1990, there emerged a new phenomenon of violence and killing that South Africa had experienced only during the days of Tschaka the Great in the eighteenth century. This time the killing was on a much larger scale, Africans killing Africans.

The province of Natal, the original home of Tschaka the Great, was turned into killing fields such as the country had never seen in this century. When the killing of Africans by other Africans combined with the killing by the military and the police the tragedy was magnified many times over. There was no place to hide, no place to run to seek refuge, death trailed the people as a shadow trails a moving object. There was no reason, no explanation, no logic for the killing. African killed African while the police stood and watched this unprecedented tragedy run its course. De Klerk claimed that he was helpless and hopeless. Although this form of violence came from different directions, the danger was that it would soon become what is known as the culture of violence.[3]

In this culture of violence, killing becomes the norm rather than the exception, the reason to be, rather than something to refrain from because moral imperatives require it. De Klerk knew that if this form of violence was not stopped, it would soon function as a direct product of the violence of apartheid. In this kind of setting he and the Nationalist Party knew that they would lose the most. This situation was another hard reality that compelled de Klerk to seek a meeting of the minds with the ANC. Only then could the culture of violence and the violence of apartheid be stopped. Any other course of action would yield no tangible result. Inwardly, de Klerk knew that if the violence of apartheid had been stopped, then the culture of violence would not have surfaced.

In February 1989, following three years of confrontation with church leaders representing many Africans arrested for committing political crimes, the Nationalist government indicated that it planned to release nearly 300 prisoners. On February 18, Adriaan J. Vlok, the notorious minister of law and order, met for two hours with a delegation of church leaders led by Archbishop Desmond M. Tutu. These leaders represented the Anglican Church, the Methodist Church, the Catholic Church, the Council of African Independent Church, the South African Council of Churches, and the Dutch Reformed Church. The presence of the Dutch Reformed Church, the official church of the Nationalist Party, proved to Vlok that these leaders had an important matter to discuss with him. Vlok had to honor their request to hold the meeting.

Following the meeting, the church leaders issued a communiqué stating the Vlok gave them an understanding that the prisoners would soon be released. The communiqué read, "We were given the assurance by

Mr. Vlok that the hunger strikers and detainees were having his personal and urgent attention. He was very sympathetic to our position and told us that he would give attention to each single detainee."[4] Vlok did not release any communiqué suggesting that he was not pleased with the substance of the discussion with the church leaders. It is also possible that before he attended the meeting, Vlok had received some instructions from de Klerk to be flexible in his discussions with the church leaders.

However, Brigadier Leon Mellet, a military spokesman, briefly described the meeting as candid, responsible, and nonpolitical. But Tutu added, "It does give our people hope. It shows that success can also be achieved through negotiations, through non-violent action. It will not advance our cause to say they have lost and we have won. We are glad that we have got to where we have got."[5] This was the first time that the Nationalist Party had come face to face with the negotiating ability of Africans. For Mellet and Vlok to come to terms with this ability would indicate a fundamental change in their approach to the question of apartheid. The fact of the matter is that Africans had always demonstrated this ability, but earlier Nationalist administrations refused to recognize it in order to justify the application of apartheid.

For de Klerk, Mellet, and Vlok this meeting represented a turning point in their attitudes toward both the ability of Africans and their view of South Africa. In 1990, during the massive violence that plagued the country from all directions, the ANC took the initiative to show that it was willing to engage in dialogue with the government. De Klerk did not wish to let the ANC capture the spotlight and allow the international community to recognize it as showing more responsibility than the government. He also did not want the ANC to think that it was showing more leadership than he was, and he did not want Afrikaners to think that his action was only a reaction to the constructive initiative from the ANC. He wanted everyone to believe that he was still in control of the political developments in the country. By allowing Vlok and Mellet to be visible, he believed that he was acting in a manner that would be consistent with the action of a statesman.

But the ANC had a plan to counteract de Klerk's move. In order to convince the country that its intentions were honorable, the ANC took six actions that would determine the course of the negotiations between itself and the government. The first action was that it appointed a top level committee led by Thabo Mbeki to investigate and report on the wave of violence in Natal. The second action was that the ANC established a joint peace committee with the COSATU to enable it to coordinate all aspects of the African struggle for their political, social, and economic development. In the process, COSATU was slowly engaging more in political activity than in economic activity.

The ANC, seemingly small in terms of military power, had designed a collective strategy to bring down the Nationalist government many times larger. The drama of life and death in the wild of southern Africa translates into lessons about the drama of life and death in the political arena between the existing powers struggling to defend their position and the deprived struggling to regain their sense of self. In 1981, a few months after the black government was installed in Zimbabwe, Robert Mugabe put this drama in the context of the struggle between the existing system and the forces of change. Asked if he was bitter about his political imprisonment for eleven years under Ian D. Smith's laager, Mugabe responded, "You cannot allow yourself to be bitter because you have a cause to fight for and those in power have their own cause to defend."[6] By the same token the ANC was becoming more active in the economy than in politics as part of its strategy to storm the laager.

The third action was that the ANC made an initiative to establish better understanding between itself and the Inkatha Freedom Party for the purpose of designing a strategy to confront their common foe, the apartheid government. The fourth action was that the ANC selected thirty Zulu and Xhosa chiefs to tour the strife-torn African areas of the major urban centers to appreciate the damage that violence was inflicting on the country as a response to apartheid. The fifth action was that the ANC sought close association with church leaders in order to coordinate their efforts. The sixth action was that the ANC set up a committee that would meet with de Klerk if he should decide to meet with its members. These actions forced de Klerk to recognize some hard realities of the situation of which he knew he was rapidly losing control.

One hard reality that forced de Klerk to seek a meeting of the minds with the ANC was the recognition of the ability of the ANC to coordinate its strategy with other African organizations based upon a common goal of isolating the Nationalist government. The Nationalist Party was now depending only on the support of Afrikaners for its political survival. At that time every other organization, including the Dutch Reformed Church, which had unconditionally supported it, had turned against apartheid. On February 2, 1990, de Klerk recognized the determination of Africans to bringing apartheid to an end.

Speaking at the opening of the second session of the ninth Parliament, de Klerk said, "I wish to focus the spotlight on the process of negotiations and related issues. At this stage I am refraining deliberately from discussing the merits of numerous political questions which undoubtedly will be debated during the next few weeks. This focus has to fall on negotiations. Practically every leader agrees that negotiations are the key to reconciliation, peace and a new and just dispensation."[7] If de Klerk's predecessors, John Vorster and Pieter W. Botha, had taken this approach to national problems, the lives of Steve Biko (1946–1977) and forty other African political activists who died under police custody in 1977 would have been saved.

De Klerk went on to surprise his listeners when he discussed what his government intended to do as a result of recognizing these hard realities. He outlined seven initiatives to give effect to the new realities of the South African political situation. The first initiative was to rescind the prohibition of the ANC, the Pan-Africanist Congress, the Communist Party, and a number of subsidiary organizations so that they could all become part of the negotiations he said were about to begin. The second initiative was that those who were serving prison sentences merely because they were members of one political organization or because they committed political offenses would be released. De Klerk's admission in this regard is very revealing. For many years it was a common practice to arrest and detain indefinitely any persons who belonged to a political party opposed to the Nationalist government. This is why he was lifting the ban on political parties.

The third initiative that de Klerk made to lay the groundwork for negotiations with the ANC was to end the emergency security regulations. Again, for years the Nationalist government had operated under the compulsion of the emergency regulations. These were applied in such a way that made it virtually impossible for those opposed to the Nationalist government to carry on normal political activity that would allow them to do business. In this connection de Klerk indicated that any restrictions imposed in terms of the emergency regulations on thirty-three organizations were being rescinded.[8] These organizations included the National Education Committee, the National Student Congress, the United Democratic Front, and COSATU.

The fourth initiative was that the cases of 380 people, most of the Africans who were still held in detention waiting to be charged, would be reviewed to see if there were mitigating circumstances that would lead to their immediate release. Because the emergency regulations under which they had been held were being ended, there would be no legal basis to continue to keep them in detention. In taking this initiative, de Klerk was fully aware that the results of the elections held on February 2, 1990, represented a shift from the Nationalist Party to the Conservative Party, which was totally against any change in apartheid or dialogue with the ANC. De Klerk felt that any other Afrikaner party did not have the full understanding that he had about the danger of trying to maintain apartheid at any cost.

The fifth initiative that de Klerk took was his recognition of the need to defuse the challenge that the Conservative Party extended in response to his intention to negotiate with the ANC. In doing so he did not want the world to doubt his sincerity or wonder whether he was able to positively influence his party and supporters to see things his way. It was quite clear to him that this challenge, the worst thus far, constituted a new set of conditions in which the Conservative Party could prove to be a real threat to the power the Nationalist Party had exercised since 1948. De Klerk knew that the swing to the right in South African politics, that is, to the right of the Nationalist Party, was likely to undercut his basic initiative unless he was successful in containing it.

De Klerk was aware that he could not do this unless the international community brought pressure to bear on him. This is why he said his government needed to move aggressively to end apartheid in order to terminate the isolation of South Africa imposed by the international community. Therefore, the sixth initiative that he took was to convince Afrikaners that the risk he was taking in restoring political activity by the formerly outlawed organizations was in the best interest of South Africa and Afrikaners themselves. These interests would be ensured by accommodation with the ANC rather than confrontation with it. He argued that the era of confrontation was over and the period of accommodation was about to begin.[9]

The seventh, and final, initiative that de Klerk took was to convince all segments of the South African community to accept the fact that the country could enter a new period of peace and progress only through dialogue and accommodation. In his address to Parliament on February 2, 1990, de Klerk argued that the removal of the ban on the ANC would eliminate the main reason the ANC was fighting. The ANC based their fight on an argument that the Nationalist government did not wish to negotiate with it, and that the ANC was deprived of its right to normal political activity by the prohibition on it. De Klerk did not concede that the reason for his government's decision to seek a negotiated resolution of the conflict between it and the ANC was the escalation of the conflict between the two sides. The intensified guerrilla warfare had been justified in the eyes of the world, and no matter how the Nationalist government tried to condemn the military action of the ANC, it knew the conflict could only increase.

De Klerk took this development into account in recognizing three conditions that compelled him to initiate a new approach. The first condition was that he and his government wished to talk to all leaders who were interested in negotiation as the best way of ending apartheid. In all of colonial Africa, the government sought a negotiated settlement only when it knew that they were about to lose a military confrontation. This is true of South Africa.

The second condition was that the lifting of the prohibition on political organizations placed everybody in a position to pursue political activity freely. In this thought process, de Klerk's view was that if these parties accepted his initiative, then they would not espouse a radical approach to the question of the country's future. In this manner he could have some controlling influence on that action.

The third condition was that the ANC itself, as a major political organization in the country, stood to benefit more than any other organization by the annunciation of its objectives and the clarity of its purpose. De Klerk concluded that its justification for continuing guerrilla warfare no longer existed.[10] In his initiative he thought that he would take away some of the ANC's rapidly rising influence and bring it to the level to which the Nationalist Party had fallen. He was unaware that the more he tried to focus on the ANC instead of seeking ways of ending apartheid, the more he indirectly gave it more power. It also meant that the international community would begin to look to the ANC for providing the leadership that was needed to perceive a future, which it represented, different from the past, which the Nationalist Party represented. In this setting the dynamics of politics of South Africa were being transformed in a radical manner quite different from what de Klerk had envisioned. An inevitable conclusion was being reached that, being part of the past and the problem, the Nationalist Party was incapable of providing the needed leadership to carve a future that would be consistent with the aspirations of all the people.

De Klerk concluded his observation of these events by making an impassioned appeal to all the people of South Africa saying,

These facts place everybody in South Africa before a *fait accompli*. On the basis of numerous previous statements that have been made there is no longer any reasonable excuse for the continuation of violence. The time for negotiations has arrived, and whoever still makes excuses does not really wish to negotiate. Therefore, I repeat my invitation with greater conviction than ever. I invite everyone to walk through the open door, take your place at the negotiating table together with the government and other leaders who have an important role to play in the cause of fairness, justice, and equality for all South Africans. The time for conflict is over, and the time for negotiation has arrived.[11]

As far as Africans were concerned, the only thing to negotiate was how to storm the laager. If peace had to come, then de Klerk must assist in the storming.

De Klerk expressed his special appreciation to those leaders who resisted resorting to violence to solve the problems the country was facing. He did not see the violence that was coming from his own government by the application of apartheid laws. He singled out Chief Mongosutho Buthelezi as an example of a leader who resisted resorting to violence. De Klerk did not mention the fact that more violence was committed in Natal where Buthelezi was in control than anywhere else during the period of the intensification of violence that made international news headlines. The continuation of violence in Natal is the reason why de Klerk lifted the state of emergency in all of South Africa except in Natal. The combination of violence in Natal and the violence of apartheid created a situation de Klerk did not know how to resolve. It so confounded him that he and his government did not appear to have any solution, which is why he secretly asked Nelson Mandela to help.

De Klerk then turned his attention to addressing the economic benefits he claimed the political solution would bring. He pledged to take action to ensure new economic development as a result of the confidence he hoped would result from his initiative to seek a negotiated resolution of the country's political conflict. He went on to outline five plans that he said his government was going to develop in order to meet the goals he stated. The first plan was that he was going to make efforts to reduce inflation to levels comparable to those of South Africa's trading partners.[12] It is difficult to know who these trading partners were because the international community had imposed economic sanctions as long as apartheid remained the policy of South Africa. These sanctions were so effective that, at their height in 1990, the South African economy was so weak that it had placed all people in a difficult situation. This compelled de Klerk to seek dialogue with the ANC.

The second plan was that de Klerk was going to encourage individual efforts to begin saving. Banks would be asked to create facilities to enable those who wished to open savings accounts. Employers would also be asked to assist their employees to take the initiative to save money for the future. De Klerk's rationale for this action was based on his belief that, with a political resolution of the problems the country was facing, it was now possible to address the search for solutions to the economic problems of the country. Once economic confidence was restored, it would be possible to place the country on the road of development.[13] The third plan was to initiate stringent financial measures to ensure that government spending was not excessive. The fourth was to reform the system of taxation so that people were not overtaxed. The fifth was to encourage exports as an impetus for industrialization and economic development and foreign exchange that was expected when economic sanctions were terminated.[14]

It is important to recognize the reality that, in all his claimed enthusiasm to initiate change, de Klerk knew clearly, as the *Baltimore Sun* stated, "White minority government, while accepting the concept of multiparty democracy in postapartheid South Africa, has opposed a system of one person one vote saying that a new constitution should include provisions to protect the rights of the minority group."[15] It is equally important to recognize that since he was elected to Parliament for the first time in 1972, de Klerk never thought the time would come when the power the Nationalist Party had exercised over the years would be questioned and challenged, and that he would be the one to preside over the process of reform that would end its power in favor of Africans.

By suggesting a constitutional provision to protect the rights of the minority, de Klerk was expressing a lack of confidence in his own proposals. He must have been aware that having imposed a policy of violence since 1948, members of the Nationalist Party, and Afrikaners it represented, now needed protection from the same kind of violence they meted out to Africans. This is a sad irony in the direction of events. De Klerk was not able to see the situation from its broader perspective. For this reason, there were those who thought that, in his claimed enthusiasm to bring about reform to South Africa, de Klerk was a member of a party that lived and operated by consideration of its past behavior and that he was living in the past.

## REACTION TO DE KLERK'S PROPOSALS

Reaction to de Klerk's proposals began to come in as soon as he had made them. One of those who responded is the man de Klerk had praised for what he called his courage in resisting the use of violence to address political problems, Mongosuthu Buthelezi. Buthelezi began his reaction by stating his belief that "There were many who doubted de Klerk's sincerity. They can now be assured that they were wrong. Perhaps most important of all, what Mr. De Klerk did today and how he did it creates a situation in which it should be potently clear to all that there could be no going back for him."[16] Buthelezi did not reveal the fact that the Inkatha Freedom Party he led was opposing the ANC by supporting de Klerk. Indeed, Buthelezi and de Klerk were in an alliance against the ANC. While de Klerk was setting a stage for negotiations with the ANC, he was courting Buthelezi in an effort to undermine the ANC. Because the ANC represented the interests of the African people, Buthelezi and de Klerk entered an alliance to discredit the ANC.

It is also quite surprising that Buthelezi used the same language that de Klerk was using to describe the intent of his proposals. He claimed that South Africa was thrust into the last decade of the twentieth century in which apartheid would be dismantled and the people would be given an opportunity to decide the future through negotiations. Buthelezi also claimed that if Africans failed to bring about the kind of reform they had been hoping for, they would only have themselves to blame.[17] He argued that South African heroes and martyrs should applaud the opportunity that de Klerk was providing the country. The black leaders should now realize the dreams of the struggle of the people of South Africa as a whole.

Buthelezi also praised de Klerk for making his proposals a historic occasion in that more than a century and a half of political experience was culminating in a rare opportunity of great historic importance and achievement. Buthelezi was quite static in claiming that de Klerk's proposals went far beyond the level of what any national leader before him had ever dared. However, by their increasing demands, Africans were causing de Klerk more serious problems than any of his predecessors had ever encountered.

Events of the past, such as the Sharpeville massacre of 1960, the massive treason trials of 1956, or the Soweto uprising of 1976 could not match the intensity of the pressure that Africans were applying on de Klerk to dismantle apartheid. Africans were no longer protesting the harshness of apartheid; they wanted it dismantled immediately. No previous leader had ever faced this kind of situation. Therefore, for Buthelezi to give credit to de Klerk in these circumstances was to lose sight of the real situation he was facing. Buthelezi should have given credit to the ANC for designing an effective political strategy that forced de Klerk to respond to its call to engage in dialogue with it.

Buthelezi also failed to recognize the hard reality that de Klerk's proposals were not motivated by humane considerations toward Africans, but by a desire to ensure the political survival of Afrikaners. This is why he suggested that a constitutional provision be made to protect the rights of the minority, meaning Afrikaners. He hoped that, in the process of negotiations with the ANC, he would succeed in manipulating Africans so that a new constitution would allow Afrikaners to continue to rule the country, and that a coalition government would emerge in which de Klerk and Buthelezi would share power. De Klerk's notion of sharing political power with Africans was based on this line of thinking, which turned out to be an illusion for both de Klerk and Buthelezi.

Buthelezi's enthusiasm toward de Klerk's proposals manifested itself in the hope he saw. He was moved to continue his tribute of the man he admired saying, "We are in the position where black and white can together look forward to grasping the thorny issues of the South African politics and look forward to dealing with them effectively and dealing with them together."[18] Buthelezi went on to say that when he took into account what the minister of constitutional development, Gerrit Viljoen, said in an interview after the opening of Parliament that solution to the problems of South Africa must be found in negotiations, he looked forward to seeing black leaders come forth within weeks to say that they were now prepared to negotiate. According to Buthelezi, the burden of proof of sincerity of the desire to negotiate was on the black leaders, not on the government. Was he projecting a bias against the ANC? It would be hard to see things from any other perspective. In taking the same attitude toward the African leaders as de Klerk was doing, Buthelezi was placing expectations on the ANC and none on de Klerk and the Nationalist government for the success of negotiations.

Buthelezi argued that de Klerk's proposals moved him to make a plea to all black leaders to come together in what he called the fullness of South African tradition for purposes of creating a nonracial society. He was confident that the white community was not afraid of the steps that de Klerk was taking. He saw the proposals as having a positive effect on the future of South Africa and urged Africans to put behind them the damaging effect of apartheid in order to help in constructing that future. Nowhere did Buthelezi call on Afrikaners to recognize the legitimate aspirations of Africans and the need to move rapidly in seeking an end to conditions created by apartheid over many years. Nowhere did he call for the end of negative attitudes among Afrikaners toward Africans. He knew that throughout the years Afrikaners regarded Africans as less than human beings who must be reminded of their inferior position in society.

Buthelezi made a strong plea to de Klerk to appoint a judicial body to act as an ombudsman or mediator who would review government decisions about persons who were still under political detention. He did not recognize a serious problem in his suggestion: Where would de Klerk find a judicial committee that would be fair in dealing with questions of African political detainees? De Klerk would have to name the committee from among the Afrikaner Nationalist Party members. After years of sustaining apartheid, would it be realistic to expect such a committee to be impartial in discharging its responsibility in reviewing cases of African political prisoners? Under the Nationalists, this exercise would be tantamount to the action of a patient who has been treated by Dr. Jekyll seeking second opinion from Mr. Hyde, or to expect the palace guard to investigate the conduct of the king. This cannot be done. Buthelezi must have been aware that the conduct of Afrikaners was not thought to contain any positive attributes that could be utilized for the benefit of the country at this stage in its development.

Buthelezi expressed concern that the state of emergency had not been lifted. However, he said that he understood the need for the government to maintain law and order. He claimed that if Africans stopped the violence, then the state of emergency would be lifted in due course. It is quite obvious that Buthelezi ignored the reality that Africans were only responding to the violence that apartheid had instituted. Buthelezi was therefore blaming Africans, the victims of that violence, for the continuation of the state of emergency. He concluded that the emergency placed power in the hands of the government in order to sustain law and order. This in turn protected democracy and allowed normal functions to take place for the good of all the people. It was clear that in Buthelezi, de Klerk now had a spokesman within the African population itself. This is why de Klerk said that the Nationalist Party would invite Africans to join its ranks.

Buthelezi could not miss the opportunity to praise de Klerk for the conduct of his government in all aspects of national life. He said that he welcomed the humanity that de Klerk was carrying out as his responsibility as president of South Africa. He also claimed that de Klerk knew how to deal with such issues as capital punishment in the same way as he knew how to deal with political organizations. He welcomed the assurances that de Klerk received from Viljoen that outlawed organizations would be legalized again to permit them to play a role in shaping events for the benefit of the country's future. Buthelezi found nothing lacking in the way de Klerk was carrying out his functions as president or in the continuation of apartheid. He failed to recognize the fact that apartheid had been recognized across the world as the cause of conflict and a lack of progress in South Africa. In his response to de Klerk's statement, he should have stressed the need to dismantle apartheid immediately as an imperative condition of initiating a new start in rebuilding a country shattered by its application.

The ANC had quite a difference reaction to de Klerk's proposals. It issued a statement soon after de Klerk's proposals saying that the proposals were "a recipe for national disaster,"[19] and called for something better that Africans could accept as a basis of negotiations. The Conservative Party said the proposals were "a recipe for revolution,"[20] and called for a halt in the dangerous game that it said de Klerk was embarking upon. The Pan-Africanist Congress lashed out at the proposals saying that de Klerk's action was to secure the privileges Afrikaners had considered their exclusive right since the days of Paul Kruger and which had been reinforced by Daniel Malan. The Pan-Africanist Congress called for a new start in designing an acceptable framework needed to begin negotiations.[21]

If de Klerk had reason to believe that Buthelezi was speaking on behalf of the African population in his support of the proposals, the reaction from other organizations brought him face-to-face with skepticism and criticism. Buthelezi, when he realized that other leaders questioned de Klerk's proposals, seemed to qualify his praise of de Klerk saying that he did not regard the proposals as cut and dried solutions to the problems that apartheid had created over many years. Ferdinand Hartzenberg, deputy leader of the Conservative Party, most of whose members had broken faith with the Nationalist Party, further stated why Afrikaners must reject the proposals saying, "One man one vote offers no protection to minority groups. It means black domination and oppression of whites."[22]

Hartzenberg's reaction was quite typical of the reaction of whites in Africa. When a call for fundamental political change was made, and when an African government was inevitable, the whites would demand special constitutional provisions to protect their positions of privilege. This is exactly what Hartzenberg was doing in his reaction to the proposals. But Hartzenberg must have forgotten that nowhere in Africa was this demand honored. Africans of South Africa were not about to become the first to acquiesce to such a demand. De Klerk himself was quite deliberate in trying to put into his proposals this provision. But the resistance from Africans proved to him that, if he and his government were going to have as successful negotiations with Africans, they would have to abandon this demand.

Of the major newspapers in South Africa, only *The Citizen* endorsed de Klerk's proposals. In an editorial of February 3, 1990, the paper gave reasons for its endorsement saying, "The Nationalist party seeks a participatory democracy in which constitutional South Africa is established. The principles on which it would be based cannot be faulted. We congratulate the Nationalist party on putting forward its ideas so succinctly. We think that it has devised a constitution which will offer a great deal of power to regional and local levels."[23] It is quite possible that *The Citizen* was thinking of maintaining the old system of Bantustan homelands which were based on regional and ethnic systems.

*The Sowetan*, a paper run by Africans for African readers, criticized the proposals as insufficient to address the problem South Africa was facing as a result of many years of apartheid. The paper suggested that if de Klerk was sincere about the proposals he was going to have to do better than the proposals he had made. The paper argued that the proposals were loaded with devises that meant the majority of the people were not fully represented. The paper concluded, "If the vote of some people is worth more than the vote of other people the future of South Africa is going to be a place of continuing bitterness."[24] *The Sowetan* was referring to the constitutional provisions that de Klerk had suggested to protect the rights and privileges of minority groups. This was a provision that all concerned, except Afrikaners, rejected unreservedly.

The reaction of the international community was quite mixed. In London, Archbishop Trevor Huddleston, author of *Naught for Your Comfort* and president of the Anti-Apartheid Movement who was deported from South Africa in 1957 for opposing apartheid, said he would launch a campaign in Britain against the proposals because they failed to state clearly that apartheid would be dismantled as a condition of negotiations. Huddleston and the organization he led wanted to see the political evolution of South Africa evolve in such a way that race would no longer be a factor in considering the position of the individual in society. Huddleston also urged white South Africa to move aggressively in seeking the elimination of apartheid in all its forms in order to avoid a major national conflict before time ran out.

The reaction of government officials in European capitals was generally supportive of the proposals. In London, Margaret Thatcher welcomed the proposals as a step in the right direction but indicated that there was a lot more to be done before they became the basis of negotiation for the transformation of South Africa. In Paris, Roland Dumas, the French foreign minister, expressed his hope that the proposals would make it possible to bring apartheid to an end as a condition of peace and progress in South Africa. In Lisbon, Cavaco Silva, the prime minister, welcomed the proposals as a beginning point toward democracy in South Africa. In Madrid, Fernandez Ordonez, the Spanish foreign minister, said his government received the news of the proposals with the hope that South Africa would move away from practices of the past and begin to work toward the establishment of true and genuine democracy. In Ottawa, Joseph Clark, Canadian Secretary of State for External Affairs urged de Klerk to continue the road to reform in the interest of establishing democracy for the benefit of all the people.

It is important to note that the reaction from European leaders had one thing in common: their recognition that de Klerk's proposals were a move in the right direction but did not constitute a set of conditions that would lead to the end of apartheid. Therefore, since de Klerk had made a special appeal to the international community to remove economic sanctions, he was forced to recognize that this was not likely to happen anytime soon until he presented clear evidence showing that, indeed, apartheid had come to an end. He was therefore under no illusion that leaders of European nations fully accepted his proposals as a final act of eliminating apartheid. It was up to Africans to ensure that de Klerk fully understood that the proposals only represented a starting point on the course of fundamental political change in South Africa. Africans also knew that, in publicizing the proposals in Europe, de Klerk was seeking the termination of the trade embargo that was crippling South Africa's economy and posing serious political implications for de Klerk and the Nationalist Party. Nelson Mandela appealed to the international community to keep economic sanctions in place until apartheid was dismantled.

The United States' reaction to de Klerk's proposals came mainly from newspapers. The *San Francisco Chronicle* called de Klerk's proposals a revolutionary gesture to Africans. The paper added, "In a landmark speech that shocked both blacks and white South Africans President Frederik W. de Klerk yesterday lifted the 30-year ban on the African National Congress. De Klerk's intentions went forward reopening political expression in the country and meeting the demands made by the ANC as a condition of black-white negotiations."[25] The *Los Angeles Times* reacted, "The path has been cleared for negotiating the way to a democratic South Africa."[26]

The *Baltimore Sun* concluded, "With this latest announcement South African President F. W. de Klerk has demonstrated that he is seriously committed to negotiations with anti-apartheid organizations on the political future of South Africa."[27] The *Chicago Tribune* reacted, "The world waited 40 years for the collapse of the Communist rule in eastern Europe. Today it is watching with astonishment as that dream comes true in South Africa. The impossible dream of blacks and whites for a country of liberty, democracy, and racial equality is now possible."[28] President George Bush stated, "I welcome this move and view it as a significant step on the on the road to the nonradical democratic South Africa."[29]

Like leaders of European nations, these newspapers and President Bush did not fully understand the implications of their endorsements of de Klerk's proposals. There were hidden agendas that were only understood by those who lived in South Africa. De Klerk did not designate himself liberator of Africans. He was a hard core Afrikaner who inherited both the mission Afrikaners believed was theirs to complete and the policy of apartheid, the instrument of fulfilling that mission. Like his predecessors, de Klerk believed that he was part of the sacred duty that had to be carried out with total devotion. But, on assuming the office of president in 1989, de Klerk was faced with a reality of the deterioration in the conditions of Africans to the extent that confrontation was rapidly rising. With no support base, inside or outside South Africa, he was forced to seek a negotiation with the ANC. He did this, not because he was genuinely motivated by a desire to advance Africans, but to save Afrikaners from disaster. Unlike Ian D. Smith in colonial Zimbabwe, de Klerk was able to see the writing on the wall before the curtain fell. This is what saved South Africa from a major national conflict.

## CONDITIONS OF NEGOTIATIONS

When de Klerk announced the intention of his government on February 2, 1990, to rescind the prohibition of political organizations opposed to apartheid, he did not spell out the terms he would utilize in negotiating with them to resolve the political problems that apartheid had been creating. However, de Klerk stated three conditions that his government was going to observe in mapping out a new future for South Africa. The first condition was the identification of the main types of democratic constitutions that deserved consideration as a model for South Africa. The second condition was an analysis of the ways in which relevant rights of individuals would be protected. The third condition was the evolution of methods by which a constitution would be developed suited to South Africa and to the interests of all the people.[30]

De Klerk made no mention of the intent of his government to eliminate apartheid. He knew that apartheid was the main problem that stood in the way of successful negotiations. He knew that for years Africans were fighting against apartheid because it was so oppressive, and that for the past thirty years the Nationalist government had imposed the state of emergency to preserve apartheid. He also knew that the banning of the ANC and the decision of Hendrik Verwoerd's government to withdraw from the British Commonwealth, both in 1960, were based on the need to sustain apartheid. He understood that since 1948 the Nationalist Party was returned to power in every election because it promised Afrikaners to uphold principles of apartheid. How could he fail to recognize that apartheid caused so much bitterness over the years, and that Africans would no longer tolerate it? How could he substantiate his claim that he wanted to start afresh in building South Africa based on true democracy?

In addition to these three conditions, de Klerk stated in his address to Parliament as prerequisites of holding negotiations with the ANC that he would ask the ANC to renounce the use of guerrilla warfare in seeking an end to apartheid. But without giving his assurance to end the violence of apartheid, the ANC could not give him that assurance. What this meant, therefore, is that there was a stalemate that had to be resolved before negotiations could begin. On September 5, 1990 de Klerk asked voters to approve his proposals for a new South Africa. He told them that if the proposals were not approved his government would produce new proposals. Without even engaging in dialogue with the ANC to determine if the proposals were acceptable to Africans, de Klerk told white voters, "Our promise to the voters is that we will not carry on with a plan that has been rejected by a majority in a referendum. If we lose we will go back to the drawing board for a new plan to bring the irreversible situation to its conclusion."[31] This was as clear a statement as he could ever make that the laager was about to be stormed.

De Klerk was speaking at a provincial congress of the Nationalist Party in the Orange Free State. He was attempting to address the concerns of Afrikaners who were arguing that he was moving too fast to accommodate the ANC. In October 1990 de Klerk assured Afrikaners that in any transition from white minority government to African majority rule, whites would continue to have a veto power. This meant that the institution of an African government would be meaningless because whites would exercise veto power to preserve their position of privileges. De Klerk should have known that this condition was totally unacceptable to Africans and the international community.

In February 1991 several hundred supporters of the neo-Fascist Afrikaner Resistance marched through the center of Pretoria to protest de Klerk's decision to hold talks with the ANC. The members were dressed in old Boer-style khaki uniforms and toting pistols. The 1,000 marchers then went into a city hall to hear their leader, Eugene Terre-Blanche, condem de Klerk as a traitor to the Afrikaner cause. Terre-Blanche told the cheering marchers, "This land is the Boers' land and they will have to take it from us over the barrel of the gun."[32] This extreme position by the people whom de Klerk was seeking to protect had an adverse effect on his action on the proposals. That is why at that time he was telling the whites that whatever political system evolved it must retain substantial power in the hands of whites, a condition he knew the ANC would not accept.

Recognizing that de Klerk and his government were incapable of formulating a set of conditions for negotiations, the ANC undertook to define its own conditions under which it would hold discussions with the Nationalist government. As early as August 1989, while it was still an outlawed organization, the ANC outlined three major conditions under which it would hold talks with the Nationalist government. The first condition was to demand that de Klerk remove the ban on all political organizations and restore normal political activity. Because these organizations represented people, de Klerk's continued ban of them would effectively eliminate Africans from the political process. If de Klerk refused to remove the ban, the ANC would bring into serious question his honest desire to create a new South Africa.

The second condition that the ANC defined for holding talks with the Nationalist government was that de Klerk must agree to dismantle apartheid. To do this, he must recognize it as the fountain of all problems in South Africa—political, social, and economic. He must also recognize that apartheid could not be reformed because it was a system that existed only to preserve the position of privileges of Afrikaners. Apartheid was the reason the international community imposed economic sanctions. De Klerk also had to recognize that apartheid represented an oppressive system that must end immediately because its existence stood between total equality for Africans and Afrikaners. It would mean the end of all forms of discrimination and segregation. It would also mean the introduction of the universal franchise, which meant that, if elections were held under these conditions, the Nationalist Party and de Klerk himself would be voted out of office and the monopoly of the political power they had exercised for many years would come to an immediate end. Would de Klerk be willing to negotiate with the ANC under these conditions?

The third condition that the ANC outlined for holding discussions with de Klerk and his Nationalist government was that de Klerk must end the state of emergency in order to allow freedom of political activity, freedom of the press, and freedom of movement of the people. For thirty years the Nationalist Party maintained the state of emergency for the sole purpose of making it impossible for Africans to engage in any meaningful political, economic, or social activity. Under the state of emergency the government would arrest and detain anyone identifying himself with any political organization considered to pose a threat to the government. The arrest and detention were affected without any charges being brought against them. Any individual who was arrested under the state of emergency had no recourse except to appeal to the government itself. Under the state of emergency there was no limit to which the government could go to silence its opponents.

In order to promote these three conditions and give them maximum publicity, the ANC outlined six phases that should be observed in its negotiations with de Klerk. The first phase would be to achieve a cease-fire and termination of hostility based on agreement. The second phase was to reach an agreement on a set of constitutional principles that would reflect the essential components of democracy. The third phase was to develop a mechanism for drawing up a new constitution. The fourth phase would define the role that the international community would play in the negotiations. The fifth phase was to ensure the observance of principles needed for the formation of an interim government. The sixth and final phase was to outline the procedure of negotiations themselves.

The ANC then sought the support of the OAU and the nonaligned nations in seeking their implementation. De Klerk and the Nationalist government were quite surprised by the ability of the ANC to articulate principles that were consistent with the requirements of the international community. They, therefore, found themselves unable to reject any of them. In this setting, the ANC had achieved a major victory over de Klerk and his Nationalist associates. A special meeting of the OAU was convened in Harare, Zimbabwe, to approve both the conditions and the phases giving the ANC the support it needed to hold negotiations with de Klerk and his government.

Facing opposition from the extreme elements of Afrikaners, de Klerk was operating from a weakened position. In Washington, D.C., the State Department welcomed both the ANC's conditions and the six phases it had outlined as constituting adequate conditions for holding negotiations with the government. A spokesman of the State Department, Richard Boucher, reacted, "Many of the points in the ANC document parallel our own public statements. We have urged the South African government to create a political environment conducive to real negotiations with legitimate black leaders."[33]

Boucher was enthusiastic in supporting the ANC position because its document contained constitutional principles that embraced provisions of an independent judiciary, free press, and free economic enterprise. These were the principles de Klerk, as the last custodian of apartheid, was unable to include in his own proposals. Given the enormous pressure under which the Nationalist government was operating, Roelf Botha, the Nationalist minister of foreign affairs, surprised his fellow

Afrikaners and the country by stating that de Klerk would have no problem accepting both the three conditions and the six phases that the ANC had outlined in 1989. Botha added, "We will handle this like grown-up people and as the leaders of the country which is the strongest in the region."[34] Given the support of the OAU, and of the U.S. State Department, the ANC knew that the Nationalists realized that they would reject these conditions and phases at their peril.

Only a few days before, de Klerk had said that his government would not hold direct discussions with the ANC until it renounced the use of violence. Botha's reaction meant that the Nationalists had accepted the three conditions that the ANC had outlined. It was now up to de Klerk and his government to honor them. They knew that they had no other option except to accept them and start negotiations. The ANC had thus scored a major victory even before the negotiations started. What was there to discuss if the Nationalists had accepted the ANC's prior conditions? Left with few options, de Klerk seemed ready to concede the fact that things had dramatically turned in favor of the ANC. Afrikaners who espoused extreme political views, such as Eugene Terre-Blanche, might as well begin now making major adjustments to live under an African government they had vowed would never come about in their lifetime.

## NEGOTIATIONS: STORMING THE LAAGER

By the time de Klerk made his proposals in an address to Parliament on February 2, 1990, he took all three conditions into consideration. Indeed, he began to observe the three conditions in the address saying, "I wish to put it plainly that the government has taken a firm decision to release Mr. Mandela unconditionally. I am serious about bringing this matter to a final resolution without delay."[35] Nine days later, on February 11, Mandela was actually released. Hundreds of other political prisoners had been released shortly before. These included Walter Sesulu, Raymond Mhlaba, Ahmed Kathrada, Andrew Mbugeni, Wilton Mkwayi, and Osacar Mpethu. Hundreds of exiles were to return soon. These included Oliver Tambo and Thabo Mbeki, both of whom were running the ANC operations from bases in Zambia.

Immediately on his release, Mandela made a statement in Cape Town saying in the traditional ANC salute, "Amandla! Amandla!" The huge crowd that came to welcome him roared back, "Ngawethu!" Then he went to add, "My friends, comrades, and fellow South Africans, I greet you all in the name of peace, democracy, and freedom for all. I stand before you not as a prophet, but as your humble servant and of the people. Your tireless and heroic sacrifices have made it possible for me to be here today. I therefore pledge the remaining years of my life[36] in your hands."[37] Mandela went on to thank the ANC and Oliver Tambo for refusing to give up the struggle against apartheid and for continuing to storm the laager.

Mandela also recognized the fact that de Klerk had gone further than any previous leader in taking steps to restore South Africa to its proper place among nations of Africa and the world. He added, "Mr. De Klerk is acutely aware of the dangers of a public figure not honoring his undertakings. As an organization we have our policy and strategy on the harsh reality we are still suffering under the policy of the Nationalist government. Our struggle has reached a decisive moment."[38] The final phase of the negotiations proved to be the final act of storming the laager.

On August 14, 1990, after three months of preparation, the first session of negotiations between the Nationalist government and the ANC was held in Cape Town. After this preliminary session the participants issued a communiqué stressing agreement on five essential considerations. The first consideration was the establishment of a working group to make accommodation on a definition of political offenses and to advise on norms and mechanisms for dealing with the release of political prisoners still being held. The second consideration was that the working group would define and recommend conditions of immunity from arrest for political offenses. The third consideration was that the Nationalist government would undertake to review existing security legislation to bring it into line with the new situation in order to ensure normal and free political activity. The fourth consideration was to ask the government to reiterate its commitment to work toward the lifting of the state of emergency. The fifth consideration was that efficient channels of communication between the government and the ANC be developed in order to curb the possibility of misunderstanding which could lead to conflict. The Nationalist government agreed to introduce legislation to repeal all apartheid laws.[39]

The success of this first session in the negotiations between the Nationalist Party and the ANC was measured in terms of de Klerk's willingness to meet the three conditions the ANC had outlined in 1989. From this point on, the negotiations focused on other critical issues remaining to be resolved. These included the constitution and voting rights. Ending all discriminatory laws was addressed by the introduction of legislation repealing all apartheid laws. All indications were that the ANC would easily prevail as de Klerk seemed more than willing to end apartheid. The absolute power that Afrikaners had exercised over many years was about to come to an end before their very eyes.

## MANDELA IS ELECTED PRESIDENT: THE FINAL
## ACT OF STORMING THE LAAGER

In January 1992, as negotiations between the ANC and the Nationalists appeared to experience some problems, de Klerk and his Nationalist government suffered a series of defeats in special elections forcing them to seek the approval of white voters to continue the negotiations. In February, de Klerk announced that a national referendum would be held on March 17, 1992, to provide an answer to a single question: "Do you support the continuation of the reform process which the State President began on February 2, 1990 and which is aimed at a new constitution through negotiation?" De Klerk considered the referendum so important that his government decided to make arrangements for voters living outside South Africa to cast their ballot on March 11 and 12. The slow progress in the negotiations with ANC created a political climate which forced some members of both black and white communities to take extreme positions.

Two examples must be presented to substantiate this conclusion. The first is that Thami Mcerwa, president of the Azanian Youth Organization, opposed the negotiations because, he said, "We want total liberation, not cosmetic changes. We may go into civil war struggle, quick fix solutions will not work. As Steve Biko said, 'It is better to die for an idea that will live than to live for an idea that will die' "[40] The second example is that Pieter Rudolph, a member of the Neo-Nazi Afrikaner Resistance movement considered de Klerk a traitor to Afrikaner interests. Rudolph argued that Afrikaners inherited South Africa as a glorious national legacy. Rudolph added, "I received this land as I received my mother's milk. I am a son of Africa."[41] The extreme positions taken by the antagonists placed South Africa at the crossroads until Nelson Mandela assumed office as president following the elections held in April 1994. Rudolph and other extreme Afrikaners were overwhelmed by the rapid pace of events they could not understand nor control.

The sad part of it all is that de Klerk agreed to be part of a national referendum that allowed only whites to vote on an issue of great national importance. Since he claimed to be committed to bringing about social reform, what better opportunity for him to start bringing Africans into his confidence than initiating a process for their involvement in the referendum? This is why on March 12, 1992, seventeen people and, on March 13, another twenty-four people were killed in violence related to the forthcoming referendum. Reporting from Johannesburg on March 13, Alan Pizzey put the conflict between the Afrikaner psychology and the determination of Africans to bring about fundamental political change in its proper context, saying, "There is still a belief among Afrikaners that God has ordained them as the master race of South Africa. But Africans believe that the future belongs to them."[42] This conflict evinces the tragedy of apartheid.

On March 18, 1992, when the referendum results showed that the "yes" vote had carried the day by a margin of 2:1 out of the total white electorate of 2.8 million voters, de Klerk went into a state of euphoria as he reacted, "Today, we have closed the chapter on apartheid."[43] While generally pleased with the outcome of the referendum, Nelson Mandela had a more somber reaction, saying, "Because I still cannot vote in my country, I cannot say that apartheid is gone."[44] De Klerk also saw the result, coming on his fifty-sixth birthday, as "the real birthday of the real South Africa."[45]

In a similar manner Allister Sparks, the South African author of *The Mind of South Africa* (1990), recognized the perils of a national crisis cast in the context of the determination of Africans saying, "The danger now is that the right-wing may turn to violence. White South Africa has rejected apartheid and must now embrace a non-racial approach to its problems. The talk of power-sharing is code word for white veto. The Africans are quite capable of grasping this reality and demand that South Africa move into the realm of a completely non-racial society."[46] Gary Player, a South African professional golfer, added, "Change is the price of survival."[47] But Pieter W. Botha, 76, reacted, "I cannot support a reform process that leads to the suicide of my people."[48] It was not possible for the old, tired horse to see things from their proper perspective. After failing to recognize the need for change during his own administration, how could he possibly accept change initiated by others?

With the referendum over, the task of negotiations resumed, giving de Klerk freedom to make more concessions to the ANC. But on April 5, violence in black townships broke out on a larger scale than before the referendum. As hundreds were killed, Mandela called for a UN peacekeeping force arguing that the South African security forces were behind the violence and that was the only way to contain it. But de Klerk rejected both the call and the charge arguing that the violence was caused by Africans themselves in the struggle for power. On April 11, in a strange turn of events, de Klerk tried to campaign in a black neighborhood outside Cape Town in an effort to recruit Africans into the ranks of the Nationalist Party. As he tried to make a speech, he was jeered and shouted down, but he managed to say, "Apartheid has been buried and will remain buried. The creation of the new South Africa has begun."[49] One angry African reacted, "We are still discriminated against, we still cannot vote. What are you campaigning for?"[50]

Unconvinced of his sincerity, ANC called de Klerk's action "a case of political opportunism."[51] De Klerk was forced to cancel the rest of the speech and hurriedly moved out of the neighborhood. The spiral of conflict took an ominous and tragic turn on June 18, 1992, when thirty-nine Africans were massacred in cold blood at Boipatong, reportedly by members of Inkatha Freedom Party headed by Buthelezi with what ANC identified as assistance from the government.[52] Although de Klerk denied the charge, "a black mine-security guard told a government-appointed commission that police from a former paramilitary unit had joined in the Boipatong killings."[53] Negotiations between ANC and the government were suspended as the result of the killings to allow the parties to assess the situation and to determine the next move. Instead of dealing forthrightly with the situation that his government had created, de Klerk threatened to reimpose the notorious state of emergency, an easy strategy the apartheid government had utilized for so many years to control Africans.

On August 3, 1992, over a million African workers went on strike for two days in protest against the refusal of the government to end apartheid. This action paralyzed major industries and services. On September 18, twenty-eight Africans were massacred in the Bantustan Homeland of Ciskei while protesting peacefully against the puppet regime of Brigadier Oupa Gqozo, who was promoted to his position in the government of South Africa for his service against the demand of Africans to dismantle apartheid. According to *Time*, when 60,000 chanting ANC supporters moved closer to the capital, "trigger-happy troops of the Ceskei army began shooting directly into the crowd. After two prolonged bursts of gunfire, 28 people lay dead in pools of blood, another 400 were wounded"[54] dragging the country closer to the edge of a major civil conflict.

On November 25 Mandela and Buthelezi, recognizing that the government was exploiting the difference between them, decided to hold a meeting to resolve the crisis between them. The attack and killing of five whites in a restaurant near Cape Town on December 4, 1992, by an unidentified group of African nationalists added a perilous twist to an already dangerous situation. There is no question that dramatic as they were, these events placed South Africa at the crossroads because of conflict between the rise of the African mind and the determination of Afrikaners to maintain apartheid.

There is no doubt that the racial confrontation apartheid created over the years was destined to intensify with the passage of time. This situation has actually led to one thing—a major racial war that has produced a national tragedy such as the one that occurred in Zimbabwe from 1966 to 1979. Apartheid has been a cancer that has destroyed the delicate tissue of South African vitality, human resources without which no nation can prosper. Even Brian Nel, an Herstige Nationale Party organizer, seemed to agree when he said ironically in 1980, "The cancer of apartheid is spreading and is going to follow you wherever you go."[55]

In the determination of the Afrikaner to sustain apartheid at all costs and in the determination of the oppressed Africans to rise and envisage the restoration of their mind lie the seeds of the destruction and the tragedy of the South African system. Although the world community has exercised its moral duty to help Afrikaners see the tragic course they have charted for the country, apartheid has extended beyond the boundaries of South Africa and must therefore be viewed from a global perspective. By 1992, the international community came to realize that, in apartheid's oppression of the black masses of South Africa, humanity as a whole was inescapably enslaved. This is the reality that de Klerk took into account in deciding to hold serious discussions with the ANC on a new constitution that would bring true democracy to South Africa.

After months of negotiations, the parties finally agreed to hold free elections on April 16–18, 1994. Immediately the ANC designed a strategy to "capture at least 67 percent of the 22.4 million eligible voters."[56] This would mean that the ANC would take 328 of the 490 seats in Parliament. As the election campaign got underway, it was clear that de Klerk was hoping for no more than a respectable showing. He was pleased that he had made it possible to turn over power to Africans in a way that would ensure the future of the whites in a new country. He was sure that an African government would not match the brutality of apartheid by utilizing similar methods.

As was expected, when the election results were known on May 2, the ANC won with more than the two-thirds majority it had needed to form the first black majority government in the history of South Africa. Nelson Mandela, the man who spent twenty-seven years in prison for opposing apartheid, emerged as the new man in the incredible saga of the transformation of South Africa. With a sense of duty and humbled by it all, Mandela responded, "It is not the individual that matters, but the group. I come to you as a servant, not a leader above others. We must together begin to mobilize our minds and build a better life for all South Africans. We are here to honor our promise. If we fail we betray the trust placed on us by our people. As we form the government of national unity, we must set the tone for the future."[57]

Conceding defeat, de Klerk pledged the support of his party to the new government that Mandela was about to lead, saying, "After three hundred years all the people of South Africa are now free."[58] When Mandela was inaugurated on May 9, the entire African continent had eliminated the last vestiges of colonial domination, raising Africans to a new level of hope for the future. Mandela made an impressive inaugural address as he reflected upon the thoughts of Africans about themselves and the future of their country saying, "Our deepest fear is not that we are inadequate. Our deepest fear is that we are powerful beyond measure. It is our light, not our darkness, that most frightens us. As we let our own light shine we unconsciously give other people permission to do the same. As we are liberated from our own fears, our presence automatically liberates others."[59] This position was the final act of storming the laager. However, cautioning his fellow South Africans, Mandela warned them not to have too high hopes because the task of rebuilding a country devastated by apartheid was not an easy one. But the transformation of the African continent was now complete.

However, the confession made on January 28, 1997, by five former police officers that they were responsible for the deaths on September 12, 1977, added a painful chapter in the annals of those who were determined to go to any length to defend the laager. That these five police officers now asked for amnesty added a tragic twist to the saga of the defense of the laager. The confessions came as a result of the action that Mandela took in naming Archbishop Desmond Tutu chairman of the Truth and Reconciliation Commission to investigate abuses by the apartheid government in order to put the past behind and look to the future. Writing for the *Christian Science Monitor* of January 30, 1997, Judith Matloff quotes Alex Beraine, deputy chairman of the commission, who explained the reason for the inquiry, saying, "Our investigative work, combined with the prospects of amnesty, has persuaded those who say they were involved in perpetrating the acts to come forward for the first time"[60] in this national effort to heal the wounds caused by apartheid. The commission made it clear that those who were willing to confess their part in the deaths would be granted amnesty, and those who did not confess would be charged of crimes against humanity.

On February 20, 1997, the author wrote a letter to Bishop Tutu to say, "The emphasis of the investigation should not be forgiveness. Rather, it must be to hold those responsible for those atrocities accountable for their action. If nothing happens to them other than forgiveness, it will perpetuate the pain the Africans have endured and those guilty of these gross offenses will go off laughing. Nothing is more harmful to the future of the country. Further, all levels of the guilty parties should be brought to justice from the lowest rank of the police force and the military to the president. The idea that only those on the front line are guilty can make a mockery of the investigation. It is virtually impossible for those who committed these crimes to do so without support from above."[61] As a religious leader who was taught the principle that "to err is human to forgive is divine," Bishop Tutu and the commission have not fully understood the implications of focusing on forgiveness. He did not even understand that South Africa needs to hold its own Nurenberg trials in order to begin the real process of healing for the nation.

The line of defense taken by the 1,500 applicants rejected for amnesty is that they were merely following orders in a situation that they saw as a virtual state of war.[62] Still elusive were applications from many senior cabinet members of the Botha and de Klerk governments. Only former law and order minister, Adriaan Vlok, applied for amnesty. Vlok did this amidst reports that that General Pierre Steyn, former defense force chief of staff, had submitted a report to de Klerk recommending that some sixty officers, including senior military officials, be investigated for gross abuse of power, and that his refusal to do anything about the report constituted a coverup. But de Klerk denied the charge. On May 19, 1997, the author watched on television in Mutare, Zimbabwe, a parliamentary debate in Cape Town on the activities of the Truth and Reconciliation Commission (TRC). A Member of the Inkatha Freedom Party (IFP) severely criticized the TRC and its chair saying, "The TRC has become an unconventional circus of horrors presided over by a weakly clown craving for the front-page spotlight. Bishop Tutu is responsible for the failures of the TRC."[63] On June 9, 1997, the author wrote a letter to Bishop Tutu to say:

I have just returned from a research trip to Africa. On May 19, while watching on television a parliamentary debate on the activities of the Truth and Reconciliation Commission in my hotel room in Mutare, Zimbabwe, I was shocked to see a member of the IFP characterize you as "a clown craving for the front-page spotlight." It was sad for me to come to the conclusion that the IFP has been an instrument of Nationalist party policy. I could not have possibly imagined what the IFP would hope to gain by such an attack of a commission whose work is critical to the future of South Africa. I would suggest that the commission's work is so important that it should be expanded to include investigation of other atrocities committed by the Nationalist government in the past. The Sharpeville Massacre, the murder of Steve Biko and others, the death of President Samora Machel, etc., are very important and need to be investigated and the facts put before the people. Unless these facts are fully known and disclosed, South Africa, like many other countries of Africa, will languish in the mire of the past.[64]

It would appear that those who were criticizing the commission were trying to defend the laager. Could the national process of healing be initiated in a climate of seeking to preserve memories of the laager?

## SUMMARY AND CONCLUSION

The discussion in this chapter leads to two basic conclusions. The first conclusion is that if the apartheid system of South Africa had recognized the fact that it would not last forever, the agony the country endured for so many years would have been spared and efforts would have been directed toward building a dynamic society in which race was not a criterion to determine a person's place. This is why in 1990 F. W. de Klerk, the leader of the last colonial system in Africa, decided to change tactics and embark on a new direction, holding discussions with Africans.

The second conclusion is that by the time the Nationalist government recognized the effect of apartheid, Africans had concluded that the road to their restoration passed through the gate of their determination to eradicate the conditions that had oppressed them for so long. There was no room for compromise anymore. This situation constituted an environment which spelled the demise of de Klerk's government itself. The transformation of South Africa in April 1994 shows that Africans all over the continent had become masters of their own destiny because they had reached a level of development that was beyond the ability of the Nationalist governments to control. When Mandela was installed as president, de Klerk was moved to say that now all the people of South Africa were free. The storming of the laager was now complete and its defenders ceased to exist.

## NOTES

1. F. W. de Klerk. "The Birth of the New South Africa" (Pretoria: Government Printer, 1990), p. 13.

2. De Klerk's father, Jan, and grandfather were prominent in the politics of South Africa as members of the Nationalist Party. Jan's sister married J. G. Strijdom, an Afrikaner of extreme racial views who served as Prime Minister of South Africa from 1952 until his untimely death in 1958. De Klerk's grandfather, "Oom Jan," was a friend of Paul Kruger (1825–1904), "Oom Paul," president of the ill-fated Boer Republic of the Transvaal established before the end of the South African war in 1901. In 1972 F. W. de Klerk adopted their political philosophy as his own modus operandi until 1989, when he was forced by conditions to modify it. But, like Mikhail Gorbachev of the Soviet Union, de Klerk was unaware of the extent of the change he initiated. In fact, de Klerk liked to compare himself with Gorbachev.

3. For a detailed discussion of this concept, see Dickson A. Mungazi, *The Mind of Black Africa* (Westport, CT: Greenwood Press, 1996), p. 210.

4. *New York Times*, February 16, 1989.

5. Ibid.

6. PBS, "Not in a Thousand Years: From Rhodesia to Zimbabwe," a documentary film, 1981. The remarks were made in answer to a question asked by a reporter during a tour of the prison.

7. F. W. de Klerk, address to Parliament, March 23, 1990, Cape Town, Government Printer, 1990, p. 14.

8. F. W. de Klerk, address to Parliament, February 2, 1990.

9. De Klerk, "The Birth of the New South Africa," p. 16.

10. F. W. de Klerk, address to Parliament, February 2, 1990.

11. Ibid., p. 29.

12. Ibid., p. 30.

13. The experience in Zimbabwe seems to offer de Klerk some lessons that he

appears to have utilized in making his initiative. Following the end of the RF, the international community felt obligated to remove the economic sanctions that had been imposed in 1966. In 1980 Zimbabwe experienced unprecedented levels of economic development. De Klerk hoped that the post-apartheid South Africa would experience the same economic growth.

14. De Klerk, address to Parliament, p. 31.

15. *Baltimore Sun*, September 26, 1990.

16. Mongosuthu Buthelezi, response to de Klerk's proposals, February 2, 1990.

17. Ibid.

18. Ibid.

19. The ANC in a statement in *This Week in South Africa*, Los Angeles: South African Consulate General, February 3, 1990.

20. Ibid.

21. Ibid.

22. Ibid.

23. *The Citizen*, an editorial, February 3, 1990.

24. *The Sowetan*, an editorial, February 3, 1990.

25. *San Francisco Chronicle*, February 3, 1990.

26. *Los Angeles Times*, February 3, 1990.

27. *Baltimore Sun*, February 3, 1990.

28. *Chicago Tribune*, February 3, 1990.

29. George Bush, reaction to F. W. de Klerk's proposals, February 3, 1990.

30. F. W. de Klerk, address to Parliament, February 2, 1990.

31. F. W. de Klerk, address to Provincial Congress of the Nationalist Party, the Orange Free State, September 5, 1990.

32. *Washington Post*, February 7, 1991.

33. Richard Boucher, "Response to ANC Conditions and Phases of Negotiations with the South African Government," *Christian Science Monitor*, August 21, 1990.

34. Roelf Botha, response to Boucher, *Christian Science Monitor*, August 21, 1990.

35. F. W. de Klerk, Address to Parliament, February 2, 1990.

36. Mandela was born on July 18, 1918. This means that when he made the statement on February 11, 1990, he was 72 years old. For details of this fascinating man, see his autobiography, *Long Walk to Freedom: The Autobiography of Nelson Mandela* (Boston: Little, Brown, and Company, 1994).

37. Nelson Mandela, address to the people who came to greet him on his release from prison on February 11, 1990.

38. Ibid.

39. Nationalist Party and the ANC, in a communiqué issued at the end of the first session of negotiations between the Nationalist government and the ANC, May 4, 1990.

40. Steve Biko was the leader of the Black Consciousness movement who was murdered in 1977 by the South African police.

41. Ibid., p. 39.

42. Alan Pizzey, reporting for CBS from Johannesburg, March 13, 1992.

43. Alan Pizzey, "South Africa: Day of Decision," March 18, 1992.

44. Ibid.

45. Bruce W. Nolan, "South Africa Says Yes," *Time*, March 30, 1992, p. 34.

46. Allister Sparks, South African journalist, during an interview with Ted Koppel, on ABC's *Nightline*, March 18, 1992.

47. Ibid.

48. Ibid.

49. ABC–TV, "South Africa," during *The Evening News*, April 11, 1992.

50. Ibid.

51. Ibid.

52. Alan Pizzey, reporting from South Africa for the CBS–TV News Service, June 28, 1992.

53. *Time*, July 6, 1992, p. 19.

54. *Time*, September 21, 1992, p. 16.

55. *New York Times*, December 12, 1980, p. 11.

56. *Time*, February 21, 1994, p. 35.

57. Nelson Mandela, address to South Africa, May 2, 1994, following the ANC's victory in the elections held April 26–28, 1994, as reported by CNN.

58. Ibid.

59. Nelson Mandela, inaugural address, Cape Town, May 9, 1994.

60. Judith Matloff, "In South Africa, To Forgive is To Find Out," in *Christian Science Monitor*, January 30, 1997, p. 1.

61. Dickson A. Mungazi, Letter to Desmond Tutu, Chair, Truth and Reconciliation Commission, Pretoria, February 20, 1997.

62. The defense of following orders advanced by those accused of crimes against humanity is a familiar one. It was used by the Nazi defendants at the Nuremberg trials from 1945 to 1949, but to no avail.

63. South Africa Broadcasting Corporation, "Parliamentary Debate on Truth and Reconciliation Commission," May 18, 1997.

64. A letter to Bishop Desmond Tutu regarding debate in the South African Parliament on Truth and Reconciliation Commission, June 9, 1997. Francis Meli in his study, *South Africa Belongs to Us: A History of the ANC* (Harare: Zimbabwe Publishing House, 1988, p. 177), lists names of seventy-six Africans who died while in political detention in South Africa from 1963 to 1985. Certainly the causes of these deaths need investigation if South Africa hopes to put the past behind it.

# 8

# De Klerk and Smith as the Last Defenders of the Laager: Summary, Conclusion, and Implications

Mental emancipation is both the instrument and modality of political and economic emancipation and cannot be taken for granted.
Robert Mugabe, July 19, 1983

Our resort to the armed struggle in 1960 was merely a defensive action against the violence of apartheid.
Nelson Mandela, February 11, 1990

## DE KLERK AND SMITH IN PERSPECTIVE

This book is based upon similarities and differences that characterized the political behavior of Ian D. Smith of Zimbabwe and Frederik W. de Klerk of South Africa. That these two men were the last colonial political leaders of their respective countries presents an opportunity to compare their political behavior. Among the differences that have been presented is the fact that Smith focused his political behavior on developing an educational policy for Africans. He designed this strategy for a very important reason. Smith saw education as a principal factor that would determine how Africans would ensure their political development. He believed that the political development of Africans would adversely effect the political power of whites.

De Klerk based his political behavior on his response to the nature of politics in South Africa, especially as it was defined by the Nationalist Party, which had been in power since the elections of 1948. He knew that the enactment of the Bantu Education Act in 1953 became the cornerstone of the system of apartheid, the fortification of the laager. Therefore, while there are differences between Smith and de Klerk's approach to politics in their respective countries, they shared a common belief in the role of education in determining the character of national politics as a definite strategy to shape the character of society. The institutionalization of the political process became their ultimate defense of the laager.

The announcement that de Klerk made on February 2, 1990, in the South African Parliament that Nelson Mandela, after spending twenty-seven years in prison, would soon be released unconditionally and that the ANC and other political parties would be legalized again caught everyone by surprise. Was de Klerk abandoning the laager? When Mandela's actual release occurred on February 11, there was a belief that the answer was "yes" because de Klerk would not continue to defend without losing the struggle. What Mandela said in Cape Town soon after his release underscores the importance of what this book has attempted to present, that is: fundamental political change becomes a necessary condition for the advancement of Africans. De Klerk recognized that this was a better strategy to defend the laager. When political change is directed toward improving the conditions governing human life, it then serves the purpose for which it was intended, serving the needs of all people. Once this happened, Africans would no longer feel that the laager posed real danger to their lives because it had stopped having the significance that it once had. For all practical purposes, the laager had ceased to exist.

With direct reference to the destructive influence of apartheid, Mandela spoke to the thousands who came to welcome him saying that he stood before them, not as a prophet, but as their humble servant. He appreciated the fact that the efforts they had made resulted in his release. These efforts, and the release itself, constituted a combination of activities that became an act of bringing the laager down. Mandela concluded, "Our resort to the armed struggle in 1960 was merely a defensive action against the violence of apartheid. Our armed struggle still exists today. We have no option but to continue. We call on our white compatriots to join us in the process of eradicating apartheid."[1] This was an act of bringing down the laager.

An examination of the application of apartheid evinces the determination of Africans to end it in all its forms. Not only was there complete racial segregation, but the Nationalist government, even under F. W. de Klerk, also believed that white students must be educated to fill positions of political dominance. As minister of education under Pieter W. Botha, de Klerk formulated educational policy that was intended to maintain this position, which is why he entered politics for the first time, winning a seat in Parliament in 1972. When Botha appointed him minister of education in 1978, de Klerk began to apply his political philosophy to the development of his educational policy that became an instrument of defending the laager at critical point in the history of South Africa. As a result, in 1984, for example, the government spent ten times as much on white education as it did on African education.[2] In the same year, student-teacher ratio was 24:1 for whites and 47:1 for Africans. In 1979, only 5,000 Africans were enrolled in institutions of higher education out of a total population of 22 million compared to 11,825 white students out of a total population of 4.3 million.[3] There is no question that the result of this policy was to limit the political development of Africans. This became an effective weapon, with Afrikaners successfully defending the laager. But it was to be short-lived.

In deciding to release Nelson Mandela, de Klerk must have fully recognized that it was time for change, time to abandon the defense of the laager, and that apartheid would be maintained at the peril of escalating a devastating national conflict and isolation from the international community. Neither the international community nor the Africans of South Africa could accept the continuing violence of apartheid any longer. Speaking in Soweto at a reception held in his honor on February 12, 1990, Mandela expressed the determination of Africans to end apartheid. With special reference to education as an important factor of the political development of Africans, Mandela warned, "The educational crisis in our country is a crisis in politics. Education under apartheid is a crime against humanity."[4]

The chief weapon of defending the laager had to be eliminated. A conclusion has been reached in this book that the problems of national development in all of southern Africa could not be resolved until solutions to the problems of educational development could be found. This is the reality and the perspective that a prominent educator in Zimbabwe had in mind when he concluded, "The thrust for national development in southern Africa cannot be undertaken without meeting the challenge of educational development. Educational development is the foundation upon which national developmental programs are built."[5] If Africans knew this, it is quite obvious that the defenders of the laager also knew it. Their tactical decision to abandon it would indicate a change in the conditions and circumstances of that defense. On the part of the defenders of the laager, change did not imply abandonment, it simply meant a change in method.

## DE KLERK'S ROLE IN THE PROBLEMS OF SOUTHERN AFRICA

The release of Nelson Mandela must also be seen in the context of the fundamental political change that had been taking place in southern Africa as a whole. Under de Klerk, South Africa was actively involved in the brutal civil wars in Angola and Mozambique. The instability that came out of this involvement gave de Klerk temporary power to control southern Africa as a region. In the same way, the opposition activities brought about by dissident elements in Zimbabwe following independence in 1980 also gave him additional power to influence developments in southern Africa. Before and after the Nkomati Accord, South Africa's periodic raids into neighboring countries in military pursuit of ANC guerrillas created conditions that destabilized the region and placed it at a crossroads. Also, South Africa's efforts to weaken SADCC, so that the black countries in southern Africa would continue to depend on it for economic survival, caused enormous difficulties for the region as a whole. From the futility of these activities as a form of defending the laager, de Klerk knew that the time had come to abandon it. Strategies that had yielded political benefits now reinforced the the determination of Africans to storm the laager.

From 1987 to 1989, the apartheid government was pressured to accept the U.N.'s terms contained in Resolution 435 of 1978 for the independence of Namibia, which was achieved finally on March 21, 1990. This event, more than any other, proved to de Klerk that his government, by its own action, was escalating conflict between South Africa and the international community. He had to take a hard look at the application of apartheid. The fact of the matter is that de Klerk could not come to terms with Africans in South Africa without persuading Afrikaners to come to terms with their neighbors. But South Africa would not come to terms with its neighbors without coming to terms with the ANC's cessation of its destabilizing activity in the region.

The increase in sales of firearms by 60 percent among whites in April 1990 is a development that did nothing to resolve the problems caused by the application of apartheid. De Klerk's conscious decision to stop military aid to Afonzo Dhlamini's Renamo in Mozambique and to Jonas Savimbi's Unita in Angola appears to have constituted a set of elements essential for regional peace. Above all, de Klerk and his government were less than successful in persuading their fellow Afrikaners to accept the reality that it was in their own best interest to accept, without further delay, the principle of majority rule under the universal practice of one person, one vote. The application of this principle in the elections of April 1994 constituted a final attack of the laager.

This is the view that the author expressed when he wrote a letter to de Klerk on February 15, 1990, saying,

It is very important for you to lift the state of emergency in order to allow Africans to place their confidence in your sincerity to negotiate in good faith. To try to negotiate with them under the influence of the state of emergency is to try to have them function with their hands tied on their back. It is vitally important for the whites of South Africa to recognize that the principle of majority rule must prevail. History shows that whenever a minority rules over the majority, abuse of power and oppression become inevitable. The support that South Africa has been giving to Jonas Savimbi in Angola and Afonzo Dhlamini in Mozambique has also created a violent situation in all of southern Africa. Regional peace is important for South Africa itself and its action to stop periodic raids into frontline states can go a long way in resolving major problems of the region."[6]

The psychology that had been operative in the defense of the laager had to change if Afrikaners hoped to have a meaningful future in postapartheid South Africa.

The massive demonstrations that were staged throughout South Africa on February 17, 1990—the first time that political demonstrations were allowed and in which thousands of Africans participated—demanded fundamental political change to accommodate the aspirations of all people. That the demonstrators demanded equal political rights, better housing, better salary, better work conditions, and an end to apartheid in education underscores the need for change in South Africa. The refusal of the government to recognize the importance of extending these basic human rights is what placed the country and the region at the crossroads. The simple fact is that Africans were not allowed to vote in national elections until April 1994. They could not hold public office outside the Bantustan Homelands. This was the basis of their legitimate demand for the immediate end to apartheid.

In 1963 Kwame Nkrumah (1909–1972),[7] the powerful and influential president of Ghana from 1957 to 1968 and whose influence was profoundly felt throughout Africa, predicted that no matter how much the designers of apartheid wanted it to continue, the policy was destined to fail because it was offensive to human values and justice. Nkrumah concluded, "History has shown that if we look below the surface it can be shown that the position of the South African government is fundamentally weak. There has been significant repudiation of the regime by a section of the intellectual class, significant in the context of the South African situation, where even the slightest liberalism in race relations brings down the wrath of the government. It is the cloud the size of a man's hand seen by the Prophet Elijah, the inevitable approach of the storm."[8]

Nkrumah's prediction seems to show why there were massive demonstrations in Washington, D.C., on that same day, February 17, 1990. It was not surprising that the demonstrators demanded President George Bush ensure that the United States would not lift economic sanctions against South Africa until apartheid had been dismantled and a nonracial society had been created. The demonstrators also demanded that President Bush withdraw his invitation to de Klerk to visit the White House for discussions, suggesting the conclusion that Americans understood the imperative need for fundamental change before South Africa was readmitted into the circle of the international community.

## COLONIAL CONDITIONS AND THE WIND OF CHANGE

The decade between 1970 and 1980 witnessed a spiraling demand for more and better education in southern Africa than at any other period in the history of the continent. However, in the decade between 1980 and 1990, the emergence of new attitudes toward political development as a prerequisite of social and economic development emerged. During the decade between 1960 and 1970, the African nations were still struggling to shake off the effects of European colonial rule as they attempted to carve for themselves a new national identity. But they quickly realized that the thrust for political development could not be undertaken without the thrust for educational development.

There is no question that the problems of African nations can be traced to the establishment of the colonial governments in the nineteenth century. As an outcome of the Berlin Conference of 1885, European nations placed more importance on securing raw materials than on the development of Africans to create better human relationships for the future to suit the social conditions in a new era. For this reason the colonial governments considered it essential to limit educational opportunity for Africans so that they could be more effectively controlled politically by training them to function as laborers.

This situation suggests that Africans could not achieve educational success during the colonial period to accomplish corresponding political, social, and economic development. The unrepresentative character of the colonial society, such as existed in South Africa and Zimbabwe when de Klerk and Smith were in office, did not permit Africans to play a significant role in their operations and functions until the end of the colonial systems. In 1963, William H. Lewis put Africans' struggle for meaningful political change in the context of the conditions created by the colonial systems, saying, "This is a time of testing in Africa. The old signposts are being torn down. The hallmarks of colonialism are disappearing. In the crucible of social and political change new human formations are beginning to take shape. In some respects this is a supremacy of an important transitional period, one signifying the end of innocence. Now, in the throes of national building and modernization, Africa is fashioning new values, identities and orientation."[9] Both de Klerk and Smith were later caught in the drama of this change of perception among Africans.

Apart from the cultural, political, and social consequences resulting from the policies pursued by colonial governments in southern Africa, there have been serious economic consequences which have had an enormous impact on the efforts of emerging nations in the region to make changes to ensure development. Because the most important reason European nations embarked on a colonial adventure in Africa was an economic one, it would be unrealistic to think that, after years of pursuing economic policies placing Africans at a disadvantage, the effect would suddenly disappear at the time African countries achieved political independence.[10] It is this reality that nations of southern Africa must take into consideration in their effort to improve their quality of life and to ensure national development.

A conclusion has also been reached in this book that political development and educational development are closely related. There is a belief among some leaders of southern African nations that their economic problems originated from the system of monopoly which, in essence, meant that the colonial governments controlled major aspects of the economy. These leaders, therefore, wrongly conclude that the nationalization of major industries is the answer to all their economic problems. They are not able to see all the adverse effects of nationalization—corruption by government officials themselves, rampant inflation, decline of the currency, stagnation in economic productivity, and a lack of incentives—which might arise. These are the problems that the African leaders are unable to solve in order to invest in education so that the standard of living of their people might improve. These are the realities that require change in the political process.

In 1960, Harold Macmillan (1894–1986), the British prime minister from 1957 to 1963, put the imperative of fundamental political change in Africa in the context of the influence of events that had global implications. Speaking to the joint session of the South African Parliament in Cape Town, Macmillan warned the colonial governments of the consequences of refusing to accept this kind of change saying,

In the twentieth century, especially since the end of the war in 1945, the process which gave birth to the nation states of Europe have been replicated all over the world. We have seen the awakening of national consciousness among people who for centuries lived in dependence upon some other power. The wind of change is blowing through the continent of Africa. Whether we like it or not, this growth of national consciousness is a political fact. We must accept it as a fact, and our national policies must take account of it. Its causes are to be found in the pushing forward of the frontiers of knowledge in the service of human needs and in the spread of education."[11]

De Klerk and Smith believed that they had what it would take to defy the gravity of history that Macmillan so eloquently described. But events proved both of them wrong.

The importance of Macmillan's speech lay, not in the results that he predicted would ensue from Africans' response to the colonial establishments, but in awakening a new level of consciousness among Africans that this was a period of change. They regarded the speech as an invitation to mobilize all their mental and intellectual resources to respond to a popular call to initiate the process for fundamental political change. For Africans of 1960, the call for this change signaled the beginning of a new era in their perception of themselves as a people with a destiny and in shaping new directions to the kind of future they had wanted and hoped for since 1945. They also regarded the colonial rule and all that it represented as something that must have no part in influencing that future. By the time de Klerk and Smith were most powerful, Africans were in no compromising mood. This spelled conflict in the near future.

The rapid pace of events that were taking place in South Africa and Zimbabwe from 1994 to 1996 must be seen in the context of developments that were taking place in all of southern Africa. An editorial in *The Journal of Social Change and Development* echoed Macmillan's concept of the wind of change in discussing the nature of political change that was taking place in the region. The journal states:

The years 1994 and 1995 will go down in the annals of the history of southern Africa as the years that saw the end of the overt dictatorships, white minority rule and the demise of *de jure* one party states. The doors of apartheid South Africa were closed in April 1994 to usher in majority rule under President Nelson Mandela. The same year also saw the end of the thirty years of dictatorial reign of Kamuzu Hastings Banda in Malawi. Mozambique under President Yoaquim Chissano is on the road to recovery. In Zimbabwe the April 1995 general elections were a non-event. The most notable event was voter apathy. Millions of Tanzanians went to the first multi-party elections in decades during the first quarter of 1995.[12]

Indeed, these are encouraging signs for a troubled region. But the continuing tragedy in Zaire has remained the curse and the scourge of the region as a whole. As of March 1997, the civil war there had caused enough concern for the U.S. government to consider sending a military unit to rescue Americans who were likely to be caught in the struggle. Over the past thirty years of his dictatorial rule, Mobutu Sese Seko has failed to recognize the fact that he brought more suffering to the people of Zaire than the colonial government, including that of Leopold II from 1885 to 1908. Peter Graffi and Marguerite Michaels have described Moboto's reign of terror saying:

Mobutu rose to head Zaire's army upon independence in 1960, then seized power five years later. In the decades since he has kept his balance by continually shunting friends and enemies in and out of favor. He has been known to have a man arrested and tortured before awarding him a prestigious and lucrative cabinet post. Over the years Mobutu has also devoted considerable energy to enriching his own coffers, dipping into the national treasury as it it were a kind of personal cash machine.[13]

Graffi and Michaels go on to say that Mobutu has used national resources to buy homes, ranches, and other forms of personal property in France, Belgium, Spain, Monte Carlo, and Portugal. Mobutu is one of the richest men in the world while Zairians have become among the poorest in all of Africa. This is why Laurent Kabila has been leading a guerilla warfare against Mobutu saying, "Mobutu must relinquish power. That is our condition for a cease-fire."[14]

## THE THRUST FOR DEVELOPMENT
## AFTER DE KLERK AND SMITH

The naming of the Truth and Reconciliation Commission in South Africa to investigate abuse of power by the Nationalist Party was an effort to view all relevant aspects of the past in order to plan the future. Part of this endeavor came from de Klerk himself, when, during a Parliamentary debate in Cape Town, broadcast on May 18, 1997, he admitted, "Apartheid was wrong. I apologize in capacity as leader of the Nationalist Party to the millions of South Africans who suffered from removal from their land, businesses, and homes, who over decades suffered the indignities and humiliation of racial discrimination, who were prevented from exercising their full democratic rights in the land of their birth, who were unable to reach their full potential because of job reservation. Let me state clearly that the Nationalist Party and I accept full responsibility for all our policies, decisions, and actions."[15]

If Ian D. Smith had accepted responsibility for the extremely oppressive nature of the policies of his government, and had apologized in the manner that de Klerk did, a better climate of reconciliation would have prevailed in Zimbabwe for the benefit of all. Instead Smith stormed out of the Lancaster House conference and called the proceedings madness. In their struggle for self, the Africans of South Africa and Zimbabwe recognized the importance of shaping policies to ensure their development based on their knowledge of the abuses of the past. The major assumption of their new struggle is that national political independence was a necessary condition for development. This strategy had the important feature of taking the increased political consciousness into consideration. It was quite obvious to Africans that no economic development could take place to benefit the people in countries that were still under colonial rule. They based their new endeavor on the knowledge that political institutions must be transformed to serve the needs of the people and to strengthen national institutions.

But, in order to ensure an effective political development to suit the needs of the emerging nations, Africans also recognized that fundamental change had to be initiated in important features of education itself, such as organization, administration, and planning. In most countries of southern Africa, change in the administration of education has not kept pace with rapidly moving events. The growth of school population, increase in spending for education, and planning for the future are all aspects of the administration of education that must be taken into account to ensure innovation.[16] It is important to remember that seeking to improve the administration of education does not mean increased bureaucracy. It is equally true to say that no country in southern Africa has sufficient financial resources to do all the things that need to be done to improve education.

In seeking to improve the administrative component of the thrust for educational development as a condition of political development, nations of southern Africa must be aware of the need to ensure careful financial planning to avoid duplication and waste. To ensure an effective system of administration of education, nations of southern Africa need to observe three basic operational principles. The first principle is that participation and consultation at all levels must form the thrust for change. This will help determine how the schools will be run, the courses offered and the general conduct of the school personnel. There must be consultation in the formulation and the implementation of policy in all its dimensions to ensure that the people are involved in their own educational development. Unless those responsible for the thrust for educational innovation take this principle into account, their efforts may yield limited results.

The second operational principle is to regard education as a unified system which, while intended to serve the needs of local students and suit local conditions, must embrace the thrust for national development as its principal objective. This involves taking national problems into account, which, when properly addressed by the educational process, will give breadth and new meaning to national purpose. A unified system will necessitate coordination of all school activity, formal and informal, academic and vocational. This approach to a unified system will enable those undertaking educational innovation to set educational objectives that are consistent with larger national goals. It will also enable those in positions of responsibility to define arrangements to fulfill those objectives and to ensure proper progression.

The third operational principle is that nations of southern Africa must endeavor to improve education "in terms of both the learning outcomes and the efficiency with which they use resources."[17] To establish this objective, professional efficiency is needed in managing the course of improvement in order to realize the relationship that must exist between investment, planning, and educational outcomes. The utilization of specialists in various segments of education, such as financial outlay, must not be delegated to individuals who have had no professional training and experience because educational development is far too important to be undertaken by amateurs. It must be emphasized that in observing these principles, nations of southern Africa must realize that they entail the practice of democracy in that those who are a part of the process in its development are intimately affected by a national program and must be part of its formulation and implementation. The signing of the new constitution at Sharpeville[18] by Nelson Mandela on December 10, 1996, symbolized the beginning of a new era of hope and national endeavor in South Africa just as in Zimbabwe in April 1980. This act became the final act of storming the laager.

In embracing these essential elements of democracy in an endeavor toward educational development, nations of southern Africa must constantly remain aware that throughout human history, "it is actually the people who have constituted a dynamic motivational force behind cultural, social and economic development,"[19] as a result of educational development. This suggests that the development of the people must become both the focus of educational process and the major means of achieving it. Any national policy that does not take both into account is void of any real political and economic meaning. This also suggests that the people must be educated in such a manner that makes them adequately prepared to utilize the educational opportunity that results from effective programs.

It has also been stated that the social, economic, and political transformation of southern Africa must seek to reduce the enormous differences that exist between rural areas and urban areas. Throughout the region, people fall into two groups: the rural people, most of whom are engaged in subsistence agriculture, and the people who reside in urban areas. In 1982 about 80 percent of the population in Zimbabwe was rural. This means that without viable means of economic activity, the development of rural areas was haphazard at best. With 80 percent of the population denied a viable means of economic development, Zimbabwe was forced to have a false sense of progress. When national resources are directed toward the development of 20 percent of the population in urban areas,[20] the countries of southern Africa cannot prosper with this serious imbalance between urban conditions and rural conditions. The political dynamics of a nation are cast in this kind of environment.

As part of a developmental strategy, the nations of southern Africa need to understand that the advancement of their interests and talents must entail mobilizing natural resources to finance educational innovation. Because this cannot be done where the educational process is weak, objectives are poorly stated, and plans inadequately outlined, the governments must provide an adequate institutional encouragement that is essential for the establishment of national organizations in which popular participation is open to all. This collective action enables participants to identify areas of focus to ensure innovation. This would make it possible to create new socioeconomic structures in which people can utilize national resources and harness new deposits of energy for the benefit of all. Educational innovation, to serve its proper purpose, must be initiated in the context of these realities.

As a product of socioeconomic growth, educational development must at all times be anchored on principles relative to the ultimate aspirations of the people in an environment of established democratic values, "set in a dynamic framework of a developing economy,"[21] and cast in a setting of free trade with minimum government control. This provides motivation and incentives for the flow of capital needed for investment to diversify industry. The exploitation of national resources, however, must be undertaken in the context of national commitment to preserve the environment and a fair system of distribution of resources. Legislation must be passed, such as Zimbabwe did in 1985, to make corruption a criminal offense. Free trade and private enterprise also enhance the flow of capital where there is no abuse. It is here where the government can play a critical role.

## NEW POLITICAL APPROACH TO NATIONAL DEVELOPMENT

From the first election campaign that followed the successful conclusion of the Lancaster House Conference held in London in December 1979, a clear indication can be noted of the type of educational process that would take place in independent Zimbabwe. The Lancaster House Conference officially turned over the reigns of government from the RF to the Africans even though Ian D. Smith boycotted it feeling that it betrayed the white man in Zimbabwe. In March 1980 the Zimbabwe African National Union-Patriotic Front (ZANU–PF), one of the three major political parties that contested the elections, published its *Election Manifesto* in which it outlined its educational plans for Zimbabwe.

That ZANU–PF was the only party to do so underscored the importance of the role that it was destined to play in both the political and the educational process in Zimbabwe. The ZANU–PF emphasized the importance of educational innovation right at the beginning of a new era in the politics of the nation which demonstrates the essential nature of the task that lay ahead and the importance of the new educational programs that it felt must be initiated in order to eliminate the effects of ninety years of colonial rule. While this was no small task, ZANU–PF seemed ready to accept the challenge.

A close study of the essential planks of that election platform shows exactly the kind of changes that ZANU–PF would introduce in the educational system if it was returned to power. Let us briefly examine these. A ZANU–PF government would introduce a uniform educational system to immediately abolish the distinction between African education and white education, forming a single system for all students. In essence, ZANU–PF was saying that racial discrimination in the educational process, a cornerstone of the RF's educational policy, would end as soon as it took office. A ZANU–PF government would also introduce a system of education that would meet the needs of the individual students and, at the same time, fulfill the developmental objectives of the nation. This kind of education would be intended to develop in the young generation a nonracial attitude, a common national identity, and loyalty based upon the fundamental freedoms of the individual.[22] The new system of education would be established so that free and compulsory primary and secondary education would be introduced in stages beginning with the primary sector. Discrimination based upon gender, a common but unintended practice in traditional culture in Africa, would also be eliminated because education was a basic right that belonged to all and because education would be intended to "become a major instrument for the development of society."[23]

To ensure that the mental processes were fully developed, a ZANU–PF government would introduce a new developmental program that would offer a supportive educational environment from preschool to university. The preschool education would be provided for children from three to five years of age. While this level of educational practice was designed to enable informal learning to take place, it would also help children at an early age to begin to develop their mental capacity as a critical requirement for future members of society. Under a ZANU–PF government, primary education would be built upon the foundation of the preschool program. It would emphasize self-development based on literary and psycho-motor abilities and would be designed to help the learner acquire capabilities needed to create a frame of mind comprehensive and broad enough to understand the importance of social issues, and to analyze them from the perspective of well-informed citizens.

A ZANU–PF government would build new secondary schools,[24] "upon the primary base and, while moving toward a comprehensive character, would sharpen the child's mental power and increase his aptitude."[25] What ZANU–PF seems to suggest here is that in trying to help students become critical human beings, education would seek to promote an indispensable quality of individuality, diverse in content and deep in perception. These are the elements that produce the truly liberated nation that ZANU–PF and Africans were seeking as a manifestation of their ability to eliminate the colonial legacy which had handicapped their development. Indeed, this was the ultimate development, the intellectual revolution that could give meaning to the social transformation of society.

A ZANU–PF government also recognized that, for the economy to improve, Zimbabwe required a strong force of skilled artisans and technicians. Therefore, a ZANU–PF government would remind the people that the RF had deliberately denied them an opportunity for this level of educational development and would ensure that both adequate facilities and opportunity would be provided for students who felt they could realize their potential and their personal educational ambitions in this way. Hence, technical and vocational education would be provided as an alternative method of realizing their individual freedom and so help in promoting national liberation. A ZANU–PF government would be committed to the training of young Zimbabweans as electricians, mechanics, aircraft technicians, printers, welders, builders, designers and other specialized technicians. A ZANU–PF government would "launch the Zimbabwe Institute of Technology which would offer courses at the university level."[26]

Along with these important aspects of educational innovation, a ZANU–PF government would also introduce a massive teacher training program in order to elevate the level of professional training and to improve the quality of teaching at all levels of education. A ZANU–PF government would seek to expand the university facilities and emphasize courses that would be necessary for national development. The fact that, at the time of independence, Zimbabwe had a literacy rate of only 30 percent would influence a ZANU–PF government's commitment to "run an all-embracing adult educational system beginning with literacy classes. This would be in keeping with our policy of fighting underdevelopment in order to develop the inherent talents of the people so as to enable all citizens to live a fuller life."[27] No doubt, ZANU–PF concluded that this is how individual freedom and national liberation are achieved. The two cannot be separated because one is an important condition of the other.

This election manifesto had a profound effect on the voters. It put ZANU–PF in the front-line of the election race and made it the favorite to win. It actually won the election with a landslide fifty-seven seats in a Parliament of a hundred members. Therefore, as soon as it took office on April 18, 1980, ZANU–PF kept the promise it had made during the campaign to initiate a fundamental educational innovation as it had specified in the manifesto. This new approach to educational innovation seems to show that political independence is an important condition for educational innovation.[28] But one must not conclude that the kind of educational innovation that Zimbabwe initiated after independence resulted in a golden age of education because, while possibilities for innovation were there, serious problems had also to be resolved.

When ZANU–PF took office on April 18, 1980, it knew that major changes had to be made in its educational system. The decisive victory that Africans scored in the battlefield against the RF forces now set the stage for a new and more challenging struggle for national development through educational innovation. Speaking on May 18, 1980, during the opening of the first session of the Zimbabwean Parliament, President Canaan Banana[29] outlined what his government planned to do to initiate a new educational system. Banana went on to say, among other things, that his government would spend $300 million on educational innovation in the 1981 fiscal year. Banana added, "In the field of education, it is the intention of my government to pursue vigorously the reopening of the many schools in the rural areas which were closed as a result of the war and to introduce free education on a phased basis beginning with the primary sector."[30] This means that universal free education would be introduced to Zimbabwe for the first time in its history. Clearly Banana and his fellow Zimbabweans knew that the white students had enjoyed free and compulsory primary education since 1935.

What Banana said about the need for fundamental educational innovation, in reality, confirmed of what Dzingai Mutumbuka, the Zimbabwean minister of education and culture, had said in London in December 1979 at the conclusion of the Lancaster House Conference. Mutumbuka clearly outlined the extent of educational innovation that he said would be necessary to restore Zimbabwe from the harmful effects of the colonial era. Suggesting that the struggle for political liberation from the RF political domination was an education in itself, Mutumbuka went on to add, "It is against this background that a new alternative system of education must be developed, designed to produce a new man, richer in the consciousness of humanity whereby life can become better for all."[31] Mutumbuka might also have added that for life to be meaningful, independent Zimbabwe must seek to eliminate the conditions that colonialism created and to restructure a new social environment that makes the kind of educational system he was talking about possible. He might also have added that because human action originates from ideas, human "consciousness of humanity" is therefore a product of an educated and truly liberated individual. National leaders must at all times take this reality into account in designing a national policy if future conflict is to be avoided.

## ADULT LITERACY CAMPAIGN:
## A SEARCH FOR INDIVIDUAL DEVELOPMENT

Mutumbuka's concept of "consciousness of humanity" was evident in the effort that the ZANU–PF government, of which he was a member, was making to transform the life of Zimbabweans as part of its commitment to individual self-fulfillment and national development. Zimbabwe fully realized that, unlike political liberation, the liberation of the mind of the individual is an absolute necessity if the negative effects of the colonizer's action are to be eliminated. This can only be done through functional literacy, which creates an environment for educational process in which the thrust for individual self-determination and national advancement go hand in hand. The RF educational system never perceived education this way but post–RF Zimbabwe felt compelled to make a new start in this direction. In realizing that functional literacy was essential for both individual self-fulfillment and national advancement, the ZANU–PF government was recognizing an important factor of Zimbabwe's developmental struggle. Without this level of education, a nation often suffers the painful pangs of underdevelopment. No matter what else it tries to do, its efforts are futile as long as the people remain illiterate. This fact was recognized by the prime minister himself, Robert Mugabe, whose government launched a national adult literacy campaign on July 18, 1983.

Mugabe fully acknowledged the fact that the campaign was not aimed merely at some illiterate adults, but at all adults outside the formal educational process. In emphasizing the value of the individual's mental liberation as an important condition of national development and freedom, Mugabe warned his countrymen that it would be impossible to achieve a new political and economic independence while the mental processes themselves are still oppressed by a lack of adequate education. Mugabe then added, "To set the mind free, to make observation and analysis accurate, to make judgment informed, objective and fair, and to make the imagination creative, are as important a cause of struggle as the struggle for political and economic emancipation. Mental emancipation is both the instrument and modality of political and economic emancipation and cannot be taken for granted."[32]

While Mugabe urged his fellow Zimbabweans to recognize the impossibility of ensuring their political and economic independence unless they were mentally emancipated, he recognized that such new innovations in perceiving national issues took longer to accomplish than they would like. This is why he also recognized that his call for universal adult literacy was a major task that demanded the allocation of major national resources in order to be achieved. Indeed, Mugabe was painfully aware that any national drive toward full emancipation would be futile as long as more than 70 percent of the population remained illiterate. With only 30 percent literacy[33] in 1983, it is clear that Zimbabwe had not developed its human potential as fast as it should have done, and Mugabe and his government had seen the negative effects of this underdevelopment. Although the literacy rate had slightly increased by 1983, still it was too low to allow a greater pace of national development. Poverty and illiteracy were more powerful deterrents of national advancement than the RF forces.

As a national leader, Mugabe also recognized that the inability of the citizens to develop their mental capacity perpetuates ignorance of the ideas that are expressed by others. The result of this is that the mentally oppressed are always exploited by conditions that they cannot control. Sooner or later, the conditions that oppress the individual will oppress the nation. Thus, Mugabe noted, "It was therefore not by accident that the white settler regimes of our colonial past denied the majority of the African people the opportunity of going to school."[34] Three questions arise to indicate the nature and the extent of the problem that Zimbabwe faced in this endeavor: Could Zimbabwe effect a 100 percent literacy in five years? What would it take? Did Zimbabwe have the resources necessary to attain this objective in such a short time? Experience in other Third World nations would suggest that this was not likely to be achieved within the time limits that Mugabe had projected.

There are two basic elements that formed the core of the new Zimbabwean thrust for universal adult literacy which must be understood. The first is that literacy would be the most visible evidence that the concept of equality in the educational process had indeed been realized, and that the government, unlike the RF before it, was fully committed to it. Adult literacy was the ultimate manifestation of the concept of self-fulfillment, which is an important prerequisite of national development. To make this happen, Zimbabweans must have recognized that an enlightened and truly liberated nation can only emerge from enlightened individuals. Many Africans have yet to come to grips with this reality. Without an enlightened citizenry, a nation will always be oppressed by a combination of forces such as social ills, racial bigotry, tribal conflict, and political dissension, all of which Zimbabwe experienced in its struggle for development.

This seems to suggest that, since illiteracy is a harmful legacy the recently colonized must spare no efforts to eliminate through educational innovation, individuals must see themselves in relationship to their society. Therefore, the second element is that the government of Zimbabwe, recognizing that education is a right that belongs to all, sought to direct its energies and resources to the full development of the human potential. This endeavor was undertaken in the full knowledge that, ultimately, the state will benefit from free and educated individuals. To emphasize this fact, Mugabe rhetorically asked, "How can a good farmer improve his farming if he cannot read instructions on the use of fertilizers? How can people themselves run their own factories and shops if they cannot count their money and write their budgets?"[35]

This fact was expressed eloquently by an African principal of a high school in Harare in 1983 when he said,

Every state stands to benefit more than anyone else from its educated citizens. All governments have therefore a stake or a major interest in the education of their people. The more the people get educated, the more they help to create a happy society. Progressive governments recognize that by educating their people they are actually creating conditions of social and political stability. This is so because education implants self-consciousness which is the basis of individual freedom and national liberation. Without individual freedom and self-determination, there is no national liberation. The interests of the government, both short-term and long-term, are invariably linked to the educational development and freedom of the people.[36]

To demonstrate its commitment to the kind of educational innovation that it had outlined during the election campaign, the ZANU–PF government established several agencies that were charged with the task of coordinating efforts to achieve universal literacy. The National Coordination Council (NCC) assumed the major responsibility of implementing national policy. The major function of NCC was to mobilize resources, monitor progress being made, and conduct periodic assessment of needs. But resources were so seriously limited that the various agencies did not quite know how best to fulfill their responsibilities.

President Banana aptly stated his belief that the educational policies of his government must seek to promote and facilitate "the growth of every Zimbabwean regardless of his status, sex, race, culture, or age."[37] Yet, these are among the cultural factors that have dictated differences in the way people are treated in Africa generally, and Zimbabwe has been a victim of them all. To eliminate this negative aspect of its quest for a new national identity through educational innovation, this legacy of the RF had first to be eliminated.

## CONCLUSION

From the preceding discussion, it would seem that the development of politics in South Africa and Zimbabwe after de Klerk and Smith took two essential aspects into consideration. The first consideration was the recognition of the vital importance of the individual, whom educational development must help in becoming aware of himself and his potential in a larger social order. Self-awareness implies engaging in those activities that seek to promote individual advancement as a foundation upon which to build national advancement. Self-awareness demands the availability of equal opportunity for all, without which, the individual cannot engage in self-fulfilling activity. This is the reality which Albert Memmi said enables the recently colonized in any country to assert themselves in relation to the definition of their needs.[38] This results in a political behavior that satisfies the individual and the nation.

The second aspect is that when the government recognized the importance of individual self-determination, it responded by formulating policies that facilitated individual effort. Memmi concluded that this effort would ultimately translate into national development.[39] The relationship that exists between the educational development of the individual and fulfilling other needs constitutes an article of faith in developing nations and has inspired the quest for a new society fully committed to a political, social, and economic development. This line of thinking is what Memmi takes into consideration when he concludes that for the recently colonized, "the important thing to do is to rebuild, to reform, to communicate, and to belong"[40] as a fulfillment of themselves. It is this definition of liberation, both political and mental, which gives birth to a new society, a true symbol and a manifestation of their search for a new social system.

There are other considerations that are important to note. Although Zimbabwe tried to become a one-party state in December, 1987, the people opposed it so strongly that is was not implemented. This author is of the opinion that the introduction of this form of government is an action that all nations of Africa must avoid at all costs. As a young nation struggling to find a path into the future, Zimbabwe must be cautious and fervent in avoiding a form of government that entails political characteristics of its colonial past. Checks and balances are an essential component of any nation that is struggling for advancement.

Without checks and balances, corruption and other irregularities by government officials go on uncorrected and citizens pay the ultimate price. In this regard Zimbabwe has experienced the agony of efforts to introduce a one-party form of government just as other countries of Africa have. The crisis related to the thinking of a one-party government began to unfold in July 1988. While President Robert Mugabe was on a mission on behalf of the Organization of African Unity (OAU) to find a peace formula which would end the brutal civil war in Mozambique, political events in his own country posed a potential for a major national crisis. In 1988, when Edgar Tekere, a leading member of the ruling ZANU–PF, resigned from the party in protest against the possibility of the introduction of a one-party system of government—a system that

Mugabe himself had indicated in 1980 he would prefer, a climate of new conflict was immediately created.

That Tekere was also protesting against what he saw to be widespread corruption among top government officials accentuated the climate of national conflict. In April 1989, when a commission of inquiry appointed by the government under the chairmanship of Justice Sandura uncovered wide-spread corruption by six senior government officials,[41] Zimbabwe moved closer to the most serious political crisis since it gained independence. The fact that this scandal had far deeper political implications than appeared on the surface suggests the critical nature of the crisis caused primarily by the desire to adopt a one-party system of government.

Realizing the political damage the scandal had inflicted on his ability to discharge his responsibility to the country as a senior government official, and as one of the six corrupt officials, Maurice Nyagumbo—veteran politician, a dedicated nationalist and a close associate of President Mugabe—took his own life to spare his family further embarrassment and national disgrace. Mugabe himself was deeply saddened by both the extent of the damage the scandal had done to the country and by the death of a man who had done so much for his people during the struggle for independence. But this national tragedy did not diminish the resolve of the people to resist the introduction of a one-party system of government. On the contrary, it intensified it.

This was not all. When, on August 4, 1989, minister of education and culture Dzingai Mutumbuka was fined $105,000 for his role in the corruption, events moved much closer to a major national crisis.[42] At that point, a new wave of political tension emerged from an unlikely place, the University of Zimbabwe itself. In August 1989, professors issued a statement criticizing the government for taking action that they said constituted a set of conditions that made "it impossible for the institution to discharge its proper constitutional responsibilities and functions as a university."[43]

The arrest and detention of law professor Kempton Makamure appeared to be a culmination of incidents the faculty members believed constituted harassment by the government in retaliation for their opposition to what was widely reported to be government corruption and degenerating political and economic conditions. That these developments were a sequel to the university student's demonstrations in September 1997 against reports of continued corruption by government officials suggests the critical nature of the crisis. When "the students called for academic freedom and their inalienable rights and demanded the university administration to lift its tacit ban on the student magazine, Focus,"[44] relations between the university and the government became

more seriously strained even though, by provisions of the national constitution, the national president is also the chancellor of the university.[45]

The conclusion that the national political climate in Zimbabwe was
deteriorating rapidly in 1989 is substantiated by a series of events that
took place in quick succession. Displeased with the efforts the government was making to restore the confidence of the public, students at the
university engaged in a variety of activities that the government concluded hovered on defiance of the law. On August 9, Joshua Nkomo,
senior government minister, and Faye Chung, minister of education and
culture,[46] went to the university in an effort to diffuse the situation. They
held a meeting with the students and tried to establish a climate of dialogue. In an impassioned and emotional appeal, Nkomo pleaded with
the students, saying, "We do not want a confrontation with our children.
We have gone gray because we have a heritage to protect, and that heritage is yourself. Therefore, dialogue must be started. You cannot solve
problems by shouting. Knowledge is not shouting. Some of your behavior is not Zimbabwean."[47]

When the 2,000 students responded by demanding that Nkomo make
assurances that the government would not turn the country into a one-
party state and that the Zimbabwe Unity Movement (ZUM), which had
been recently formed under the leadership of Edgar Tekere, be allowed
a platform to express its political views for the benefit of strengthening
democracy, Chung's patience ran out as she responded, "Senior Minister
Nkomo has been invited here not to be insulted. If this is what we call
our future leaders, then I must say that this university is full of rubbish,
and the government will not waste money on rubbish."[48] This exchange,
caused primarily by difference of opinion about the idea of a one-party
state, created a situation with a new potential for explosive outcome. By
1991, conditions at the university had deteriorated so badly that Walter
Kamba, the vice-chancellor, was forced to resign.

When the government refused to grant ZUM leaders permission to
hold political meetings at the university, the students were once more in
a restive mood. Fearing a general breakdown of law and order, the government temporarily closed the university for two weeks in October
1989. A few weeks later the government granted ZUM permission to
hold political meetings throughout the country, thus easing the political
tension that was disrupting national programs and sending a clear message that the government must abandon the idea of one-party state. For
a period of time in 1989, the entire country was held in suspense over
what the future held politically. The elections held on March 24, 1990,
show that the intent of the government to turn the country into a one-
party state was not shared by many people. Not only did seven political
parties contest the elections but also, throughout the country, various

forms of violence were reported related to the question of a one-party state.

In a statement issued on the day of the elections, the Catholic Church's Justice and Peace Commission criticized the government's intention to install a one-party system against the wishes of the people, saying, "The use of firearms against political opponents is a shocking development. The rising incidence of violence and intimidation is already calling into question the freeness and fairness of the elections."[49] Mugabe considered the elections so crucial that he did not find time to attend the independence celebration for Namibia on March 21. By June, the increasing demands on teachers combined with rapidly rising enrollments, inadequate salaries, and declining conditions of service forced teachers to go on strike threatening to derail the course of national development that Zimbabwe had charted at the inception of independence.

In 1992 Zimbabwe was facing serious problems in its development. The Zimbabwean dollar had declined to such a low level that, combined with the worst drought since 1896, the economy had been destroyed, putting thousands out of employment and posing serious political implications for the country. Christine Sylvester sums up the problems that Zimbabwe faces as it struggles for development: "Zimbabweans are experiencing pressures to assert and at times to invent cultural authenticity through ethnic identification, traditional religion, racial politics, and artistic themes. Ironically, this is an aspect of modernity's engulfment of difference by submerging it in a discourse of integration, unity, and commonality. Yet positions in between and marginal to old and new also struggle for space in Zimbabwe's inherited matrix of identities, as does a state that is itself multi-centered and cross-pressured."[50]

These were problems that Zimbabwe never anticipated in the aftermath of the collapse of the RF. But they were created by the government's wish to institute a one-party system, which often has a potential for abuse. Yes, President Mugabe and his government are extremely sensitive to the need to protect the rights of all people. But a future government may not be so sensitive and the precedent which might be established would not serve the needs of the country well. That Mandela has not encountered these problems is because he has not attempted to introduce a one-party system of government. Hopefully, he will not try to do so in the future.

To guard against the possibility of a new social malaise, nations of Africa in general must remember that in such political ideology as the one-party state or a president for life, new forms of colonialism may emerge to impose new conditions of oppression perhaps worse than those Africans endured under European colonial governments. This author rejects, unreservedly, the arguments advanced by many African national leaders that democracy is too costly and is divisive. On the contrary, the practice of democracy ensures that all people express their political views freely. In his study, *Tomorrow is Another Country: The Inside Story of South Africa's Road to Change*, Allister Sparks, the author of *The Mind of South Africa*,[51] and a South African, concludes that the transformation of South Africa from a minority rule to majority government represents "the dawn of a new millennium, a new country with new horizons and divisions. There will be enormous new challenges, too, but the democratic structures are there to resolve and grow through them. For the graffito says building a new nation is a continuous process. The construction never ends."[52] That is the ultimate manifestation of national liberation that the combination of education and democracy makes possible in any country.

## IMPLICATIONS

The discussion in this chapter and in this book suggests three implications about the relationship that exists between educational development and political development in South Africa and Zimbabwe. The first implication is that the primary intent of both is to ensure the development of the individual in a larger social context. Development of the individual means self-actualization. This includes self-sufficiency, security in one's personhood, and fulfillment of those goals that are unique to the individual. It means the promotion of one's interests consistent with one's talent. It means freedom to set goals and objectives and to establish priorities. It means the ability to generate an environment that gives one freedom of choice to pursue study programs of one's interests. It is only when one's educational needs have become fulfilled that one plays a role in helping one's society fulfill its needs.[53] This is how the elements of national development are put in place. The underlying principle in the relationship between these elements is that there must be successful educational innovation to make it possible. This suggests the conclusion that the end of the colonial laager has presented Africans with a new opportunity that they must utilize to ensure their development.

The second implication is that a truly politically independent nation can only arise from a truly independent population, which can only emerge from educated individuals. Many nations of Africa, including southern Africa, have yet to realize this truth. Without an educated population, nations will always be oppressed by a combination of forces such as social ills, racial bigotry, tribal or ethnic conflict, and political dissent—all of which southern Africa has experienced. The conclusion, therefore, is that educational innovation is in the best interest of the nations themselves. The important thing for South Africa and Zimbabwe to keep in mind is that educational development is an important condition of political development. The two cannot be separated. About this important principle in the relationship between the two, Paulo Freire concludes that the "ability to communicate ideas of self-consciousness"[54] forms an essential part of an education designed to ensure self-fulfillment as an important step toward creating an environment of national development. This means that cooperative efforts must constitute a viable channel to successful development.

The third implication is that the greatest threat to national development comes from the desire of some governments to institute one-party systems. The possibility of a one-party system has existed in Zimbabwe since 1980. Government leaders seem to neglect to recognize the fact that in Africa the philosophy of one-party government has shown evidence to prove that it robs the people of a genuine desire to promote ideas of individuality as a condition of national development and replaces their confidence for the future with an abyss of despair. What has been discussed about Zimbabwe substantiates the accuracy of this conclusion. In this kind of social and political setting, the educational process has only peripheral meaning because individual incentive and self-motivation, which are important characteristics of human achievement, are rendered meaningless by the government's desire to have its own philosophy and policy prevail at the expense of the goals of the individual. Since he assumed the office of president on May 9, 1994, Nelson Mandela has maintained the importance of a multiparty democracy. The difference between South Africa and Zimbabwe is the attitude of the people.

Therefore, the introduction of a one-party system of government is often an indication that the government has something either to hide from or to fear in its own people. Thus, the introduction of a one-party system of government cannot be considered a step in the direction of national development. After forty-five years in office, the Nationalist Party of South Africa has found this to be true the hard way. While the Nationalist Party ruled supreme for nearly half a century, both the educational process and human interactions suffered a severe setback. The sustenance of democracy is too important to be tampered with because the survival of any nation and the course of national development depend on it. No matter how government officials see it, the one-party system of government is nothing less than a form of dictatorship.

This is why, for example, massive demonstrations staged against the government of Kenneth Kaunda in Zambia led to an attempted military coup in June 1990. Since he took office in October 1964, Kaunda has not only instituted a one-party rule, he has also alienated Zambians by creating a political environment that has denied Zambians a role in the affairs of their country. That is exactly what Hastings Banda did in Malawi from 1964 to 1994. In 1994 both Kaunda and Banda were voted out of office as a result of being forced to accept the principle of free elections. Both men stood condemned by both their own people and the international community. They left office in disgrace, instead of as national heroes who tried to serve their respective countries.

In August 1989 a leading African educator in Zimbabwe, Edward Mazaiwana, expressed some views that are important to the development of African countries in general. He suggested that initiative for national development is undertaken by recognizing the interests of the people. Expansion in education is meaningless unless it is anchored in democratic principles. He added that problems of economic development, transportation, and population increase must be approached from the perspective of recognizing that whatever is done must be done in the interests of the people. This is how national development can take place.[55] National leaders of any country in Africa must reject defending the laager in the same way the colonial establishment did. South Africa and Zimbabwe, be well advised and be wise!

## NOTES

1. Nelson Mandela, in a statement made in Cape Town soon after his release from Victor Verster Prison, SABC, February 11, 1990.

2. United Nations, *A Crime against Humanity: Questions and Answers on Apartheid in South Africa* (New York, 1984), p. 16.

3. Ibid., p. 17.

4. Nelson Mandela, speaking in Soweto during a reception held in his honor, February 12, 1990, SABC.

5. An African educator in Zimbabwe, during an interview with Dickson A. Mungazi, August 10, 1989.

6. Dickson A. Mungazi, in a letter to F. W. de Klerk, February 15, 1990. On March 12, 1990, S. P. Basson, de Klerk's administrative secretary, wrote to "acknowledge receipt of your letter."

7. For a detailed discussion of Nkrumah's role in the decolonization of Africa, see, for example, Dickson A. Mungazi, *The Mind of Black Africa* (Westport, CT: Praeger, 1996).

8. Kwame Nkrumah, *Africa Must Unite* (London: Panof Publications, 1963), p. 14.

9. William H. Lewis, *Emerging Africa* (Washington, DC: Public Affairs Press, 1963), p. 5.

10. Ibid., p. 7.

11. Harold Macmillan, "Commonwealth Independence and Interdependence," a speech given to the Joint Session of the South African Parliament, Cape Town, February 3, 1960. By courtesy of the British Embassy, Harare, Zimbabwe.

12. "A Wave of Democratic Elections Sweeps the Sub-continent of Southern Africa," *The Journal of Social Change and Development*, an editorial. Harare, Zimbabwe, No. 38/39, January 1996, p. 1.

13. *Time*, March 24, 1997, p. 58.

14. Ibid., p. 57.

15. F. W. de Klerk, during a parliamentary debate on the Truth and Recon-

ciliation Commission, in Cape Town. South African Broadcasting Services, May 18, 1997.

16. Botswana, *Report of the National Commission on Education* (Gaberone, April, 1977), p. 185.

17. Ibid., p. 186.

18. Sharpeville, a short distance south of Johannesburg, is where seventy Africans were massacred by the police on March 21, 1960, for protesting against apartheid. The signing of the new constitution there stressed the importance of the massacre as a critical historical event and the promise of the future.

19. Zimbabwe, *Transitional National Development Plan*, Vol. 1, 1982, p. 18.

20. Ibid., p. 19.

21. Ibid., p. 20.

22. ZANU–PF, "Election Manifesto," March 1980. Courtesy Zimbabwe National Archives.

23. Ibid.

24. See discussion later in this chapter.

25. ZANU–PF, "Election Manifesto," March 1980. Courtesy Zimbabwe National Archives.

26. Ibid.

27. Ibid.

28. Albert Memmi, *The Colonizer and the Colonized* (Boston: Beacon Press, 1965), p. 138.

29. Banana served as president from 1980 to 1987, when the office of prime minister, which Robert Mugabe held, was eliminated and when Mugabe assumed the office of executive president.

30. Zimbabwe, Government Policy Statement Number 5: A Presidential Directive, May 18, 1980. Courtesy Zimbabwe National Archives.

31. Dzingai Mutumbuka was Minister of Education and Culture, Zimbabwe, 1980–1989. Mutumbuka resigned from the government in July 1989, following his trial and conviction in the national scandal. Dzingai Mutumbuka, "Zimbabwe's Educational Challenge," paper presented at the World University Services Conference, London, December 1979. Courtesy Zimbabwe National Archives.

32. Robert Mugabe, "Literacy for All in Five Years," speech given in launching the National Adult Literacy Campaign, July 18, 1983. Courtesy Zimbabwe National Archives.

33. World Almanac and Book of Facts, 1983. Mugabe himself claimed that the literacy rate in Zimbabwe was 60 percent in 1983.

34. Robert Mugabe, "Literacy for All in Five Years," July 18, 1983.

35. Ibid.

36. A high school principal, during an interview with the author, in Harare, Zimbabwe, August 8, 1983.

37. Canaan Banana, *Theology of Promise: The Dynamics of Self-Reliance* (Harare: The College Press, 1982), p. 59.

38. Memmi, *The Colonizer and the Colonized*, p. 138.

39. Ibid., p. 139.

40. Ibid., p. 135.

41. For the names of these officials and the extent of their involvement in the scandal, see *Herald*, April 13, 1989.

42. Zimbabwe, *Herald*, August 4, 1989.

43. Zimbabwe, *Parade News Magazine*, August 1989, p. 44.

44. Ibid.

45. See Dickson A. Mungazi, *Colonial Policy and Conflict in Zimbabwe: A Study of Cultures in Collision, 1890–1979* (New York: Taylor and Francis, 1992) for discussion of reasons why this practice must be changed.

46. Faye Chung became minister of education on August 4, 1989, when Dzingai Mutumbuka was forced to resign from his government position following his conviction on charges of corruption.

47. Zimbabwe, *Herald*, August 11, 1989.

48. Ibid.

49. Karl Maier, "Opposition May Thwart Mugabe's Bid for One-party System," *Washington Post*, March 29, 1990.

50. Christine Sylvester, *Zimbabwe: The Terrain of Contradictory Development* (Boulder, CO: Westview Press, 1991), p. 160.

51. For a parallel study, see Dickson A. Mungazi, *The Mind of Black Africa* (Westport, CT: Praeger, 1996).

52. Allister Sparks, *Tomorrow is Another Country: The Inside Story of South Africa's Road to Change* (Chicago: University of Chicago Press, 1995), p. 239.

53. Dickson A. Mungazi, "Educational Innovation in Zimbabwe: Possibilities and Problems," *The Journal of Negro Education*, 52, no. 2 (1985).

54. Paulo Freire, *Pedagogy of the Oppressed*, trans. M.B. Ramos (New York: Continuum, 1983), p. 62.

55. Edward Mazaiwana, interview with Dickson A. Mungazi, Harare, Zimbabwe, August 15, 1989.

# Selected Bibliography

## BOOKS

Andrews, F. C. *John White of Mashonaland*. New York: Negro Universities Press, 1935.

Anglin, Douglas, ed. *Conflict and Change in Southern Africa: Papers from a Scandinavian Conference*. Washington, DC: University Press of America, 1978.

Austin, Reginald. *Racism and Apartheid in Southern Rhodesia*. Paris: UNESCO, 1975.

Ayadelette, F. *The American Rhodes Scholar*. Princeton: Princeton University Press, 1946.

Banana, Canaan S. *Theology of Promise: The Dynamics of Self-Reliance*. Harare: The College Press, 1982.

Barber, James. *Rhodesia: The Road to Rebellion*. London: Oxford University Press, 1967.

Battle, M., and Charles Lyons. *Essays in African Education*. New York: Teachers College Press, 1970.

Berens, Denis, and Albert B. Planger, eds. *A Concise Encyclopedia of Zimbabwe*. Gweru: Mambo Press, 1988.

Bond-Stewart, Kathy. *Education*. Gweru: Mambo Press, 1986.

Brooks, Edgar. *Native Education in South Africa*. Pretoria: Van Schaik, 1930.

Brownlee, Margaret. *The Lives and Work of South African Missionaries: A Bibliography*. Cape Town: The University of Cape Town, 1952.

Bull, Theodore. *Rhodesia: Crisis of Color*. New York: Quadrangle Books, 1967.

Carter, Gwendolyn, and Patrick O'Meara. *Southern Africa: The Continuing Crisis*. Bloomington: Indiana University Press, 1987.

Cash, Wilbur Joseph. *The Mind of the South*. New York: Alfred A. Knopf, 1941.

Challiss, Robert John. "The Educational Policy of the British South Africa Company in Southern Rhodesia, 1899–1904." Master's thesis, University of Cape Town, 1968.

Chidzero, B. T. *Education and the Challenge of Independence*. Geneva: IEUP, 1977.

Chirenje, Mutero. "The Afro-American Factor in Southern African Ethiopianism, 1890–1906." In *Profiles of Self-determination: African Responses to European Colonialism, 1652 to the Present*, edited by David Chanaiwa. Northridge: California State University, 1976.

Christie, Ian D. *Samora Machel: A Biography*. London: Panof Books, 1989.

Clark, E. *Quebec and South Africa: A Study of Cultural Adjustment*. London: Oxford University Press, 1934.

Clements, Frank. *Rhodesia: A Study of the Deterioration of a White Society*. New York: Frederick Praeger, 1969.

Cohen, Robin, ed. *Democracy and Socialism in Africa*. Boulder, CO: Westview Press, 1991.

Cook, Peter. The Education of a South African Tribe: The Bomvanal. Ph.D. diss., Columbia University, 1934.

Cooper-Omer, J. D. *The Zulu Aftermath: A 19th Century Revolution in Bantu Africa*. Evanston, IL: Northwestern University Press, 1966.

Cory, Robert, and Dianna Mitchell, eds. *African Nationalist Leaders in Rhodesia's Who's Who*. Bulawayo: Books of Rhodesia, 1977.

Cousins, H. *From Kaffir Kraal to Pulpit*. London: S. Patridge, 1899.

Cowan, Lang, James O'Connell, and David Scanlan, eds. *Education and Nation-Building in Africa*. New York: Praeger, 1966.

Cox, Courtland. *African Liberation*. New York: Black Education Press, 1972.

Curle, Adam. *Education for Liberation*. New York: John Wiley and Sons, 1972.

Curtin, Philip. *The Images of Africa: British Ideas and Action*. Madison: University of Wisconsin Press, 1964.

———. *Africa South of the Sahara*. Morristown, NJ: Silver Burdett, 1970.

Davidson, Basil. *The Black Man's Burden: Africa and the Curse of the Nation State*. New York: Times Books, 1992.

Davidson, Francis. *South Africa and Central Africa: A Record of Fifteen Years of Missionary Labors among the Primitive Peoples*. Elgin, IL: Brethren Publishing House, 1915.

Davies, Horton, ed. *South African Missions, 1800–1950*. London: Thomas Nelson, 1954.

Davis, Richard. *Bantu Education and the Education of Africans in South Africa*. Athens: Ohio University Center for International Studies, 1972.

de Klerk, F. W. *Address to Parliament of the Republic of South Africa*. Pretoria: Government Printer, 1990.

Demon, Donald, and Balam Nyeko. *Southern Africa since 1800*. London: Longman, 1984.

Diffendorfer, Ralph, ed. *The World Service of the Methodist Episcopal Church*. Chicago: Council of the World Board of Benevolences, 1928.

Dodge, Ralph E. *The Revolutionary Bishop: An Autobiography*. Pasadena, CA: William Carey Library, 1986.

———. *The Unpopular Missionary*. Westwood, NJ: Fleming H. Revell, 1964.

Drake, Howard. *A Bibliography of African Education South of the Sahara*. Aberdeen, TX: The University of Aberdeen Press, 1942.

Dugard, John. *The Southwest Africa/Namibia Dispute*. Berkeley: University of California Press, 1973.

Eicher, J. C. *Educational Costing and Financing in Developing Countries*. Washington, DC: World Bank, 1984.

El-Ayouty, Yassin. *The Organization of African Unity, Ten Years After* (Comparativer Perspective.) New York: Praeger, 1975.

Fafunwa, Babs. *History of Education in Nigeria*. London: George Allen and Unwin, 1974.

Fletcher, Basil. *The Background of Educational Development in the Federation*. Salisbury: The University of Rhodesia and Nyasaland, 1959.

Fortune, George. *African Languages in Schools: Select Papers from the 1962 and 1963 Conferences on Teaching African Languages*. Salisbury: University College of Rhodesia and Nyasaland, 1964.

Fraser, D. *The Future of Africa*. Westport, CT: Negro Universities Press, 1911.

Freire, Paulo. *Pedagogy of the Oppressed*. Translated by M. B. Ramos. New York: Continuum, 1983.

Gelfand, Michael. *African Background*. Cape Town, South Africa: Juta and Company, 1965.

———. *Diet and Tradition in African Culture*. London: E and S Livingstone, 1971.

———. *Growing Up in Shona Society*. Gweru: Mambo Press, 1979.

Gibbs, Peter. *Flag for the Matebele: An Entertainment in African History*. New York: The Vanguard Press, 1956.

Gordon, Robert. *The Bushman Myth: The Making of a Namibian Underclass*. Boulder, CO: Westview Press, 1991.

Green, J. S. *Rhodes Goes North*. London: Bell and Sons, 1936.

———. *The Planting of Christianity in Africa*. London: Murray, 1952.

———. *The Planting of Christianity in Africa*. London: SPCK, 1959.

Grundy, Kenneth. *South Africa: Domestic Crisis and Global Challenge*. Boulder, CO: Westview Press, 1991.

Hailey, William. *The African Survey*. London: Oxford University Press, 1957.

Hapgood. *Africa in Today's World Focus*. Boston: Ginn and Company, 1971.

Harden, Blaine. *Africa: Dispatches from the Fragile Continent*. New York: W. W. Norton and Co., 1990.

Hargreaves, J. D. *Decolonization in Africa*. New York: Longman, 1988.

Hassauig, Schioldberg. *The Christian Missions and the British Expansion in Southern Rhodesia, 1888–1923*. Ann Arbor: The University of Michigan Microfilms, 1960.

Henderson, Lawrence. *Angola: Five Centuries of Conflict*. Ithaca, NY: Cornell University Press, 1979.

Hendrikz, E. A. "Cross-Cultural Investigation of the Number Concepts and Level of Number Development in Five-Year-Old Urban Shona and European Children in Southern Rhodesia." Master's thesis, University of London, 1965.

Herbstein, Dennis. *White Man, We Want to Talk to You*. London: Oxford University Press, 1979.

Hindley, George. *Fifty Years with Ford*. Bulawayo: Duly and Company, 1961.

Hirschman, David, and Brian Rose. *Education for Development in Southern Africa*. Johannesburg, South Africa: South African Institute of International Affairs for the Foundation of Foreign Affairs, 1974.

Hirst, Paul. *Knowledge and the Curriculum: A Collection of Philosophical Papers*. London: Poutledge and Kegan Paul, 1974.

Holleman, J. F. *Shona Customary Law*. Cape Town: Oxford University Press, 1952.

Hortrell, Muriel. *African Education: Some Origins and Developments in 1953*. Johannesburg, South Africa: South African Institute of Race Relations, 1964.

Houtandji, Paulin. *African Philosophy: Myth and Reality*. Bloomington: Indiana University Press, 1982.

Huddleston, Trevor. *Naught for Your Comfort*. New York: Oxford University Press, 1956.

Innes, Duncan. *Our Country, Our Responsibility*. London: Africa Bureau, 1969.

Irvine, Sanders H. *Selection for Secondary Education in Southern Africa*. Salisbury: The University College of Rhodesia and Nyasaland, 1965.

Jaster, Robert. *The Defense of White Power: South African Foreign Policy under Pressure*. New York: St. Martin's Press, 1989.

Jowitt, Harold. "The Protectorate of Southern Africa." In *The Yearbook of Education*. Salisbury: Government Printer, 1954.

July, Robert. *A History of the African People*. New York: Scribner and Sons, 1974.

Kalso, Milton. "A Study of Selected Aspects of Three Elementary School Programs in the United States with Implications for Rhodesia." Ed. D. diss., The University of Oregon, 1969.

Kane, Norah. *The World's View*. London: Cassell and Company, 1954.

Kapenzi, Geoffrey. *A Clash of Cultures: Christian Missionaries and the Shona of Rhodesia*. Washington, DC: University Press of America, 1978.

Kaplan, Irving. *Zaire: A Country Study*. Washington, DC: The American University Press, 1979.

Kaunda, Kenneth. *Zambia Shall Be Free*. New York: Frederick Praeger, 1963.

Kimble, H. T. *Emerging Africa*. New York: Scholastic Books, 1963.

Kitchen, Helen, ed. *The Educated African: A Country Survey*. New York: Praeger, 1971.

Knorr, Kenneth. *British Colonial Theories*. Toronto, Canada: University of Toronto Press, 1974.

La Guma, Alex, ed. *Apartheid: A Collection of Writings on South African Racism by South Africans*. New York: International Publishers, 1971.

Lardner-Burke, Desmond. *Rhodesia: The Story of Crisis*. London: Albourne, 1966.

Legum, Colin. "The Nkomati Accord and Its Implications for the Front-Line States and South Africa." In *Confrontation and Liberation in Southern Africa: Regional Directions after the Nkomati Accord*. Edited by Ibrahim S. Msabaha and Timothy M. Shaw. Boulder, CO: Westview Press, 1987.

Lewis, Leonard. *Equipping Africa: Educational Development in British Colonial Africa*. London: Edinburgh House Press, 1968.

Lovejoy, Paul, ed. *African Modernization and Development*. Boulder, CO: Westview Press, 1991.

Lugard, Frederick. *Dual Mandate in British Tropical Africa*. London: Blackwood, 1926.

Lyons, Charles. *To Wash and Aethiop White: British Ideas about Black African Educability, 1530–1960.* New York: Teachers College Press, 1975.

Makulu, Henry. *Education, Development and Nation-Building in Independent Africa.* London: SCM Press, 1971.

Malherbe, Ernest. *Education for Leadership in Africa.* Durban, South Africa: Natal Technical College, 1960.

———. *The New Education in a Changing Empire.* Pretoria: Van Schaik, 1963.

Mandela, Nelson. *Long Walk to Freedom: The Autobiography of Nelson Mandela.* Boston: Little, Brown and Company, 1994.

Martin, David, and Phyllis Johnson. *The Struggle for Zimbabwe.* Harare: Zimbabwe Publishing House, 1981.

Mason, Reginald. *British Education in Africa.* London: Oxford University Press, 1959.

Maxey, Kees. *The Fight for Zimbabwe: The Armed Struggle in Southern Rhodesia.* London: Rex Collins, 1975.

McHarg, James. "Influences Contributing to the Education and Culture of the Natives People of Southern Rhodesia, 1900 to 1961." Ed.D. diss., Duke University, 1962.

McIntyre, W. *Colonies into Commonwealth.* New York: Walker and Company, 1966.

Memmi, Albert. *The Colonizer and the Colonized.* Boston: Beacon Press, 1965.

Mlambo, E. *Rhodesia: The Struggle for a Birthright.* London: Hurst and Company, 1972.

Mnyanda, B. J. *In Search of Truth.* Bombay: Hind Kitabs, 1954.

Mugomba, Agrippah, and Mougo Nyaggah. *Independence without Freedom: The Political Economy of Colonial Education in Southern Africa.* Santa Barbara, CA: ABC–Clio, 1980.

Mungazi, Dickson A. "The Change of Black Attitudes Toward Education in Rhodesia, 1900–1975." Ph.D. diss., The University of Nebraska, 1977.

———. *The Cross between Rhodesia and Zimbabwe: Racial Conflict in Rhodesia, 1962–1979.* New York: Vantage Press, 1981.

———. *The Underdevelopment of African Education: A Black Zimbabwean Perspective.* Washington, DC: University Press of America, 1982.

———. *To Honor the Sacred Trust of Civilization: History, Politics, and Education in Southern Africa.* Cambridge, MA: Schenkman Publishers, 1983.

———. *The Struggle for Social Change in Southern Africa: Visions of Liberty.* New York: Taylor and Francis, 1989.

———. *Education and Government Control in Zimbabwe: A Study of the Commissions of Inquiry, 1908–1974.* New York: Praeger Publishers, 1990.

———. *Colonial Education for Africans: George Stark's Policy in Zimbabwe.* New York: Praeger Publishers, 1991.

———. *Colonial Policy and Conflict in Zimbabwe: A Study of Cultures in Collision, 1890–1979.* New York: Taylor and Francis, 1992.

———. *The Mind of Black Africa.* Westport, CT: Praeger Publishers, 1996.

———, and L. Kay Walker. *Educational Reform and the Transformation of Southern Africa.* Westport, CT: Praeger Publishers, 1997.

Murray, Victor. *The School in the Bush: A Critical Study of the Theory and Practice of Native Education in Africa.* London: Longman, 1938.

Naylor, W. S. *Daybreak in the Dark Continent*. New York: The Young Peoples'
     Missionary Movement, 1905.
Nkrumah, Kwame. *Africa Must Unite*. London: Panof Publications, 1963.
Obasamjo, Olusegun, and Hans d'Orville, eds. *Challenges of Leadership in African
     Development*. New York: Taylor and Francis, 1990.
O'Callaghan, Marion. *Namibia: The Effects of Apartheid on Culture and Education*.
     Paris: UNESCO, 1979.
———. *Rhodesia: The Effects of Apartheid on Culture and Education*. Paris: UNESCO,
     1979.
Oldham, James. *White and Black in Africa*. New York: Green and Company, 1930.
Oliver, Stephan. "Recent Adaptations of Education in Rhodesia." Master's thesis,
     The University of South Africa, 1948.
Omari, C. K. *The Family in Africa*. Geneva: World Council of Churches, 1974.
Parker, Franklin. *African Development and Education in Southern Rhodesia*. Colum-
     bus, OH: Kappa Delta Pi, 1960.
———. "Early Church-State Relationship in African Education in Rhodesia and
     Zambia." In *World Yearbook of Education*. New York: World Almanac
     Books, 1966.
Peck, A. J. *Rhodesia Accuses*. Boston: Western Islands Press, 1966.
Ranger, Terence. *Revolt in Southern Rhodesia, 1896–1897*. Evanston, IL: North-
     western University Press, 1967.
———. *The African Voice in Southern Rhodesia, 1898–1930*. Evanston, IL: North-
     western University Press, 1970.
Raphaeli, Nimroid. *Public Sector Management in Botswana*. Washington, DC:
     World Bank, 1984.
Raynor, William. *Tribe and Its Successors: An Account of African Traditional Life
     after European Settlement in Southern Rhodesia*. New York: Frederick Prae-
     ger, 1962.
Rea, Frederick. *Missionary Factor in Southern Rhodesia*. Salisbury: Historical As-
     sociation of Rhodesia and Nyasaland, 1962.
Richards, J. R. "Personality Factors and Main Subject Choice in Colleges of Ed-
     ucation in England and Rhodesia." Master's thesis, The University of
     Manchester, 1972.
Riddell, Roger. *From Rhodesia to Zimbabwe: Education for Employment*. Gweru:
     Mambo Press, 1980.
Rogers, C. A., and C. Franz. *Racial Themes in Southern Rhodesia: Attitudes of the
     White Population*. New Haven, CT: Yale University Press, 1967.
Rolin, Henri. *Les Los at l'Administration de la Rhodesie*. Bruxelles: l-Etablissment
     Emil Bruylant.
Samkange, Stanlake. *What Rhodes Really Said about Africans*. Harare: Harare Pub-
     lishing House, 1982.
Schweitzer, Albert. *Our Task in Colonial Africa*. New York: Harper Brothers, 1948.
Shamuyarira, Nathan. *Crisis in Rhodesia*. London: Deutsche, 1964.
Sparks, Allister. *The Mind of South Africa*. New York: Alfred Knopf, 1989.
———. *Tomorrow Another Country: The Inside Story of South Africa's Road to Change*.
     Chicago, IL: University of Chicago Press, 1995.
Sparrow, G. *The Rhodesian Rebellion*. London: Brighton, 1966.

Stack, Louise, and Donald Morton. *Torment to Triumph in Southern Africa*. New York: Friendship Press, 1976.

Steiner, Elizabeth. *Educology of the Free*. New York: Philosophical Library, 1981.

Sylvester, Christine. *Zimbabwe: The Terrain of Contradictory Development*. Boulder, CO: Westview Press, 1991.

Tichawapedza, Fungai. *The Zimbabwean Woman in the Struggle for Liberation*. Washington, DC: ZANU Office, 1978.

Tutu, Desmond. *Crying in the Wilderness: The Struggle for Justice in South Africa*. Grand Rapids, MI: William R. Eerdmans Publishing Company, 1982.

Walker, L. Kay, and Dickson A. Mungazi. *Colonial Agriculture for Africans: Emory Alvord's Policy in Zimbabwe*. New York: Peter Lang Publishing, 1997.

Williams, G. Mennen. *Africa for the Africans*. Grand Rapids, MI: Eerdmans, 1969.

## Government Documents in Zimbabwe

### Ordinances

*Ordinance Number 6: The Repression of Theft of Stock*, 1893.
*Ordinance Number 5: Imposing the Payment of Native Taxes*, 1894.
*Ordinance Number 18: The Appointment of the Director of Education*, 1899.
*Ordinance Number 3: Responsibilities of the Director of Education*, 1903.
*Ordinance Number 7: Control of Native Schools*, 1912.

### Annual Reports of the Director of Education

1924, 1925, 1930, 1932, 1933, 1938, 1940, 1945, 1954.

### Reports of the Director of Native Education

1926, 1928, 1929, 1932, 1934, 1935, 1954, 1959, 1960, 1961, 1962, 1962, 1965, 1966, 1969, 1970, 1974, 1975, 1976, 1977, 1978.

### Reports of the Commissions of Inquiry

*Commission of Inquiry into Education* [Marshall Hole, Chairman], Ref. A/5/08, 1908.

*Commission of Inquiry into Industrial Development of Natives* [Herbert Keigwin, Chairman], Ref. A/7/20, 1920.

*Commission of Inquiry into Native Affairs* [James Graham, Chairman], 1911.

*Commission of Inquiry into Native Education* [Alexander Kerr, Chairman], 1951.

*Commission of Inquiry into White Education* [Alexander Russell, Chairman], Ref. A/2/17, 1916.

*The Report of the Commission of Inquiry into African Primary Education* [L. J. Lewis, Chairman], 1974.

*The Report of the Commission of Inquiry into Discontent in the Mangwende Reserve* [James Brown, Chairman], 1961.

*The Report of the Commission of Inquiry into Native Education* [A. V. Judges, Chairman], 1962.

*The Report of the Commission on Higher Education in the Colonies* [Justice Asquith, Chairman], the British Colonial Office, Ref. Cmd.6647, 1945.

*The Report of the Land Commission* [Morris Carter, Chairman], Ref. CSR/3/26, 1925.

### Parliamentary Debates (Rhodesia)

1955, 1960, 1962, 1963, 1964, 1967, 1969, 1970, 1971, 1972, 1973, 1977, 1978, 1983.

### Ministry of Information, Press Statements, and Speeches by Government Officials on Education

Chung, Faye (Minister of Primary and Secondary Education). "Pre-school Training Graduates." Ref. 317/88/GB/SD/BJ, July 25, 1988.

Chung, Faye. "The Importance of Local Production of Science Textbooks." Ref. 80/89/CB/MA. March 9, 1989.

Chung, Faye. "The Role of Booksellers in Educational Development." Ref. 223/89/CB/EM/SM, July 13, 1989.

Chung, Faye. "Women Are Educated Less than Men." Ref. 230/89/CB/SM/SR, July 25, 1989.

Culverwell, Joseph (Minister of State for National Scholarship). "Take Education Seriously." Ref. 59/88/SL/BC, February 23, 1989.

Culverwell, Joseph. "U.S. Sponsored Students Graduate." Ref. 78/89/CB/MA, March 1, 1989.

Hughes, Aminia (Deputy Minister of Transport). "Be Selfless and Dedicated Teachers." Ref. 482/88/SM, October 28, 1988.

Karimanzira, David (Minister of Social Services). "Educate the People on the Dangers of Agrochemicals." Ref. 399/88/EMM/CB, September 14, 1988.

Karimanzira, David. "Educate Farmers on Better Livestock Production." Ref. 472/88/EMM/SM, October 25, 1988.

Karimanzira, David. "Government to Provide More Extension Staff." Ref. 235/89/EMM/SM/SK, July 25, 1989.

Kay, Jack (Deputy Minister of Lands, Agriculture, and Rural Settlement). "Zimbabwe is SADDC's Breadbasket." Ref. 384/EMM/SG, August 29, 1988.

Ministry of Higher Education. "Learner-Tutor Course Applications." Ref. 459/88/CB/SM, October 17, 1988.

Ministry of Information. "Vacancies for Zimbabwe-Cuba Teacher Education Course." Ref. 460/88/CB/SM, October 17, 1988.

Ministry of Public Construction and National Housing. "Three Hundred Million Dollars Boost Rural Housing." Ref. 19/89/BC/SK, January 23, 1989.

Muchemwa, Felix (Minister of Health). "State Certificated Nurses Graduate in Masvingo." Ref. 29/80/RN/SD/BJ, July 21, 1988.

Mujuru, Joyce (Minister of Community and Cooperative Development). "Women's Role in Nation Building." Ref. 4/1/89/SG/SM, June 6, 1989.

Mutumbuka, Dzingai (Minister of Higher Education). "Marymount Teachers Graduate." Ref. 365/88/03/MM, August 20, 1988.

Mutumbuka, Dzingai. "The Role of Professional Bodies in National Development." Ref. 427/88/CB/EMM, September 22, 1988.

Mutumbuka, Dzingai. "The University of Zimbabwe Staff Development," Ref. 405/88/CB/ME, September 14, 1988.

Mutumbuka, Dzingai. "Training Institutions Play Vital Role in National Development." Ref. 447/88/CC/ES, October 7, 1988.

Mutumbuka, Dzingai. "The Importance of Revising History." Ref. 15/89/CB/SK, January 23, 1989.

Nkomo, John (Minister of Labor). " A Call for Educational Program." Ref. 356/88/SK/EM/SG, August 17, 1988.

Nyagumbo, Maurice (Minister of Political Affairs). "Zimbabwe Objects to Education of U.N. Transitional Assistance Group." Ref. 7/89/BC/SM, January 13, 1988.

## Other Government Documents

*The African Education Act*, 1959.

*The Anglo-Rhodesian Proposals for a Settlement*, 1971.

*Campaign for Full Literacy in Five Years*, Office of the Prime Minister, 1983.

*Circular Number Six on African Education*, 1970.

*The Dynamics Expansion in African Education*, April 20, 1966.

*The Education Policy of the Rhodesia Labour Party*, 1945.

*The Education Policy of the United Rhodesia Party*, 1939.

*The Five-Year Education Plan for Africans*, 1956.

*The Kandowe Declaration: Emphasis on Education*, 1983.

*The Land Tenure Act*, 1969.

*Native Affairs Development Association*, 1969–1973.

*The Rhodesia Front Party Constitution*, 1962.

*Policy Statement Number 5: Presidential Directive for the Development of Education in Zimbabwe*.

## Southern Africa
### Church Publications

The Catholic Church. *Pastoral Letter: Violence in Southern Africa*. London: S.C.M., 1970.

Christian Century Foundation. *Christian Century*. October 8, 1969.

Christian Council of Rhodesia. *The Church and Human Rights*, an annual report, 1965.

———. *Annual Report*. Salisbury, 1969.

Heads of Denominations. *Memorandum to the Ministry of African Education*, Salisbury, February 26, 1970.

———. *Resolution to the Ministry of Education*. Salisbury, April 28, 1970.

Lamont, Donal. *An Open Letter to the Prime Minister*. Old Mutare: Old Mutare Methodist Archives, October 26, 1976.

Methodist Church. *The Christian Advance* (2) Number 1, 1918.

———. *Official Journal of the Methodist Church*. Old Umtali: Rhodesia Mission Press, 1905, 1907, 1919, 1927, 1964, 1969, 1970.

———. *Umbowo*, Old Umtali: Rhodesia Mission Press, 1964, 1974.

National Council of Churches, *Africa is Here*. New York: Board of Foreign Missions, 1952.

Pelley, Donald. *A Short History of St. Augustine's Mission*. St. Augustine's School Records Office, 1903 (Mimeographed).

United Methodist Church. *Southern Africa*. New York: Board of Global Ministries, 1986.

United Methodist Church. "Resolution Warning the Government of Southern Rhodesia against Unilateral Declaration of Independence," in *Official Journal of the Methodist Church*. Old Umtali: Rhodesia Mission Press, 1963.

## Newspapers and Magazines

*African Daily News, The*. January 16, 1961; February 20, 1964.

*African Weekly*. December 13, 1944; April 18, 1948; August 28, 1946; December 12, 1945.

*Bantu Mirror, The*. February 19, 1947; July 20, 1948; March 3, 1949.

*Journal of Social Change and Development in Southern Africa, The*. no. 38/39. Harare Zimbabwe, January 1996.

*Moto*. July 1963, September 1963, April 1964, December 1965, September 1966, February 1967, May 1983.

*Newsweek*. July 2, 1979.

*Rhodesia Herald*. August 24, 1902; September 7, 1917; November 12, 1968; April 5, 1967; November 12, 1968; August 15, 1970.

*Teacher in New Africa*. 1964, 1965, 1966, 1969.

## Unpublished Materials

British Methodist Church, The. The Education Policy of the Methodist Church. Waddilove, February 8–9, 1946. Mimeographed.

Chimbadzwa, Josiah. *The Seed is Planted*. A tape recording made by Rev. E. Sells, 1968. Old Mutare Methodist Archives.

Dodge, Ralph E. Letter dated March 18, 1959, addressed to Garfield Todd, former prime minister.

————. "The Church and Law and Order," an essay, 1963.

————. "The Church and Freedom," an essay, 1963.

————. "The Church in Africa," an episcopal address in *The Official Journal of the Methodist Church*. Old Mutare: Rhodesia Mission Press, 1963.

————. A newsletter addressed to Methodist Missionaries, February 24, 1964.

————. Letter dated July 17, 1964, addressed to William Harper, RF Minister of Internal Affairs.

————. "The African Church Now and in the Future," an unpublished essay, 1964.

Floyd, Jean. "A Kraal School in Uzumba Reserve," an essay on African education. Old Mutare Methodist Archives, 1956. Mimeographed.

Harper, William (RF Minister of Internal Affairs). Letter dated July 22, 1964, addressed to Ralph E. Dodge.

Hassing, Per. Letter addressed to Dr. James Matthews, an official of the Methodist Church in New York, written from Old Mutare Methodist Center, April 2, 1959: Old Mutare Methodist Archives.

Jowitt, Harold. "The Reconstruction of African Education." Masters thesis, The University of Cape Town, 1927.

Kachidza, Henry. Letter dated August 1, 1964, addressed to the World Council of Churches in Geneva.

Methodist Church, "A Warning against the Declaration of Independence," a press statement, May 17, 1964.

Mungazi, Dickson A. Letter to Bishop Desmond Tutu, Chair, Truth and Reconciliation Commission, Pretoria, South Africa, February 20, 1997.

Nkomo, Joshua. Letter dated July 18, 1964, addressed to Ralph E. Dodge.

Rhodesia Socialist Party, The, *The Policy of the Rhodesia Socialist Party*. Mutare, 1970. Mimeographed.

Shephard, D. E. (private secretary to the Minister of Internal Affairs), letter dated July 22, 1964, addressed to Ralph E. Dodge.

Todd, Garfield. Telegram dated July 17, 1964, sent to Ralph E. Dodge.

ZANU–PF. *The Election Manifesto of the ZANU–PF: A Statement of Goals and Principles*. Harare: ZANU–PF Office, 1979.


## Other Government Documents and Materials

Birley, Robert. "African Education," an address given to Cape Western Region Conference on Education. Johannesburg: South African Institute of Race Relations, 1956.

Botswana: *Botswana Update*. Gaberone, 1982.

Botswana: *Education for Kagisano: Supplementary Report of the National Commission on Education*. Gaberone, July, 1979.

Botswana: *Education Statistics*. Gaberone: Government Printer, 1979.

Botswana: *Report of the National Commission on Education*. Gaberone, April, 1977.

Botswana: *Ten Years of Independence*. Gaberone, 1976.

British South Africa Company Records: The Diary of Leander Starr Jameson: AV/AJ/11:Folios 109–11, Zimbabwe National Archives.

———. Earl Grey, 1896–1898: Folio: AV/1/11/1/11:547–548. Zimbabwe National Archives.

———. Earl Grey. EG:1/1/11:Folio 547, Zimbabwe National Archives.

Chabala, R. M. (administrative secretary to President Nelson Mandela), letter to Dickson A. Mungazi, January 28, 1997.

Huggins, Godfrey. (Prime Minister of Colonial Zimbabwe, 1933–1952, and of the Federation of Rhodesia and Nyasaland, 1953–1956), *Education Policy in Southern Rhodesia: Notes on Certain Features*, 1939.

———. "Partnership in Building a Country," a political speech, December 21, 1950.

———. "Partnership in Rhodesia and Nyasaland," a speech given during a campaign for the establishment of the Federation of Rhodesia and Nyasaland, May, 1950.

———. "Taking Stock of African Education," an address to the Rhodesia Christian Conference, Goromonzi, August 26, 1954.

———. "Taking Stock of African Education," an address to the Southern Rhodesia Missionary Conference, Goromonzi, August 26, 1954.

———. "The Education Policy of the Rhodesia United Party," a statement of policy and principles. Salisbury: Government Printer, 1939.

Jowitt, Harold. "The Protectorate of Southern Africa." In *The Yearbook of Education*. Salisbury: Government Printer, 1954.

Mozambique: Samora Machel, "Educate Men to Win the War, Create a New Society, and Develop a Country," a speech given at the Second Conference on Education and Culture, September, 1970.

————. "Leadership in Collective, Responsibility is Collective," a speech given to the Joint Meeting of Frelimo Instructors, February 2, 1972.

————. "The Liberation of Women as a Fundamental Necessity for Revolution," an address given at the opening of the First Conference of Mozambique Women, March 4, 1973.

Mozambique: "Documento Informativo," Ref. Doc/Inf.01/11, Maputo, 1979.

Mozambique: Ministry of Information. *Education in Mozambique*, Maputo, 1982.

Rhodesia: *African Education*, Ref. 738, 1973.

Rhodesia: *Parliamentary Debates*, August 26, 1977; August 27, 1974; August 30, 1974.

Rhodesia: *Report of the Commission of Inquiry into Racial Discrimination* [Vincent Quenet, Chairman], Ref. 27015/36050, April 23, 1976.

Rhodesia: *Education: An Act* , No. 8, 1979.

South Africa: *South Africa Broadcasting Corporation on Political Rights*, Ref. SABC/ TV,1/90, February 2, 1990.

South Africa: "President F. W. de Klerk's Visit to the United States of America, September 1990." Washington, DC: South African Embassy. 1990.

South Africa: "President F. W. de Klerk: First Year in Office." Pretoria: Government Printer, 1990.

South Africa: "South Africa: The Events of February 1990." Washington, DC: South African Embassy, 1990.

South Africa: F. W. de Klerk, "The Birth of the New South Africa." Pretoria, Government Printer, 1990.

South Africa: "The National Economy of South Africa, 1989–90." Pretoria: Government Printer, 1990.

South Africa: *Proclamation over Southwest Africa*, November 27, 1918.

Southern Rhodesia: *Ordinance Number 1*, 1903.

Southern Rhodesia: *Legislative Debates*, 1923–1961.

Southern Rhodesia: *Annual Reports of the Director of Native Education*, 1927–1960.

Southern Rhodesia: *Annual Reports of the Secretary for African Education*, 1962– 1979.

Tanzania: *Education for Self-Reliance*. Dar es Salaam: Government Printer, 1967.

Zambia Information Service: *Zambia in Brief*. Lusaka, 1975.

Zambia: *Educational Reform: Proposals and Recommendations*, October, 1977.

Zambia: K. D. Kaunda. *Blueprint for Economic Development: A Guide on How to Clear Obstacles*. October 8, 1979.

Zimbabwe-Rhodesia: *Report of the Constitutional Conference*, Ref. R2R3, London: Lancaster House, December 21, 1979.

Zimbabwe: *Annual Digest of Statistics*. Harare: Government Printer, 1988.

Zimbabwe: *Annual Report of the Secretary for Education*, 1980–1989. Harare: Government Printer, 1989.

Zimbabwe: B. T. Chidzero (Minister of Finance and Planning). *Budget Statement*. July 27, 1989.

Zimbabwe: *Constitution of Zimbabwe, The*. Harare: Government Printer, 1985.

Zimbabwe: *Constitutional Amendment* No. 23, 1987.

Zimbabwe: "Not in a Thousand Years: From Rhodesia to Zimbabwe," a documentary film, PBS, 1981.

Zimbabwe: *Prime Minister Opens Economic Conference*, September 5, 1980.
Zimbabwe: *Prime Minister's New Year's Message to the Nation*, December 31, 1980.
Zimbabwe: Ministry of Education. *Arra Kis: School Library News*. Harare. Vol. 6, No. 60, July, 1986.
Zimbabwe: Mugabe, Robert [Prime Minister]. *Address to the Organization of African Unity*, Document No. 2. Freetown, Sierra Leone, July 4, 1980.
Zimbabwe: Mugabe, Robert."Literacy for All in Five Years," a speech given to launch the National Adult Literacy Campaign, July 18, 1983. Zimbabwe National Archives.
Zimbabwe: ZAPU. *Primary School Syllabus*, August, 1978.

## Newspapers and Magazines

Barr, F. C. "Native Education in Rhodesia." *Month* 35 (June 1966): 352–59.
Bevan, L. E. "Education of Natives in the Pastoral Pursuits." *NADA* 2 (1924): 13–16.
Birmingham, David. "The United Kingdom Studies Symposium on African Studies." *The Journal of Modern African Studies* (April, 1970): 138–40.
Cannon, J. "Cecil Rhodes and Religious Education." *The Methodist Quarterly Review* (October 1924): 634–37.
Carruthers-Smith, E. E. "African Education in Bulawayo from 1892." *NADA* (1971): 81–93.
Charles, S. J. "Southern Rhodesia." *Practical Education and School Crafts* (July, 1964): 201–3.
*Chicago Tribune*. October 1, 1981.
*Christian Science Monitor*. "Future Leaders Learn Next-door: Namibians Study at U.N. School in Zambia, September 7, 1989."
Currie, J. et al. "Indirect Rule in Africa and its Bearing on Educational Development." *Overseas Education* (1933): 82–84.
Davidson, Basil. "African Education in Bantu Central and Southern Africa." *Presence Africaine* (1956): 106–12.
*Economist*. June 24, 1989; September 30, 1989.
Fletcher, Basil. "Educational Enterprise in Africa." *School and Society* (May 23, 1959): 242–43.
Fritz, Mark. "African Democracy Takes a Backward Leap." *Arizona Daily Sun* (Flagstaff), November 21, 1993.
Good, Robert. "Intelligence and Attainment in Rhodesia." *Overseas Education* (April 1956): 17–27.
*Herald*. (Zimbabwe). July 4, 1983 through August 11, 1989.
———. "Mozambique Looks to the World for $450 Million Aid," April 13, 1989.
———. "Secondary Schools Hit by Shortage of Qualified Teachers," July 15, 1989.
———. "Apartheid Cannot Be Condoned," July 10, 1989.
———. "Worry over School Zoning," July 17, 1989.
———. "Mozambique Peace Drive a Concern," July 20, 1989.
———. "Concept of Education with Production Explained," July 24, 1989.
———. "University of Zimbabwe gets $400 Million from Federal Republic of Germany for Developing Equipment," July 28, 1989.

———. " Nkomo's Economic Objectives are a Priority in Resettlement," July 28, 1989.

———. "Sanctions that Would Bite," August 11, 1989.

———. "Nkomo Lectures University Students," August 11, 1989.

———. "President Calls for Revolutionary Land Reform Programs," August 12, 1989.

———. "Compensation for Teachers Who Joined Freedom Struggle," August 17, 1989.

Huggins, Godfrey. "Rhodesia Leads the Way: Education for Europeans in Southern Rhodesia." *Times Educational Supplement* (February 14, 1931).

Irvine, Sanders H. "Education for Citizenship." *NADA* (1961): 74–83.

Jackson, H. M. "Native Education in Southern Rhodesia." *African Observer* (1934): 28–32.

Junod, H. A. "Native Language and Native Education." *The Journal of African Society* (1905): 1–14.

Kazembe, Phillip. "Shona in the Schools." *Teacher in New Africa* (June, 1967): 16–18.

Lacey, C. "Christian Racism in Rhodesia." *Christian Century* (March 1972).

Lewis, Thomas. "The Problem of Semi-Educated African." *Overseas Education* (January, 1942): 265–73.

Lloyd, B. W. "School Library Facilities for Africans in Southern Rhodesia." *Overseas Education* (April, 1960): 36–41.

*Los Angeles Times.* "Africa's Future Riding the Train to Nowhere." (July 17, 1990).

Maier, Karl. "Opponent May Thwart Mugabe's Bid for a One-Party System." *Washington Post* (March 29, 1990).

Milton, Alan. "Teachers for Rhodesia's Tomorrow." *South African Outlook* (August 1966): 129–30.

*Moto* (Gweru). (August 1983–August, 1989).

Mungazi, Dickson A. "Educational Innovation in Zimbabwe: Possibilities and Problems." *The Journal of Negro Education* 54, no. 2 (Spring, 1985): 196–212.

———. "Application of Memmi's Theory of the Colonizer and the Colonized to the Conflicts in Zimbabwe." *The Journal of Negro Education* 55, no. 4 (1986).

———. "A Strategy for Power: Commisions of Inquiry into Education and Government Control in Zimbabwe." *The International Journal of African Historical Studies* 22, no. 2 (1989).

———. "To Bind Ties between the School and Tribal Life: Educational Policy for Africans under George Stark in Zimbabwe." *The Journal of Negro Education* 58, no. 4 (1989).

———. "Apartheid in South Africa: Origin, Meaning, and Effect." Audio-Visual Services, Education, Northern Arizona University, Ref. AC/ECC/2/90, February 22, 1990, Documentary Film.

———. "Educational Policy for Africans and Church-State Conflict During the Rhodesia Front Government in Zimbabwe." *The National Social Science Journal* 2, no. 3 (June, 1990).

Murphree, Betty Jo. "The Acculturative Effects of Schooling on African Attitudes and Values." *Zambezia* (1970).

Murphree, Marshall. "A Village School and Community Development in Rhodesia Tribal Trust Land." *Zambezia* (1970).

*Newsweek.* July 1, 1979; January 27, 1986.

*New York Times.* Desmond Tutu, "Judge de Klerk by His Actions." October 20, 1989.

*New York Times.* "Students Fail Zimbabwe and Pay Heavy Price." November 16, 1989.

*New York Times.* "Higher Controls Seen in Zimbabwe." December 10, 1989.

*New York Times.* "The Old Men Versus the Public: Africa's Iron Hands Struggle to Hang On." July 15, 1990.

Ngonyama, Suzan. "The Education of the African Girl." *NADA* (1954): 57–58.

Parker, Franklin. "African Community Development and Education in Southern Rhodesia, 1920–1935." *International Review of Missions* (July 1962).

———. "Education in the Federation of Rhodesia and Nyasaland." *The Journal of Negro Education* (1961) 286–93.

*Sunday Mail, The* (Zimbabwe). "Teachers Form Union," August, 1989.

*Time.* "South Africa Scan: Facts and Reports," 1989.

*Time.* August 17, 1981; March 5, 1990; July 9, 1990; Sepember 4, 1990; November 4, 1946; March 24, 1997.

*Washington Post.* February 3, 1989; August 1, 1989; May 7, 1990.

*World Almanac and Book of Facts, The,* 1983, 1990, 1992, 1995.

## Other Materials and Documents

### UN Documents on Namibia:

United Nations. Council for Namibia. *Meetings Held in Algeria* May 28–June 1, 1980.

United Nations. Council for Namibia. *Meetings Held in Panama City,* June 2–5, 1981.

United Nations. Council on Namibia. *Arushu Declaration and Program of Action on Namibia,* May 14, 1982.

United Nations. *A Trust Betrayed: Namibia.* New York.

United Nations. Decree Number 1. *For the Protection of the Natural Resources of Namibia.* New York, September, 1974.

United Nations. *Namibia: A Unique UN Responsibility.* New York, December, 1981.

United Nations. *Nationhood Program for Namibia.* New York, 1981.

United Nations. *Objective: Justice: Walvis Bay, an Integral Part of Namibia,* a statement on the future of Namibia, April 24, 1978.

United Nations. *Plunder of Namibian Uranium.* New York, September, 1974.

United Nations. *United Nations Council for Namibia: What it is, what it does, how it works.* New York, March 1983.

UNESCO. *International Conference in Support of the Struggle of the Namibian People for Independence,* Paris, April 25–29, 1983.

### On Southern Africa in General

ABC-TV: *20/20: The Agony of Mozambique,* March 2, 1990.

Africa Action Committee. *Uhuru for Southern Africa.* Kinshasa, December 15, 1984.

Afro-American and African Studies. *Africana* 2, no. 1 (1985).

Anad, Mohamed. *Apartheid: A Form of Slavery.* New York, U.N. no. 37/71, 1971.

Ayittey, George. "In Africa Independence Is a Far Cry from Freedom." *The Wall Street Journal*, March 28, 1990.

Basson, S. P. N., letter to Dickson A. Mungazi, March 12, 1990.

British Council of Missionary Society. "Violence in Southern Africa: A Christian Assessment," October 28, 1970.

British Methodist Church in Zimbabwe. *The Waddilove Manifesto: The Educational Policy of the Methodist Church*, February 9, 1946.

Carlson, Brian. "American Education: A South African Perspective in the Process of Desegregation." *Kappa Delta Phi* (Summer, 1988).

Center for Applied Research. *Social Implications of the Lagos Plan of Action for Economic Development in Africa, 1980–2000*. Geneva, November 1981.

Central Committee for SWAPO. *Swapo: Political Program of the Southwest Africa People's Organization*. Lusaka, July 28–August 1, 1976.

Churchill, Winston, and Franklin Roosevelt. *The Atlantic Charter*, August 14, 1941.

Congolese National Liberation Front (CNLF). *The Struggle for Liberation*. New York, 1975.

*Continued Policy of Discrimination*. Harare, 1963.

Davidson, Basil. *Africa: New Nations and Problems*. Arts and Entertainment, 1988. Documentary film.

Dodge, Ralph E. "The Church and Political Community," 1963.

———. "A Political Community," May 1964.

Evans, M. *The Front-Line State, South Africa and Southern African Security: Military Prospects and Perspectives*. Harare: University of Zimbabwe, 1989.

Gordimer, Nadine. *Gold and the Gun: Crisis in Mozambique and South Africa*. Arts and Entertainment, 1990. Documentary film.

Landis, Elizabeth. "Apartheid and the Disabilities of Women in South Africa." New York: United Nations Unit on Apartheid, 1975.

League of Nations Covenant: Article 22, January 20, 1920.

League of Nations:*The Mandate for Southwest Africa*, May 7, 1920.

Loveridge, F. G. (Senior Education Officer in the Ministry of African Education, Zimbabwe). "Disturbing Realities of Western Education in Southern Africa." Harare, March 13, 1963.

M'Bow, Amadou-Mahtar, Unesco Director-General. "Unesco and the Promotion of Education for International Understanding." An address to the New York African Studies Association Conference, Albany, New York, October 29, 1982.

Macmillan, Harold. "Commonwealth Independence and Interdependence." An address to the Joint Session of the South African Parliament, Cape Town, February 3, 1960.

Malianga, Morton. "We shall Wage an all out war to Liberate Ourselves," April 30, 1966.

Mandela, Nelson. "A Statement made in Cape Town soon after his Release from Victor Verster Prison." SABC, February 11, 1990.

———. Inaugural Address. Cape Town, May 9, 1994.

———. "Speech given in Soweto during a reception held in his honor," February 12, 1990.

Mazaiwana, Edward. Interview by author. Harare, Zimbabwe, August 15, 1989.

McHarg, James. "Influences Contributing to Education and Culture of Native People in Southern Rhodesia." Dissertation, Duke University, 1962.

McNamara, Robert. "The Challenge of Sub-Sahara Africa." In *John Crawford Lectures*. Washington, DC, November 1, 1985.

Mnegi wa Dikgang. *Education with Production* 5, no. 2 (June 1987).

Molotsi, Peter, Fordham University. "Educational Policies and the South African Bantustans." Paper presented at the New York Association of African Studies, Albany, New York, October 29–30, 1982.

Morton, Donald. "Partners in Apartheid." New York Center for Social Action: United Church of Christ, 1973.

Mungazi, Dickson A. Letter to President F. W. de Klerk, February 15, 1990.

Mungazi, Dickson A. Letter to Bishop Desmond M. Tutu, Chair, Truth and Forgiveness Commission, February 20, 1997.

Mutumbuka, Dzingai. "Zimbabwe's Educational Challenge." Paper read at the World University Services Conference, London, December 1979.

Muzorewa, Abel T. Interview with Dickason A. Mungazi, Harare, Zimbabwe, July 28, 1983.

New York Friends Group, Inc. *South Africa: Is Peaceful Change Possible?* New York, 1984.

Office on Africa Educational Fund. *The Struggle for Justice in South Africa.* Washington, DC, February, 1984.

Organization of African Unity. "A Communique on Mozambique." Nairobi, Kenya, August 8, 1989.

"Prospects of a Settlement in Angola and Namibia." A Statement by the parties [Representives of the U.S.A., Angola, SWAPO, Cuba].

Public Broadcasting System. "Not in a Thousand Years: From Rhodesia to Zimbabwe." Documentary film, 1982.

Rhodesia Front Government. *The Dynamic Expansion in African Education*, Ref. INF/NE/Acc.40/2710, April 20, 1966.

Riddell, Roger. *From Rhodesia to Zimbabwe: Alternatives to Poverty.* Gweru: Mambo Press, 1978.

Sithole, Ndabaningi. Interview with Dickson A. Mungazi, Harare, Zimbabwe, July 20, 1983.

Smith, Arthur, Minister of Education in Rhodesia. Interview with Geoffrey Atkins of the Rhodesia Broadcasting Service, on educational policy for Africans, January 31, 1968.

Smith, Ian D. Interview with Dickson A. Mungazi, Harare, Zimbabwe, July 20, 1983.

Smuts, J. C. *The League of Nations: A Practical Suggestion.* Paris: UNESCO, 1918.

South African Ministry of Information. "South Africa Stops Native Students from Territorirs from Attending its Schools." Press release, November 2, 1950.

Southern Rhodesia. United Federal Party, *Information Statement*, Ref. UFP/SR/9, 1961.

Sullivan, Leon. "Meeting the Mandate for Change: A Progress Report on the Application of the Sullivan Principles on U.S. Companies in South Africa." *Fight Against Apartheid.* New York: UNESCO, 1984.

Tanzania. *Basic Facts about Education.* Dar es Salaam: Government Printer, 1984.

Tanzania. *Education for Self-reliance*. Dar es Salaam: Government Printer, 1967.

The Anglo-Rhodesian Relations: Proposals for a Settlement, Ref. Cmd/RR/46/
71, November 25, 1971.

Thompson Publications. *Parade*. Harare, August, 1989.

TransAfrica. *Namibia: The Crisis in U.S. Policy toward Southern Africa*. Washington,
DC, 1983.

UNESCO. "Education in Africa in the Light of the Lagos Conference." Paper
Number 25, 1976.

United Nations. *Program of Action against Apartheid*. New York, October 25.

United Nations. *A Crime against Humanity: Questions and Answers on Apartheid in
South Africa*. New York, 1984.

United Nations. Unit on Apartheid. 1971. *Bantustan Policy: A Fantasy and a Fraud*.
Prepared by Leslie Rubin, Number 12/71.

University of Cape Town. "A Call for Post-doctoral Research Fellows, 1991." *The
Chronicle of Higher Education*, March 16, 1990.

Washington Office on Africa. *Resources on Namibia*. Washington, DC, March 1982.

Watson, P. *The Struggle for Democracy*, a documentary film, PBS, 1988.

World Bank. *Accelerate Development in Sub-Sahara Africa: An Agenda for Action*.
Washington, DC: World Bank, 1983.

———. "Alternatives to Formal Education: Unesco Conference on Education."
Harare, June 28–July 3, 1982.

World Council of Churches. *Involvement in the Struggles against Oppression in
Southern Africa, 1966–1980*. Geneva, n.d.

ZANU. *Liberation through Participation: Women in the Zimbabwean Revolution*. Harare: ZANU, 1981.

———. *Zimbabwe: Election Manifesto* 1979.

Zimbabwe Conference of Catholic Bishops. *Our Mission to Teach: A Pastoral Statement on Education*. Gweru: Mambo Press, 1987.

# Index

## About the Author

DICKSON A. MUNGAZI is Regent's Professor of History at the Center for Excellence in Education at Northern Arizona University. He is the author of numerous books on African political history and education, including *The Mind of Black Africa* (Praeger, 1996), and *Educational Reform and the Transformation of Southern Africa*, coauthored with L. Kay Walker (Praeger, 1997).

ISBN 0-275-96030-7

HARDCOVER BAR CODE

ISSCW  B
S649M

MUNGAZI, DICKSON A.
    THE LAST DEFENDERS
OF THE LAAGER  : IAN D.
SMITH AND F.W. DE KLERK

ISSCW    B
         S649M

HOUSTON PUBLIC LIBRARY
CENTRAL LIBRARY